Penguin Books

Nairn's London

Born in 1930, Ian Nairn was first given the chance to write
about architecture by the *Architectural Review*, after two
false starts in mathematics and the R.A.F. He went on to
write on buildings and places throughout the world for
the *Daily Telegraph*, the *Observer* and, finally, the *Sunday
Times*. By temperament he was much happier among
working journalists than professional men, and listed
flying and pubs – the only kind of building he would have
liked to design – among his hobbies. He is also the author
of *Outrage*, *The American Landscape*, *Modern Buildings
in London* and *Nairn's Paris*. He paid his wife the
compliment of saying that 'she would certainly have been
in *Nairn's London* had she only been made of brick or
stucco'. Ian Nairn died in 1983.

Peter Gasson was born and brought up in north-east
London. He first encountered Ian Nairn's writing during
a vacation job in a Westminster architect's office, and read
Nairn's London while studying English language and
literature at Magdalen College, Oxford. Visiting every
entry in *Nairn's London*, as he has done in the course of
preparing this new edition, is the fulfilment of a long-
cherished ambition.

Ian Nairn

Nairn's London

Revisited by Peter Gasson

Penguin Books

PENGUIN BOOKS

Published by the Penguin Group
27 Wrights Lane, London W8 5TZ, England
Viking Penguin Inc., 40 West 23rd Street, New York, New York 10010, U.S.A.
Penguin Books Australia Ltd, Ringwood, Victoria, Australia
Penguin Books Canada Limited, 2801 John Street, Markham, Ontario, Canada L3R 1B4
Penguin Books (N.Z.) Ltd, 182–190 Wairau Road, Auckland 10, New Zealand

Penguin Books Ltd, Registered Offices: Harmondsworth, Middlesex, England

First published 1966
Reprinted 1967
Revised edition 1988

Printed and bound in Great Britain by
Butler & Tanner Ltd, Frome and London

Set in Monotype Plantin

To John Nash,
who provided so much of the material,
and to Tony Godwin,
who gave me the chance to write about it

Contents

Preface

This guide is simply my personal list of the best things in London. I have all the time tried to be rigorous – not any old Wren church or view or pub, but the good ones – and I have all the time tried to get behind conventional aesthetics to an internal reality of which beauty is only one facet. What I am after is character, or personality, or essence.

Whether this grandiose programme has achieved anything more than a collection of subjective maunderings, I am not sure. Too often words which seemed appropriate in the heat of the moment turn out to be trite clichés. Too often my perceptions have been blunted by the fact that I have lived in London for ten years, looking hard at buildings all the time. It is sometimes hard to recapture from the consciousness the first delight in a building which you may have seen a hundred times. There are bound to be too many superlatives, and too many of the same superlatives: I can only plead with the reader to regard this as an anthology and treat each embarrassing rapture as complete in itself.

The guide goes up to the edge of the built-up area – a little further all round than the Greater London Council – and contains about four hundred and fifty entries. This is an astonishing number. In spite of everything, London contains many more and more varied masterpieces than Rome or Paris, just as the National Gallery can produce more and more varied excitements than the Louvre or the Vatican galleries. Nothing will ever quite fit to the accepted waves of Continental influence; and the true Londoner will never quite fit in any pattern at all, even an English one.

The book is organized into what seemed to be common-sense areas. Within them, the order does indicate a route of a sort; but this is not intended to be a package tour. The references are to *London A to Z* and one-inch ordnance survey maps sheets 160, 161, 169, 170, and 171; the survey references are indicated thus: O.S.; all others are *A to Z*. The topographical clues are all straightforwardly keyed in to them, though they may take a little looking for – that is part of the game. I have always tried to give modern buildings the benefit of the doubt, and I have always been more responsive to townscape than to individual buildings. A few buildings and places, such as the Royal Festival Hall, which could hardly be left out but seemed to me to be not living up to their reputation, have gone into square brackets.

Everything in the book is accessible. Locked churches are out unless the keys are freely given. The vicar's wife of one Middlesex church (*not* in the guide) refused to let me in even after I had explained my harmless purpose: 'The plausible ones are always the worst,' she said.

This kind of experience is subhuman, and I have no wish to subject readers to it.* Private property is respected unless the owner regularly opens his house to the public – there are some superb eighteenth-century interiors in the West End, but they are highly inaccessible. However, public authorities, where they own a town or country house, I have considered fair game, for they are our servants as well as our masters. Outstanding works of art are mentioned in houses and the smaller galleries. But the masterpieces in the four main collections (National Gallery, Tate, British Museum, Victoria & Albert) would fill a book on their own, and I have not tried to describe them. On the other hand, the best monuments in Westminster Abbey, which is almost a national sculpture gallery, are described in detail. A list at the end of the book groups places and buildings by date and type for those who want to specialize.

This, quite obviously, is not a normal guide and is not trying to be one. If you want straightforward general information, the best bet is probably the *Blue Guide*. For architectural information, there is nothing to beat *The Buildings of England*; in writing this book I personally have been very glad that the series covers almost all of the area, with only Kent to come.

Finally, as the objects selected will make quite clear, the book has no barriers. I just don't believe in the difference between high- and lowbrow, between aristocracy and working class, between fine art and fine engineering. All are tilting-horses erected by paper men because they can't or daren't recognize the golden thread of true quality. This book is a record of what has moved me, between Uxbridge and Dagenham. My hope is that it moves you, too.

* On the same principle, many theatres are excluded because they discourage – without prohibiting – casual visitors. It seems too much of an imposition to ask visitors to endure a bad play in order to see a good auditorium.

Preface

For this new edition, no changes (apart from one or two minor corrections) have been made to Ian Nairn's irreplaceable and intensely personal text, as originally published in 1966.

Sadly and inevitably, a few whole entries, and a number of details elsewhere, are now out of date. All the sites have therefore been revisited and checked, and later information has been provided in the form of numbered notes at the end of relevant entries (all footnotes are the author's own). Additional material has been set in smaller type. The numbered notes are not intended as a complete record of developments and demolitions in London over the past twenty-odd years; there is material for a substantial new book on this alone. Their purpose is to draw attention to major differences, save readers from looking for buildings which have disappeared, and point the way to places which have become difficult to find. The aim is to enable a new generation of readers to enjoy seeing London as nearly as possible as Ian Nairn saw it twenty years ago. (Any opinions expressed or implied in the notes are, of course, those of the annotator, and would not necessarily have been shared by Ian Nairn.)

Some of the changes since 1966 are of a general nature, and are best dealt with here rather than in the main text.

In central London, many of the **churches** are open except, ironically, on Sundays. In the suburbs they are almost always locked, and the only reasonably sure way of seeing inside is to attend a service. The mention of a church interior, therefore, does not mean that access can still be gained to it on a casual visit. The notes occasionally give opening times, or warn of particular difficulties.

The survival rate of **pubs** is remarkable: only two losses in the whole book. This is not to say that they are quite the same places they were twenty years ago. Décor can be changed subtly by using well-worn fabric to preserve atmosphere; conversely décor can stay substantially the same and atmosphere mysteriously disappear. The notes draw attention to the more obvious changes: the most frequent is the knocking together of separate bars into one homogenized space.

Large-scale **cleaning** of major public buildings began in the early 1960s amid some controversy, and has continued ever since. The rawness of newly-scrubbed brick and stone has now been tempered by a decade or so of weathering and even, in some cases, of replacement grime. But readers should bear in mind that in 1966 many of the buildings described in this book were still covered by a thick layer of London soot, while a few were newly and glaringly white.

The **modern buildings**, necessarily, date mostly from the 1950s and 1960s; indeed nearly all of them had been included two years earlier in Ian Nairn's *Modern Buildings in London*. The period is now at the nadir of fashion in many circles, and some of the buildings themselves have not worn too well. But the examples chosen were the best of their date, and their reappearance here may help towards a further reappraisal.

Buildings put up since 1966 are very briefly described in the notes if they are adjacent to, or significantly affect, the 1966 entries. They represent only a very small selection of the enormous number built in London in the past two decades. Readers wishing to explore the subject further could start with the recent R.I.B.A. guide, *Modern British Architecture since 1945*, which is not as self-congratulatory as one might expect.

According to the Retail Price Index, **prices** are now between six-and-a-half and seven times what they were in the mid 1960s, but this is based on a selected shopping basket of items. Some prices have risen much more, particularly those for London property, which have lately reached such phenomenal levels as to threaten the economic and social cohesion of the metropolis.

Map references have been up-dated to the modern *London A to Z* standard edition, and to the Ordnance Survey 1:50,000 Landranger series.

For straightforward **general information**, including opening times, the *Blue Guide* is still available. It is up-dated and reissued regularly, and has generated a separate volume on museums and galleries. The newer Michelin green guide is less comprehensive but good value, with excellent coloured maps and plans. *The Buildings of England* is still incomparable for **architectural information** of all periods: the London volumes in print at the moment cover the cities of London and Westminster and the London boroughs south of the river, with north-west and north-east London still to come.

More has survived of Nairn's London than might have been expected when the book was first published, as the frenetic rebuilding of the 1960s and early 1970s gave way to a period of slower growth and increased concern for conservation. But there are signs that a new wave of rapid change is breaking, and that it may be timely to repeat the warning and invitation on the back cover of the original edition:

As this book is published, some of its entries are disappearing; go and see the rest quickly. Read, visit, look, assent or differ, agree or argue. What we do guarantee is that your reaction will not be one of indifference.

P.G.

Note on the Illustrations

The photographs for illustrations 1, 2, 3, 22, and 23 are by W. J. Toomey; those for illustrations 8 and 9 are by Eric de Maré and we thank the Gordon Fraser Gallery for permission to reproduce them; all other photographs are by the author.[1]

Numbers in square brackets in the text refer to the illustrations.

1. Photographs to illustrate changes since 1966 are by Geoff Howard.

Acknowledgements

TO THE 1988 EDITION

Even a project as modest as these few footnotes could not have been carried through without a great deal of help and guidance. I am particularly grateful to Bridget Cherry, Robert Thorne, Brian Glover, Sarah Hosking, Mr Geoffrey Hewlett, the Rt Hon. Timothy Raison, M.P., the Geographers' A–Z Map Co. Ltd, and many other corporate bodies and individuals for information, answers to queries, and/or access to buildings; to Tim and Ann Murphy and Roger and Janice O'Brien for hospitality and invaluable local knowledge; and to Mrs Peggy Warr for her immaculate typescript. Above all my thanks are due to Mrs Judy Nairn, without whose encouragement and help I could never have embarked on, let alone completed, the revision of Ian Nairn's book.

P.G.

Introduction

There are four hundred and fifty entries here: between them they define Europe's biggest city. And that is the only way to do it, because London as a single personality simply does not exist. It never has, at least from the moment when Edward the Confessor built his abbey on the marshes a couple of miles away from the original, homogeneous commercial city. All the attributes of the capital have piled on to this shallow basin of gravel like rugby players in a scrum, kicking and elbowing each other out of the way. And now with the pace of building hotted up and all the second-degree consequences working themselves out – the flood of the office workers is one, the flood of tourists is another – Central London has disintegrated. Units like the City or Fleet Street may still mean something, but by pushing out all the quiet, human places the planners and speculators have removed the only mortar which could bind them together. London is indeed a thousand villages; remove them and all that is left is a vast hulk peppered with spectacular buildings, quaint occasions, false sophistication and too many people in the Underground.

If there is a generalized sense of the capital – bright lights, red buses, swirling traffic – it is almost entirely due to the genius of John Nash, who in Regent Street gave the West End a trunk around which it could grow. Nash came from Lambeth, and he was every inch a cockney: tolerant, shrewd, cheerfully vulgar and with a remarkable eye for quick profit. Here in fact is the real basis for a coherent city – that is, its people. And a splendid, easy-going place they could make it too: a blend of Paris and Copenhagen. But everywhere the cockneys are pushed out and the cockney streets are pulled down – often with the best of sociological intentions. Just as topographical London is a vast twenty-mile saucer of people with a rim of low hills, so human London is a central goulash with its rightful inhabitants forming an unfashionable rim. The human essence of the city is now in places which are often nothing to look at: Brentford, Mitcham, Charlton, Tottenham, Plaistow, West Ham, Wembley. The old contract which bound clubman, chorus-girl and costermonger together to form a city has been torn up, and London has moved into a limbo in which professional and social contacts are scarifying and even the ordinary street contact is becoming unsympathetic. We are not yet on an American level of city-street unfriendliness, but this is only just around the corner.

My forecast may be too pessimistic: I hope so. I have lived in London for ten years and perhaps I am punch-drunk from pompous phrases in the City and neighing banalities in Chelsea. Certainly, one evening in a good cockney pub and the whole preposterous bunch of unspeakables floats off down the Thames to the Northern Outfall

Sewer. But what London desperately needs is a new Nash, a person with stature enough to see the city as a whole and humanity enough to see that it cannot possibly rediscover itself through grand gestures and centralization, but only through a multiplication of idiosyncratic and wildly different characters. Long live the thousand villages; long live the tolerant cockney spirit that allows them to coexist. London burnt in 1940 for the sake of tolerance, and the price was well worth it. It is burning again, but this time only to satisfy developers' greed, planners' inadequacy and official stupidity. We must put out the fires and start healing this great place with the love and understanding it needs. It is already three parts gone; for God's sake let us leave the rest alone, and help to make the city whole again.

1 City of London

Still as insular as if it were walled and gated. But, like all of Central
London, you feel that the character is shrinking away from a whole
city-pattern into isolated attractions which will eventually become as
phoney as the Tower. Meanwhile, there is a noble coherence between
City plan and City people – though it is hideously distended, with
three or four times as many workers as it ought to have, abandoned in
the evening and excruciating at lunch-time: if you want to eat anywhere
in comfort, do so before twelve thirty or after two. But the old City
places, where bombs, misplaced traditional or misguided modern
architecture has not got at them, are memorable: narrow, dark-
coloured, so that the occasional widening for a street or a City churchyard is something that you remember. The true City gent has a genuine
sobriety and discretion to match, best seen around the Stock Exchange,
which dovetails perfectly with the ribald slang of messenger-boys or
Billingsgate porters. But it is all slowly being flushed out by the alien
tide that flows in across London Bridge at 8.55 a.m. every Monday to
Friday; and, much more viciously, by the false idea that the upper
crust of the City has of itself. Clean the buildings, bleach the Wren
woodwork, pile on the civic banquets, but for God's sake don't actually
live there. Perhaps the new Barbican will alter things, but I doubt it:
the change has gone too deep. And when the last City pub goes gay,
and the last honest café or hairdresser has been leased away into
smartness, then the heart will have gone out of London. Because this
is the real metropolis: Westminster and the West End are just hangers-
on and could have been anywhere, but the City needs this particular
site. We are squandering its essence without a second thought, and in
one particular case – the cleaning of St Paul's – with everyone's good
wishes and a Lord Mayor's Fund.[1]

1. POSTSCRIPT 1987. There have been two radical changes to the City in the
past twenty years. The first is the transformation of the skyline, with the
National Westminster Bank and a forest of towers finally wresting dominance
from St Paul's. The second is the sudden loss of the river-based industry –
fish market, wharves, and warehouses – in the wake of which the lower part of
the City has been turned into an inhuman wilderness of office blocks, ranged
along an arterial road.
    The financial heart of the City retains much of its traditional character, in
spite of rebuilding, and in spite of the continual breaking open of the medieval
street pattern for widened roads and alien new piazzas. But it is still almost
entirely a place for work, becoming dormant every evening, and occupied at
weekends only by busloads of tourists. Early impressions are that the Barbican
has made a difference only by setting up a new alternative City alongside the
old one.

West view of St Paul's, with St Martin Ludgate   141 8J–K
Sir Christopher Wren, 1677–87

The way to come on St Paul's is along Fleet Street, and the way to go along Fleet Street is on top of a bus. That way, the dip down to Ludgate Circus and up again seems sharper. The railway viaduct, ugly in itself, does the same thing as the Lud Gate which stood on the site: it provides a check to the eye, indicating that the city centre is beyond. Whether the view would be better without it is a nice point. Probably it would, because the sight of St Paul's at the end is so grand that nothing should blur it.

Wren would probably have liked an academic formal approach. Luckily, the medieval street plan provides something far better. All the pomp is still there, but Ludgate Hill brushes past the west front at a slight angle. A closed vista is turned into an invitation to turn the corner and explore the whole building, not just to stop at one façade. Half way up, Wren put the gristly spire of St Martin Ludgate, one of the best and best-known examples of an architectural foil, balanced against the bulbous western towers and the immense dome behind. St Martin itself was untouched in the war, and is as full of atmosphere as an unrestored pub: dark luminous wood and rough plaster. It is a gauche design, with four giant columns clanking into the central space from the corners; but it is worth all the genteel light woodwork and frigid precision of restorations like St Vedast Foster Lane, and St Lawrence Jewry.

St Paul's   141 8L

Wren might have chosen grandeur, or drama or *terribilità* or excitement. Instead, there is overwhelming compassion, the common touch ennobled. No wonder that cockneys love it, and see it as a badge as well as a symbol. Here once and for all the principle of English freedom has been given spiritual form: licence and variety in the parts, conforming not by order but from free will. The necessity to combine a dome with a long, additive, Gothic-type nave may have played havoc with Wren's formal intentions★ but by doing so it went to the roots of his personality. Compromise was his nature, and in a sense far deeper than our present recourse to lowest common denominators. So each bay is both Gothic and classical, vigorously discrete and subordinate at the same time to the whole mass. So is each unit in each bay, so is each marvellously carved spray or cherub's head in each unit. All of St Paul's speaks individually and collectively at once: to all people and to this particular person: and this not by revelation as Hawksmoor or Soane – or Michelangelo at St Peter's – might have done, but by

★ His completely centralized design of 1673 would have been a miraculous toy. But could we have loved it?

inspired, judicious application. Because of its assiduous concern it floats, serene but not detached – the best kind of night-nurse – where St Peter's is still wound around with human passions. The dome is in an utter repose which transcends passion instead of ignoring it: the scale is huge and tiny at the same time. It is a stupendous, encompassing achievement of balanced feeling and maturity – and one that has come to the top again and again in this funny-shaped island just off Europe: Shakespeare's last plays, but also what England seems to have called out of people like Handel and T. S. Eliot. It is hard not to sound like a bad Churchillian parody, but in fact this is why we fought the war.

Because of this overriding humanity, and because soot and Portland stone work a funny magic on each other, St Paul's should never have been cleaned. The scrubbed parts show a small gain in clarity of detail and an immense loss in personality. This process of accumulated and misdirected good will is doubtless unstoppable, but it is sad that St Paul's of all places should have been chosen for this sacrifice of the spirit for the substance.[2]

Inside, the key to the whole design is in the segmental arches on the diagonal sides of the dome. The eye seizes on them straight away because everything else is orderly, in straight lines or semicircles. Technically, they provide part of the buttressing for the dome. Spiritually, they command the whole cathedral, as you realize when you walk up the central aisle towards the dome. The octagonal space finally bursts open, with each direction given the same weight as the other seven. The Anglican emphasis at the east end is quite clear – and is expressed admirably in the post-war *baldacchino* based on Wren's sketches. But it never dominates: one feels, without blasphemy, that the transepts and diagonals could hold a mosque or a Hindu temple. It is utterly Anglican – and very far from today's milk-and-water Anglicanism. Utterly un-Catholic, utterly un-totalitarian: a political and social gospel as well as a religious one. The details hold the same magic as the parts of the outside: that each unit is separate – the bays of the aisles, especially, crowned with a stone circle outlined in white plaster – so that you, in relation, are fallible and shrinking. Yet, at the same time, every unit adds up first arithmetically, in the sense that four bays are more impressive than two, and then geometrically, using the pun of a geometrical progression $1:2:4:16:256$ to represent the leaps of Wren's brilliant mathematical mind. The odds square themselves as each level of meaning opens up, and the progression is endless. And all the time it works inwards too. The space could be a hundred miles long: the carved detail gets perpetually sharper and more personal. The whole building comes down to the tensed bands of foliage between the pilasters on the gigantic nave piers: and the viewer expands to the global tolerance proposed by the whole building. It is an unforgettable contract.

Monuments

What a mess of marble. No wonder we are now lumbered with abstract art, after this prodigious display of incapacity. Group after group brings on nausea, boredom or the giggles; and almost all of it paid for from public funds. Flaxman's *Nelson* in the south transept stands out as a person amongst all the pudding-faces; but it is devalued by the posturing underneath (fed-up lion, Britannia, two aspiring boys). Our attempts today certainly cost less but are really no better. It is a terrible proof that committee or exchequer cannot summon up art to order.

Wellington's funeral carriage (Gottfried Semper, 1852)[3]

The crypt is not a separate shrine like a Gothic crypt: it is simply a device to keep the rest of the building up, and there is a good deal more marble down there. But there is also, right at the west end, the one object in St Paul's worth a special visit: Wellington's funeral carriage. It weighs eighteen tons and was drawn by twelve black horses, four by three. An implacable expression of Victorian grief, bowed down with heavy ornament, drum-rolls implicit in every scroll. It looks as powerful and unstoppable as a railway engine; but it was designed not by Brunel, but by the progressive German architect Gottfried Semper, one of Prince Albert's favourites.

2. Work has begun on the north side to clean off another twenty years' accumulation of London grime. The old mixture of soot and stone can still be studied nearby on St Martin-within-Ludgate.

3. Wellington's funeral carriage has been reclaimed by his family and is at Stratfield Saye House, Hampshire. As consolation, the crypt now contains the great carved wooden model of Wren's 1673 design for the cathedral.

East view of St Paul's, from Watling Street   141 8L

The rebuilt and widened Watling Street is lined by slabs of dead mutton, but it leads to a spectacular view of St Paul's. It points at the heart of the building, unguarded by any façade – the join of choir and transepts. Directly on the axis is the tower of St Augustine, one of Wren's simplest. The rest of the church disappeared in the blitz, but this battered fragment remains, cradled by the cathedral as though it was a human victim not an architectural one. The tower will soon be attached to the new St Paul's Choir School, and with care this need not destroy the loving mother-and-child effect.[4]

4. Any building attached to the tower was bound to impair the effect to some degree, but the new school was carefully designed to fit unobtrusively into St Paul's Churchyard.

'Financial Times' Building (Bracken House), Cannon Street
Sir Albert Richardson, 1959   141 8–9L

What a funny business. From a distance it looks like one more City
hulk. From the equivalent distance of my own preconceptions it seems
unbelievable that Sir Albert Richardson could have turned up trumps
with a modern office block. Yet the conviction grows with every visit
that Bracken House is a friendly, logical, lovable personality – and
there is certainly plenty of faceless stuff around to check by. The
classical details are reduced to classical essences such as pier and
lintel, as they might be in a Victorian warehouse. The wholly alien
combination of red sandstone and brown brick is effortlessly mellow;
and the indentations of the bays are the kind of handle the ordinary
passer-by or user needs to convert a building into a person. Sir Albert's
genial eccentricity is breathing all over it; but if you track down his
firm's other London buildings on the strength of this one, you will be
in for a terrible disappointment.

St Mary Aldermary, Queen Victoria Street   141 8M
Sir Christopher Wren, completed 1682

Wren treated Gothic as though it were a cantankerous old aunt: with
affectionate disrespect. This late Gothic church was rebuilt after the
Fire, with money which was left for the purpose on condition that the
old style was kept. The outside is sober enough, and the arcades would
pass muster in any abbey. But thereafter it is every man for himself.
Wren superimposed a froth of fan vaulting and saucer domes, far
better than the eighteenth century could manage when it was playing
at Gothic, and harmonized them perfectly with his cherubs and foliage,
which he contrived to introduce into the spandrels above the arcade.
The whole concoction is topped up by the outrageous expedient of
leaning the east end skew to follow the street-line, popping a plaster
roundel in the middle of the vault and leaving the unequal sides to sort
themselves out how they will. The oddest thing is in fact just how late
Gothic the result is, especially in the aisles. If the Vertues had thought
of plaster vaults, this is what they would have done with them. Here
is exactly the same bite into space, and the same sharpness. The old
aunt had her way in the end; they do.

Meeting of Cornhill, Lombard Street,   142 8A
King William Street, Queen Victoria Street,
Poultry, Prince's Street, Threadneedle Street

This roomy seven-way junction, without even a name to it, is the dead
centre of the City, just as Piccadilly Circus is the centre of Westminster.
To make such a vortex twice looks very like carelessness, though the
fault here is Wren and his jejune ideas of Baroque planning. In fact it is
an exciting place, with buses whistling off at all angles and a pedestrian
platform in front of the Royal Exchange to look at the traffic jams. The

trouble is that the City has no Piazza del Duomo to balance it. Varieties of official architecture nod in and out with well-rounded emptiness: the Mansion House (1739–53), the Royal Exchange (1841) and Sir Herbert Baker's evil superstructure to the Bank of England (1930s) which out-faces Soane's screen wall underneath. They all pay their respects to the vortex, not to each other, so that it would now be folly to try to convert this into a pedestrian square. Other places, other solutions.[5]

5. A pedestrian square was to have formed part of the Mansion House Square scheme, designed by Mies van der Rohe and finally rejected after the Prince of Wales had referred to Mies's proposed tower block as 'another glass stump'.

Bank to Monument, below ground   142 8A

Discreet notices at the entrance to Bank station suggest that you can reach the District and Circle lines. And so you can; but the route involves corridors, one of L.T.'s cavernous lifts, a walk along the whole length of Bank station and out at the other end, an escalator which is perversely going up, not down, and then another stretch of corridor. It may seem to be a nuisance or one of London's odd jokes, according to whether you are in a hurry or not. But there is no reason why it could not be dramatized to become as impressive as one of the alley sequences near Cornhill. The raw materials are all there.

(If you want to *catch* a train, nip down to Cannon Street and pick up the District and Circle at Mansion House. To add to the confusion, this station is at the juncture of Cannon Street and Queen Victoria Street, while the station actually by the Mansion House is Bank.)

St Stephen Walbrook[6]   142 8A
Sir Christopher Wren, 1672–7

God's crossword puzzle, Ximenes-by-the-Mansion-House. The clues have been so beautifully analysed by Nikolaus Pevsner in the *Outline of European Architecture* that there is no point in paraphrase. Wren here combined four church plans in one. St Stephen's is a domed space, a nave and aisles, an even array of columns around a central hall, and a Greek cross, all at once. What it lacks is something which will tear your heart out, and for that you need to go a few yards farther east, to St Mary Woolnoth. The coolness and balance at once created the intellectual marvel and prevented it from making the final leap. 'Spatial polyphony', as Dr Pevsner said, but worthy not of Purcell, who never forgot his heart, but of J. S. Bach, who sometimes mislaid his. Yet it is not heartless but heart-free, in a landscape of detachment where neither pain nor pleasure has any meaning. It is, surely, one of the mansions – though it could never be mine.

6. Reopened after restoration in 1987. It now houses the controversial Henry Moore altar-stone, described by its advocates as a 'mysterious, ethereal white presence' and by its detractors as resembling 'a giant piece of Camembert on a cheese-board'.

St Mary Woolnoth   142 8B
Nicholas Hawksmoor, 1714–30

This is the one City church that you must go in. By comparison almost
all Baroque churches on the Continent seem overloaded and hysterical.
Here, intellect and emotion are exactly matched; the whole man in the
designer was stretched to its uttermost. And the viewer is stretched
too.

Outside, Hawksmoor has taken up the awkward wedge-shaped site
so easily that you don't realize until afterwards just how odd the
building is. In other words, it transcends originality. It is the mind,
afterwards, which asks what on earth two small towers are doing on
top of an oblong, columned temple on top of prodigious rustication.

Inside [1], there is no hindsight: everything is immediate and endur-
ing. It is a square inside a square, the inner square top lit with great
lunettes concentrating everything down towards the centre and you in
it. It feels like being on the hot end of a burning glass, and it is all
done not by overpowering ornament but in purely architectural terms,
through solidity of space and resilient depth of carving. Space, here,
is made so tangible that you can experience, for the price of a bus ticket
to the City, the super-reality of the mystics or mescalin, and even be
able to see how this marvellous man achieved it – for example, by
projecting the entablature in front of the three majestic Corinthian
columns which celebrate each corner. The altar is in an arched recess at
the east end, but it is a mere direction-indicator. The real focus of the
church is yourself, wherever you are standing. If the Sainte Chapelle
or Die Wies transports outwards, this forces inwards, quintessentially
Protestant. You are forced in through yourself, and this is not a
romantic view but the strictest spatial analysis.[7]

7. The recent sumptuous restoration, with star-spangled ceiling, distracts the
eye a little.

St Mary Abchurch, Abchurch Lane   142 9B
Sir Christopher Wren, 1681–6

This is one of Wren's happiest, outside and in, and it got through the
war without serious damage. Simple brick outside, with a simple tower,
and more successful than some of his even-tempered attempts at
Baroque gusto. The inside [2] is audacious; Wren simply inscribed a
vast circle on the roof of his almost square box and allowed the corners
to work out how they would. It looks like the result of a scribble on a
menu card, and it works perfectly – for the unexciting space is given
an elegant form without interfering with the flowering of woodwork
underneath. The reredos is one of Grinling Gibbons's documented
works, made for the church, and fills its wall with regal unself-
consciousness; the sumptuous pulpit has an oversize top whose nearest
relative is a tricorn hat. The ceiling painting is dark, almost grisaille,
in the same style as those at St Paul's. Everything inside this apparently

demure box is a little bit larger than life and has room to breathe –
whereas an Italian designer of the same time would have crammed in
twice as much detail and blurred the effect.

Grocers' Hall Garden[8] 142 8A

This consists of two unpromising entrances marked IN and OUT within
a few yards of the middle of the City – on the west side of Princes
Street, opposite the Bank of England. Once in, or out, there is a
crescent-shaped courtyard, with the rich 1889-Jacobean of the Grocers' Hall all around. In the middle, a lush, well-kept lawn. There is
no special refinement in all this and there does not need to be, because
the shock of plain grass is enough. As surreal as cows coming down
Cornhill; and incredibly English, in its insistence on country in the
middle of city.

8. Most of Grocers' Hall burned down in 1965. The replacement, which
presents a blank stone face to a yard with no lawn, is not worth a detour.

Tivoli Corner, Bank of England 142 8A
Sir Herbert Baker, 1936

If the law concerned itself with aesthetics, Herbert Baker should have
been indicted for his work at the Bank of England. But this, at least,
will add up on the positive side of the final balance sheet. The Tivoli
Corner (Lothbury and Princes Street) was a proud ordonnance of
Corinthian columns, with Soane in his most academic mood. Too
proud, maybe, for there is no love in the carving. Anyway, Sir Herbert
burrowed through in his whiskery way to provide a rotunda which
eases the pedestrian's job. The centre is open, a roundel of pure air in
the heart of impure or at least compromised air. There is an inscription
around it from the Bank of England, saying 'how good we are to
give you this', but never heed that. This tiny circlet intensifies and
transfigures the sky in a way that a complete horizon never could. It
is the intense, imploring view from the prison-yard, and to be able to
share the experience without suffering the sentence is quite a dis-
pensation.

St Margaret Lothbury 142 7A
Sir Christopher Wren, 1686–1701

Most City churches have Wren fittings. This one has its fittings sited
with real drama, to charge up the even-tempered space. They were
mostly imported in the nineteenth century from demolished churches,
so that the present arrangement is in fact due to Victorian sensitivity
as well as Wren. The set piece is an openwork screen, resting on
openwork barley-sugar columns, made of two incredibly thin wooden
spirals winding round each other. In the middle, a sumptuous eagle is
hung up as though it were a poulterer's pride and joy. On the left-
hand side an equally sumptuous pulpit and sounding board has been

thrown against it. It is more like a declamatory aria than a church interior. The south aisle, shut off with screens, is like a small church in itself, a sweet-box full of goodies. The tiny font has a tiny wooden cover where the old near-pagan horror of serpents tied by their necks to a central stem has been pushed away into cherubs' heads on the ends of scrolls. Lucky, wholesome Restoration England. And on the west wall there is a bust by Nollekens of Mrs Simpson (1795), up to his best standard – a mature, understanding face with the kind of character that doesn't need beauty to help it along.

Stock Exchange[9]   142 7–8B
Thomas Allason, 1853, and J. J. Cole, 1882

To feel the City contrast at its sharpest, go from the traffic vortex at Mansion House to Bartholomew Lane, a quiet street at the back of the Bank of England. A quiet cul-de-sac opens off it – Capel Court. And at the end is a demure stuccoed front, one bay wide, which is the main entrance to the City's most important building, the Stock Exchange. This is reserve taken to the farthest limit; and it is only half of the story. The public gallery has an unprepossessing entrance in Threadneedle Street, apparently unrelated, which seems to be just a set of office stairs. Work your way through and you come out suddenly high up above what seems to be dark-coated bedlam or Piccadilly Underground in the rush hour. Three thousand five hundred members are rushing around a huge hall the size of a station concourse, and every one of them is dressed between dark blue and black. It looks chaotic but isn't, just like Nature: an unregimented and delicately balanced pattern runs through it, with the jobbers seated round the columns and the brokers moving between them. It has a life of its own, supra-human: the kind of collective vitality that corporations and local authorities try in vain to create by shouting about it. Here it comes unasked because everyone has a real stake in things.

(The gallery is open from 10.30 to 3.15 – when public business finishes – and you are not hustled. Those remote hurrying figures down below can be seen close up in the long Victorian probity of the Stock Exchange Grill,[10] across Throgmorton Street.)

9. The old Stock Exchange, described here, was demolished in the late 1960s. There is nothing demure about the new one, on the same site, but taking up about ten times as much volume. The Big Bang of 1986 ended the distinction between jobbers and brokers and made the trading floor redundant (it is due to be closed by the time this book comes out). Away from public gaze, over five thousand members buy and sell by telephone and computer.
10. It has been modernized, and is now the Long Room of the Throgmorton Restaurant.

City Club, 19 Old Broad Street   142 7C
Philip Hardwick, 1833

It looks like Wren, stuccoed and relaxed, turning the bend of the street with an assurance that is partly due to it being slightly convex on a concave site – the same order of conjuring trick as the entasis on a Greek column. It is in fact by up-to-the-minute Philip Hardwick, designer of the Euston arch – which ought to be in this book but isn't because of the actions of blind men in high places. Here he forgot fashion and simply built to the spirit of the place. This is the best possible kind of tradition; equivalent to the dark suits, dark pubs and the queer classless continuity of the City's professionals, as distinct from the chinless wonders who are 'something in the City'. As the headquarters of the City Club it is exactly right and it must resist all the current pressures for redevelopment. There could not be a more telling contrast with the Royal Exchange, only a few yards away and designed in those same 1830s, which was the first building to put on a City style as a fashion rather than an instinctive way of feeling.

(It is now in danger of demolition: I hope it still stands by the time the book comes out.)[11]

11. It was to have been demolished to make room for the National Westminster Bank tower, but in the end it was reprieved, cleaned and restored, and now nestles at the tower's foot. Natwest (by Richard Seifert & Partners, 1972–81) is the tallest office building in Britain at present, although it may be out-topped before long by a tower at Canary Wharf on the Isle of Dogs. It is also, whatever one thinks about its height, a spectacular piece of engineering, with unimaginable tons of building hung above empty space.

Cornhill alleys   142 8B

The space between Cornhill and Lombard Street is the only part of the City where the sequence of alleys really works as an alternative to the diesel-choked streets instead of being no more than a convenient short cut. The best entry is through Ball Court, next to 39 Cornhill. There are notices pointing to Simpson's Tavern, but better than any notice is the low front of the tavern itself, giving a come-on from the end of the Court. The restaurant here is one of the old school: dark ceilings, dark woodwork, marble-topped tables, high-backed seats, and polished brass.[12] Beyond, the alley slips away to one side and joins another. This is officially Castle Court, unofficially the high street of this car-free village, running parallel to Cornhill, weaving in and out of lavatory bricks and pompous pilasters: and always full of people, even in its most bewildering twists and turns. This is no quaint survival. Behind St Michael Cornhill is its market place: the church-yard, apparently a hundred miles away from the street, where you can sit quietly surrounded by offices, the Jamaica Bars – a good City wine house – and the thundering Bach-like variation on Magdalen Tower which Hawksmoor provided for St Michael in 1718.

12. The marble-topped tables have gone, but the restaurant has kept its atmosphere and its quintessential City clientele.

St Peter Cornhill   142 8B
Sir Christopher Wren, 1677–87

Three completely different personalities inextricably sewn into the
City, the opposite of the isolated-monument-on-a-pedestal. The first
view from Cornhill would be enough: three windows sliding away
from the street, shops crowding all round, and only the porch to tell
you that it isn't a special kind of tobacconist's. At the back, down St
Peter's Alley, the City's other face: a tiny churchyard, walled in with
buildings; seats and plane trees; and a brick tower so chubbily domestic
that you wonder how all these other tall buildings have strayed into
Beccles or Southwold. The third view, in Gracechurch Street, is best
of all. The east end turns up sandwiched between offices and looking
like a special kind of office in itself; one of Wren's happiest inventions,
three-above-five, with a wonderful freehand amplitude that suggests
that designer and mason thought it up between them over a pint.

Leadenhall Market   142 8C
Sir Horace Jones, 1881

A beautiful piece of Victorian planning, which needs to be noticed and
scheduled before somebody sweeps it away in an idle moment.[13] A
cross-shaped arcade in the centre of a block – a kind of London
Galleria, with four stone-and-glass fronts with grand lettering and
grand carving of capitals and corbels: all the life that was missing
from Victorian official monuments. Nothing could be neater or more
eloquent. During the day it is a riot of fish and fowl with row after row
of turkeys and chickens on hooks, right up to the cornice and the glass
roof. A cornucopia, to set against the computers and the nine-to-five
stint: where the rest of the City may make you feel small, this is larger
than life.[14]

13. Nobody has.
14. It has acquired an astonishing neighbour in the shape of Richard Rogers's
new Lloyd's building. The interior – a soaring, narrow, glass-vaulted atrium,
criss-crossed by escalators and surrounded by blue-carpeted galleries – can be
seen from the visitors' gallery, 10–2.30 weekdays. The exterior – a futurist's
vision of exposed ducts, pipework, and lift-shafts, with stairs and other services
in protruding steel canisters – can be seen at any time, but it may be years
before we are sufficiently recovered from the visual shock to make a considered
aesthetic judgement.

St Helen Bishopsgate, doorcases   142 7C
c. 1640

A funny medieval church, with parish and nunnery naves side by side;
and a funny site off Bishopsgate, with its churchyard frowned over by

a mountain of glazed white tile.[15] But no more than that. What is worth coming to see is the pair of doorcases inside, to the west and south doors. No lecturer could have arranged a neater contrast in style and in being. Both come from the uneasy 1630s or 40s. The south door, with the royal arms on it, is a jolly bit of city merchants' classicism, of a piece with the Jacobean tombs on either side of it. The west door is patrician and correctly Italian, reflecting the new Court taste. So king and parliament glare at one another. That is the contrast in style. But the burghers' door is hackneyed and weary within its style, whilst the 'royal' door is electrified, just as Inigo Jones's buildings are electrified. The proud Corinthian columns and scrolly pediment quiver with energy, as touchy as Charles himself, but without any weakness. It is a piercing exposition of a temper which put up only a handful of buildings.

15. Now also by an even taller mountain of sheer grey-blue glass: the Commercial Union building, chastest and most refined of the City's skyscrapers (by Gollins, Melvin, Ward & Partners, 1964–9).

St Ethelburga Bishopsgate   142 7C
One of the sweetest things in the City: a little medieval church sitting up as pert as a sparrow or a typist between two monuments to commerce. Five storeys of Victorian fuss on one side, the vast pre-war Bank of Indo-China on the other side.[16] And St Ethelburga's charm is augmented, not impaired, by the contrast – a pointer to what to do with old buildings when the environment takes a big leap upwards. The inside is unremarkable – just a simple, villagey nave and aisle – which perhaps is the most remarkable thing of all, here.

16. The five storeys of Victorian fuss have been replaced by a severe eight-storey grid of white concrete. The Bank of Indo-China is now the Indo-Suez Bank. The church is open only on Tuesdays and Thursdays.

Spanish and Portuguese Synagogue, Bevis Marks   142 7D
Joseph Avis, 1700
A quiet courtyard behind the street (usually locked – go to the vestry in Heneage Lane) and, once inside, a great luminous room, compassionate light streaming in through big clear-glass windows on to a set of curly brass chandeliers from Amsterdam that are almost at eye level. Nothing has fretted or worried it for two hundred and fifty years, and the force of undisturbed goodness is as tangible as the marbling on the gallery pillars. The designer was a Quaker who gave his fee to the congregation, and this is exactly what the building conveys: that the real parts of all religions are identical.

St Katharine Cree, Leadenhall Street   142 8D
1628–31

An urgent, bizarre hybrid of classical and Gothic, newly restored after
a period when its whole future was in doubt. Outside, the building has
those weird Venetian windows with Gothic tracery which cropped
up occasionally in the mid 1600s (e.g. at Berwick-upon-Tweed and
Goudhurst). But here they are complicated by overwrought blocking
in the lintels – this is true mannerism, not a stylistic bungle. And inside,
the bulgy classical arcades, whose entasis really means something and
whose soffits with rosettes stamped in them like telegrams really mean
something, lead to a creepy spidery vault, which holds the styles in a
tenuous balance. The appearance would better fit an early Jesuit
church anywhere on the Continent, but the edginess would not: this
church, built by Archbishop Laud, is Anglo-Catholic in the exact
sense. The inside effect is blurred now, with offices in the aisles and
the rest a *mélange* of fittings; but that is better than demolition: and
among the oddments is a memorable set of stations of the cross,[17] by
Arnold Daghani, a Rumanian artist now living in Israel and who had
been in a concentration camp. Done purely with the shape of the cross
and sets of hands, the integrity shines out in spite of the thin drawing –
the exact opposite of Cocteau's sophisticated doodles in the French
church at Leicester Square.

17. They have disappeared, all but one, presumed lost or stolen.

Aldgate   142 8E

One of the most dramatic contrasts in London. Just when the City
seems to be getting to its most crowded and correct, along Fenchurch
Street and Leadenhall Street, the whole thing falls away. In a few
yards the bowler hats have gone, the buildings – shoddy but very
expressive – house second-hand goods and small-scale tailors. The
streets have stalls like Tubby Isaacs's in Goulston Street, selling eels,
inscribed: 'We lead, others follow'. This is the East End with a bang,
and just around the corner are some of the roughest streets in Stepney.[18]
At the other end of Aldgate East is another moving change: the split
of Commercial and Whitechapel Roads – one going to the docks and
the estuary, the other pointed straight at the heart of East Anglia, those
long miles beyond Newmarket. It is only a traffic block now, but it
could be marvellous, given town artists and not just town planners.
Half way along on the south side is the Hoop and Grapes, a lovable
survival of the years just after the Fire. The inside, long, low and dark,
is in the old style too.

18. The City is showing signs of spilling over into Aldgate, but hasn't yet
extinguished its essential character. Tubby Isaacs's stall, complete with its
famous inscription, is still triumphantly *in situ*, a reassuring sight in a changing
and inconstant world.

LOW ROAD: BLACKFRIARS TO THE TOWER

The Black Friar, Queen Victoria Street   14I 9J
H. Fuller Clark, 1897

This is a late-nineteenth-century equivalent of the Soane Museum,
with mirrors and deception everywhere. It reaches a climax in the
Snack Bar at the back of the Saloon, with a barrel-vaulted alcove in
which real views through to the bar are expertly balanced against
multiple reflections. It is said to be one of the masterpieces of London,
and it would be if someone like Mackintosh had been the designer.
But unhappily it is tainted with a particularly musty imagination which
has clouded the space like a bad pint of bitter. The theme of bibulous
friars is flogged to death – each item inscribed 'by Henry Poole R.A.' –
the frieze is crowded with sententious axioms, the walls look like very
old gorgonzola. It is really not wild enough, always flirting with Art
Nouveau and never going the limit. When the pressure of friardom
lets up the effect is much better and also more Art Nouveau, like the
little bar on the corner. But much worth seeing, in any case: there is
nothing else like it.

Apothecaries' Hall, Blackfriars Lane   14I 9K

Nowhere better to see one colour of London's spectrum. The outside
is a heavy-lidded brick building overlooked by the new *Times* offices[19]
and nudged in front by the same viaduct which makes such a bewildering place out of Ludgate Circus. Under the entrance arch there is
complete serenity, yellow stucco unrolling itself with all the time in
the world around a courtyard. You could walk all day in New York
and not find this kind of contrast, which is one of the ways that cities
stay sane. You enjoy the calm after the hubbub; but you also enjoy the
hubbub after the calm. Maybe New Towns should have oases of noise
just as this is an oasis of quiet. The buildings are seventeenth-century
underneath, and were given their present bland covering in 1786.

19. Now Continental Bank House. *The Times* moved out to the Grays Inn
Road, and was last heard of in Wapping.

St Benet, Upper Thames Street[20]   14I 9K–L
Sir Christopher Wren, 1677–85

Or St Benet Paul's Wharf, which is where the stone was unloaded for
the Cathedral. This is probably Wren's most lovable church, and may
be the one which came nearest to his own modest personality. There
is absolutely no ostentation, yet, because of Wren's breadth of feeling,
there is no artificial thin-lipped restraint either. 'Humble brick', made
great through true humility: plain windows, hipped roofs that might
have come from an estate cottage, only an occasional sure-footed swag
of flowers for punctuation. It is now a Welsh church, and the inside is
kept simple and reverent, without any of the showiness of some of the
post-war rebuildings. So a piece of real, justifiable showiness is all the

more impressive when it happens: the door to the tower as you go out –
royal arms and doorcase combined into a superb piece of rhetoric –
everything expressed through the surface, yet everything beneath the
surface expressed too.

20. Now generally known as St Benet, Paul's Wharf, although Paul's Wharf
has disappeared. Virtually inaccessible from Upper Thames Street, which has
been realigned and runs through a tunnel, it is best approached from Queen
Victoria Street, opposite Godliman Street. The redevelopment all round has
left it in an isolated, uncomfortable position, with an elevated road whisking
round it. It is usually locked. The woodwork inside was left unstained when
the church was redecorated after a fire in 1971, and this may spoil the interior
for some visitors.

St Mary Somerset, Upper Thames Street   141 9L
Nominally Sir Christopher Wren, 1686–94

The church has gone, and the tower itself is plain; but, my goodness,
what a fiery headpiece for compensation. Four obelisks and four urns
jostling each other like jungle plants trying to reach the sunshine – the
man who goes native in Tahiti after thirty years in a bank. The design
has a force and an urgency a long way removed from Sir Christopher's
usual limpidity. It was one of the last of the city churches to be built,
and it might be a fair guess to attribute it to Hawksmoor, who was
then Wren's assistant.

Queenhythe   141 9M

The working riverside is almost inaccessible, except down slits between
warehouses with a few inches of water at the end of them. But here
there is a tiny inlet, and the result is a kind of water-square, with
warehouses on three sides, very Venetian, with the oily Thames lapping
away at old foundations [4]. Everything is urgent, and visibly expressed – the opposite of Tilbury or the styling of B.R.'s diesel
locomotives, where everything is coated with a film of unreality. Best
to see it from the west side (Abbey Wharf) where Bankside Power
Station – another slice of unreality – is out of the view. Best to reach
it from Upper Thames Street down a tiny slit called Coffee House
Lane. It smells not of urine but of coffee and spices from the warehouses.[21]

21. Not very Venetian now, with bland red-brick offices instead of warehouses.
Abbey Wharf and Coffee House Lane have been buried under new buildings.
A faint hint of the old riverside atmosphere can be caught a few yards further
west, by the Samuel Pepys Inn.

St Michael Paternoster Royal, College Street
St James Garlickhythe, Garlick Hill   141 9M and 142 9A
Sir Christopher Wren, 1686–94, steeple 1715;
and 1674–87, steeple 1713

This is one of the few parts of London where you can still get an
inkling of what Wren was about with his steeples. These two are almost
twins, the same game of diminishing stages played with evenly spaced
columns in St Michael, coupled corner columns in St James. The top
of the dome of St Paul's just gets into the picture and looks like a big
brother playing games with the youngsters. St Mary Somerset erupts
with its pinnacles down Upper Thames Street, the Monument crackles
away on the skyline in the other direction, and St Mary-le-Bow peeps
in with an inimitable gesture at the end of Garlick Lane, the steeple
far more elegant when half-concealed than clinically dissected in full
view up in Cheapside. What a city it must have been with every view
inflected, the steeples bigger than the houses and St Paul's much bigger
than either.[22]

St James has just been restored – and well;[23] but with Wren this is
no substitute for three hundred years of atmosphere. What is worth a
look is the pair of curly, openwork columns helping to keep up the
west gallery – a precocious use of iron for structure as well as ornament.

St Michael is still unattended and needs watching, for oily attempts
have already been made to remove it.[24] Since the war, it has been given
a stupid opened-out approach, with a pair of weak buildings giving
servile nods across a small desert called Whittington Garden. Ta very
much. The real City spirit is seen better in 21–2 College Hill, which
runs up to Cannon Street: two riotous doorways, one seventeenth-
century, the other probably Victorian; raucous faces and a cascade
of fruit. By comparison, today's City architects and sculptors have
forgotten how to live.

22. The townscape is much impaired by the crush of large new buildings:
neither St Paul's, nor St Mary Somerset, nor the Monument is now visible
from St James Garlickhythe.
23. Its south side has since been cruelly exposed by the dual carriageway.
24. They did not succeed; it is in use as the church of the Missions to Seamen.

Skinners' Hall, Dowgate Hill   142 9A
William Jupp, c. 1790

A late-eighteenth-century front of perfect discretion, like the centre-
pieces of Bedford Square but better done. The kind of imagination
which can get a standard design absolutely right is just as worthwhile
as the more flamboyant variety. The main part is No. 8; No. $8\frac{1}{2}$ is an
archway [5], given a simple plaster vault which again is perfectly
detailed. At the end of it is a tiny arcaded courtyard with Skinners'
Hall proper, a seventeenth-century building, on the other side.[25] You
can look in but not get in, and this somehow increases the effect rather

than spoiling it. Looking back down the passage, the traffic could be a mile away. This alternation of extreme bustle and extreme quiet is the quintessence of the City, or what's left of it.

25. The outer gate of the archway is normally locked.

St Magnus Martyr, Adelaide House, and the clock, Lower Thames Street
Sir Christopher Wren, 1671–85

142 9B

St Magnus has one of Wren's most feminine steeples, tucked away next to Billingsgate and under London Bridge. Adjacent, and much taller, is the sheer, crude backside of Adelaide House, built in 1924. So far, this is just a lucky accidental contrast, though one which the City could easily multiply with a little forethought. But what makes it special is the clock: a great face on a great scrolly bracket, dated 1709. It converts the huge cleft of air into inhabited space, the oddest kind of sympathetic frame. It could not be more effective if it appeared in the most picture-postcard view of olde London, replete with cobbled alleys and bow-fronted shops.

The Monument
Sir Christopher Wren and Robert Hooke, 1671–7

142 9B

It is indeed *the* Monument, in the true Roman line. Only the Restoration could have produced it – the short few years when ceremonial was not something apart but was at the same time larger than life and not just an enlargement of domestic forms. A century later, Caius Gabriel Cibber's allegorical relief would have gone frigid: here it grows out of the stone like the proud curl of the acanthus frames and the grave lettering. The stone itself has come alive, and it needs no spiritual gymnastics to imagine it breathing. There are three hundred and eleven steps to the top, without a halting-place; the view makes most sense to a stranger in that – unlike most London views – it shows how the city is completely formed by the river yet has turned its back on it. To anyone who knows London, it is a prose transcription of what can be apprehended poetically from Bankside or Tower Bridge approach.[26]

26. Today it also provides an eye-to-eye confrontation with a selection of the City's tower blocks.

Billingsgate, Lower Thames Street[27]

148 1C

For a few streets east of the Monument, the City of London becomes a real direct working city instead of a vast warren of office workers sitting on their fannies. Fish is what does it, and you can guarantee the townscape and the back chat by the sharp clean smell, as good as a seaside holiday. Sniff before you walk. The market itself, fussy outside and noble inside, is at the bottom end, lately spoilt by the wanton demolition of the Coal Exchange and by the over-wide road due any year now. But up the hill, the streets and alleys are undisturbed. Men with wonderful, diverse faces are cutting up fish or fishy things (blocks of ice, for example), there's a spare eel or two in the street and lots of used fish-boxes. People being different, and the place as a whole having the same direct connexion with life ('See, I work in London and I do this') as the old parts of Genoa or Naples, but without the squalor which has wrongly been equated with this kind of plan. The best bit is probably the lane which runs from Botolph Lane to the west end of St Mary-at-Hill. Market caffs which are a good place for fish and chips (one snack bar rests unselfconsciously in an old City churchyard in Monument Street). If ladies want to know whether they have genuine sex appeal instead of one of fashion's counterfeits, this is a good place to find out.

27. Abandoned by the fish trade (the market moved to the Isle of Dogs in 1982), and loomed over by a misshapen mass of blue glass, Billingsgate looks battle-scarred, defeated, and very sad. Faint, ghostly fish-smells lingered around it for a time, but they have now been driven out by the odour of masonry dust. It is being converted into offices – what else? – and offices have swamped all the little streets up to the Monument.

St Mary-at-Hill, Lovat Lane   142 9C
Sir Christopher Wren, 1670–76

A Wren church as it should be, not genteel with light woodwork and scoutmaster-saints. The architecture is nothing, here, even though it is one of Wren's most interesting plans, given a foppish restoration in 1847: the fittings are everything. Old dark wood gleams in the light, a magnificent pulpit rears up into Wren's domed space, magnificent iron sword-rests make curly patterns against the clear glass. But the lion and unicorn guarding the way to the altar have *VR* carved on them; much of this work is early Victorian, carved by W. Gibbs Rogers – the City church tradition just linking with the City pub tradition before the Gothic Revival torpedoed it.[28]

28. Some of the woodwork has been gilded. The lion and unicorn now guard the organ-loft.

33–5 Eastcheap   142 9C
R. L. Roumieu, 1877

Victorian wildness can come from half a dozen causes, from mere fashion to cantankerousness. But this is truly demoniac, an Edgar Allan Poe of a building [20]. It is the scream that you wake on at the end of a nightmare. Like Poe, and unlike Horace Walpole or a modern detective novel, the horror is no game. Acutely pointed arches shriek away in front of the windows, the wall shrinks back in half a dozen varieties of terrified chamfer. Demolition is in the air; but it must be preserved[29] – not as an oddity, but as a basic part of human temperament, and one which doesn't often get translated into architecture.

29. It has been, so far.

French Ordinary Court   142 9D

Number 42 Crutched Friars, near Fenchurch Street Station, is one of
the best eighteenth-century houses left in the City, with a swagger
steak-and-oyster doorway. Beside it a hole leads into French Ordinary
Court, neither French nor ordinary. It is in effect a big and very
dark wedge-shaped room carved out under the railway tracks, full of
mysterious and seductive smells (spices? scent?) from bonded warehouses. A fine and private place; but, as the notice says, 'Commit no
nuisance'. A footpath runs through from one corner into Fenchurch
Street.[30]

30. No. 42 Crutched Friars is still intact. French Ordinary Court is disappearing under redevelopment.

All Hallows Barking-by-the-Tower, Great Tower Street
Medieval, plus Seely & Paget, 1955–8   148 1D

Any close resemblance to the pre-war church, blitzed in 1940, is
coincidental: but in recompense this extravaganza is very attractive in
its fey way. With only the outside walls remaining, the architects put
in late Gothic arcades and a four-centred vault of rough concrete.
Under the arches are huge concrete lintels, also exposed: on them rest
mock galleries – carved in mock seventeenth-century style – which
hide the lighting! Outside, the seventeenth-century copper steeple is
brand new, to a new design – and, it must be said, a fine swashbuckling
one, more Amsterdam than Wren. The pulpit is genuine – from St
Swithin, Cannon Street – cleaned so that it looks brand new and given
a sounding board shaped like a shell. This way of designing is usually
a disaster, and there are plenty of modern buildings in Britain to prove
it. What carries it through here is child-like audacity and a real sense
of fun.

Do not miss the font cover beyond the west end of the south aisle.
It seems to float of its own accord in the little unapproachable room;
a lovely Restoration piece with a bird above three cherubs. And, for a
surprise, the arch on the right-hand side of this is Roman brick, part
of the original seventh-century church.

The Tower   148 1E

The Tower is London's one big hostage to the unreality of organized
sight-seeing. It is lucky not to have more; but the Abbey and St Paul's
are too big to be swamped and Buckingham Palace is too much used.
All the Tower's history is past, and the chance of a memorable place
to look at was lost with the preposterous mock-medieval outer walls
of the 1840s, probably by Salvin, every bit as silly as Windsor and far
less fun: all subsequent repairs have accentuated the stage-set or comic-
opera character. Now, by comparison, the bascules of Tower Bridge
feel straightforward. The White Tower itself, heartlessly made over

with yellow instead of white stone, has not a fraction of the force of its ruined brother at Rochester.

Still, if it is a joke, it is at least full-blown farce, and enough historical events have happened to make invention unnecessary. The trouble is that the atmosphere makes even the real events seem phoney: people actually went to their death through that pasteboard Traitors' Gate? Nonsense!

On a stricter level there are two things really worth seeing.* One is in the Tudor chapel of St Peter ad Vincula:[31] the wonderfully crisp canopy, of what looks like hard chalk, to the tomb of John Holland (d. 1447) and his wives. Crisp because untouched, not retouched, and every little face and curl of foliage has an angular grace that is one of the most English of English virtues. The effigies themselves are the usual puddingy shop-work.

Nice, but perhaps not enough of a draw to justify the endless crocodiles of tourists and all that armour. But the other thing should be seen by any London visitor. The Chapel of St John is on the first floor of the White Tower, which was built before 1100. Perhaps no other building in the whole of England conveys such an overwhelming effect of early Norman steamrollering mass, the force that produced Domesday Book and fixed the shires. It seems as if it were all hollowed out of one solid block, and had always been in the block waiting to be hollowed, from the heavy plain capitals to the tunnel vault.

31. To see it, you will need to attach yourself to one of the Yeoman Warders' guided tours.

St Olave Jewry, Ironmonger Lane   142 8A
Sir Christopher Wren and others, 1670 and 1880

The Wren tower is modest enough; it is what has gone on behind it that is so extraordinary. It became redundant in the last century, and a small office block was butted on to the west front, keeping exactly the same shape but transforming the use – chartered accountants instead of curates. It is now far more memorable than it would have been as a church, and one pointer to how a city can retain its monuments whilst transforming them. Opposite the churchyard, an alley runs through to King Street. It is called Prudent Passage and it is entirely lined with white glazed bricks. There is a moral here somewhere.

*A third, perhaps, is the Crown Jewels themselves. Most of them were made for Charles II, determined not to go on his travels, in 1661, and are splendidly curly, extrovert pieces. It says a lot for the age that they fit perfectly with the monumental simplicity of the huge Maundy Dish made for William and Mary.

Guildhall   141 7M

Civic display doesn't alter much. This fifteenth-century hall has the same virtues and the same drawbacks as a good modern town hall. Rich, florid, and rather empty without a floorful of diners or a courtful of witnesses. Fair enough, though something deeper and nobler is possible. The realization of the builders' intentions by Sir Giles Gilbert Scott with a set of stone bows (replacing a spindly Victorian roof which burnt in the blitz) is quite justifiable. Not so the fearful building that Sir G. G. tacked on at the back, towards London Wall.[32]

This rich but insensitive chamber contains several mounds of sculpture in the best St Paul's manner. Fair enough, again, as a background to the canapés and orotund speeches. But to fit in Nelson and the elder Pitt the stone mullions had to be stubbed off short. They were then given truly agonized corbels, leering and grimacing at the pomp underneath. Gog and Magog, remade after the war by James Woodforde in the style of Cibber's originals, strike grotesque attitudes from the west gallery. And with hindsight, so does Dance's main front, built in 1788 in a wild mixture of Gothic and classical. Things are not so simple as the after-dinner speakers might wish.

If you want to rinse your mouth after these uneasy pieces of equivocation, then go to the Guildhall Library in Basinghall Street, left and left again. On the staircase are three superb royal statues by Nicholas Stone which came from the Guildhall Chapel.[33] Queen Elizabeth is a noble mature woman, far more desirable than she was in real life. Edward VI is all precocious intelligence and gawky doubt; and Charles I, in his own life-time, is a wild joke of absolutism, a playing-card king. A big difference from all the costly platitudes in the Guildhall itself.

32. Sir Giles Gilbert Scott died in 1960, but his firm went on to design the expensive, angular new building which forms a west wing to the Guildhall and houses the new Guildhall Library.

33. The three statues are still in the old library, now the Corporation of London's Road Safety Centre. They are not normally accessible to the public but can be seen by special arrangement with the Guildhall Art Gallery, Aldermanbury, London EC2P 2EJ.

Goldsmiths' Hall, Foster Lane   141 7L
Philip Hardwick, 1829–35
Carving by Samuel Nixon

How odd that the designer of that model of Georgian sobriety, the City Club in Old Broad Street, should also have designed this. Because here, eight years before Victoria, is the perfect Victorian public building, with all of the virtues and none of the vices. Rich yet controlled, full-bodied but not overwhelming; and, above all, early enough to have the classical detail still felt with passion and responsibility. There is nothing more vibrant, even in Wren, than the superbly crisp arms and trophies threading their way amongst the Corinthian capitals of the main façade. Here was a nobler, more alive rediscovery of Italy than Barry's: the other fruits are nowhere near London, but scattered all over the northern industrial cities. The inside, which I have not seen, looks to be up to the same standard. The Company sometimes holds exhibitions here, and a visit would be well worth while for the building alone.

St Botolph, Aldersgate   141 7L

The comfortable, humane, live-and-let-live thing that a city church ought to be: one furry stock-brick body (1788 by Nathaniel Wright), one up-to-date stucco east end (1831), and a spindly tower with a really hungry cupola on top. All sorts and conditions, like the background figures in a Hogarth street scene. The inside is apparently complete and elegant late eighteenth century, but seems impenetrably locked, which is no way to go on.

Christ Church, Newgate Street   141 7K
Sir Christopher Wren, steeple finished 1704

A lovely steeple, perhaps Wren's best, with all the Baroque indecisions of designs like St Vedast Foster Lane straightened out, made square-cut and English. Wren here created out of right angles as complicated a flow as Borromini's. Three square stages: the lowest, with the belfry, has pilasters growing out of the stone; the middle has a central core and a ring of delicate columns free-standing around it; the top stage has attached columns. So here is submission, detachment and attachment, and all without a curve to its name. The church was blitzed, alas, and will not be rebuilt: the steeple remains[34] as a reproach to the glacial Grecian steeples of a century later, and also to such repetitive Wren steeples as St Bride, Fleet Street.

34. It is now attached to a Georgian Vestry House, rebuilt in 1981.

Bart's Hospital, West Smithfield   141 6K

This is one of London's peculiar places whose character needs to be safeguarded as jealously as though it were the Temple or St James's Park. The hospital, in all its classical sobriety, with never a pointed arch all through the nineteenth-century additions, faces Smithfield Market's endearing fussy face. (The pubs around here, as at Covent Garden, open in the early morning.) The open space between hospital and market turns out to be a spiral ramp, which leads down to black tunnels calling themselves Smithfield Goods Station though they look much more likely to lead straight to the Old Bailey. On the east side is the entrance to St Bart's-the-Great. A sonata for oboe, tuba, cello, xylophone, and clavichord, and good stuff too.

   Bart's itself has a grand entrance: a tough, compact building of 1702 by Wren's mason, Edward Strong Jun. This is Wren's Hampton Court style returned nearer to Holland and gaining from it, every swag and window-pediment making its point; above the arch, Henry VIII looks out with a splendid po-face.

Through the arch and on the left is another London surprise – St Bartholomew-the-Less, the hospital church. Above the door-knocker is a notice saying *Try this – it works.*[35] It does, an object lesson to all the timid lockers-up of London's churches. The building was rebuilt by Dance in 1787 and again by Hardwick in 1823, a jolly Gothic octagon, one of the most cheerful buildings in London. The plan is still Dance's, with the octagon inscribed in a square and the gloomy corners given noble blind arches – an idea which Dance took further in his church at Micheldever near Winchester. It is easy to see how much his pupil Soane must have learnt from this gruff quixotic designer whose best buildings have all disappeared. Newgate Gaol, the best of all, was a few yards away on the site of the Old Bailey.

Through the next arch is the main quad of the Hospital. On the left through an open door is a brown-and-gold stairwell, designed by Gibbs and laughably painted by Hogarth, who was completely at odds with the generalized sentiments expected of him. Perhaps you shouldn't be here, but nobody seems to turn you out: a bit of the real London.

35. No longer, but the church is still open.

St Bartholomew-the-Great, West Smithfield   141 6K

A puzzle for purists, for its effectiveness is in the austere stilted Norman arches around the apse, contrasted with the mid-Gothic tracery above. Yet nearly all of this is due to Sir Aston Webb in the 1890s, though he had good evidence for his reconstruction. The original parts are late Norman, *c.* 1140, and about the best in London. The design was exciting and overawing with its rhythm of four-arches-under-one to each bay of the triforium, but it is now far too mutilated to be felt properly. The clear glass and the impersonal arches together give an atmosphere of bleak integrity which is the strongest thing about St Bartholomew.

Nothing remarkable in the fittings, except the funny way in which the sixteenth century tried to buy its way into eternity: an oriel-windowed oratory jammed into one bay of the triforium for Prior Bolton, and a retrospective monument to Prior Rahere the founder, then three hundred years dead, diagonally opposite, forced into a bay of the choir arcade.

The outside is effectively Aston Webb's, and loveless, but the surroundings have some charm and could have more. On the north side is No. 41 Cloth Fair [83], a wonderful survival of old London, rescued from dereliction before the war by Lord Mottistone.* Wonderful not

* 'Seely' of Seely & Paget, see p. 19.

as a specimen of rustic late-seventeenth-century architecture; not even as a very pretty building (which it is), but as an embodiment of the old London spirit. Chunky, cantankerous, breaking out all over in oriels and roof-lights, unconcerned with academies, fashions or anything else other than shapes to live in. There was a lot of this in London after the Fire; this is now almost the only example left.

[Charterhouse   141 5K

A rambling nest of medieval and Renaissance buildings, an equivalent of Lambeth Palace north of the river. It is rather demonstratively private – 'trespassers may be prosecuted' etc. – and was in any case severely damaged by bombing. The patched-up parts that you can see from outside have at the moment a quality of instant picturesqueness rather like one of those deep-frozen American dinners. (Open only on Wednesdays, only in the summer, only at 2.45 p.m. prompt.)]

Golden Lane   141 4–5M
Chamberlin, Powell & Bon, begun 1953

The buildings themselves – a very high density housing estate for the City of London – are sometimes fussy and sometimes weatherbeaten. But in a way they are unimportant compared with the spaces between them. Every trick in the book is brought in, and not for cleverness's sake, but to create a real place out of statistical units of accommodation. There are half a dozen ways of crossing the site: along corridors, under buildings, down steps and up ramps. And it is all meant to be used. The space itself, continually fluctuating and flickering, new views always opening and faster than the eye can take them in, is like Span at Ham Common. But the temperament is quite different. This is no ivory tower, and these places are meant for rude human beings playing rough games. There is a new Peabody estate next door: tall blocks, asphalt between, and a list of prohibitions as long as your arm. It is difficult to credit that it is intended for the same species of animal. The architecture of Golden Lane has improved as the estate has grown, and the newest part, facing Goswell Road, has a good pub (the Shakespeare) built into the bottom of it: modern, but without the decorative affectations that plague pub designers. The faults of this estate are immediately apparent. The virtues only show up later, but they will stand repeated visits, where L.C.C. estates like Roehampton seem shallower and shallower.[36]

36. It is now end on to the Barbican, by the same architects, so their work over thirty years can be studied within a small area.

Route Eleven or South Barbican, London Wall   141 5–6M
City of London Planning Office, plus various architects, begun 1960

It is hopeless to judge this until the first-floor pedestrian network is complete. Even so, it is worth seeing as the only consistently modern part of the City. The scheme consists of five (eventually six) tall glass slabs arranged on either side of a dual carriageway, all on land which was cleared by the blitz. By Nash's standards this is a child-like pattern, but it has its moments of brittle magnificence and also its moments of surprising accident (one of them is the way in which a slab rears above the view of the Guildhall down King Street, the contrast so violent that the identity of both is kept). It could be much more exciting when there is a first-floor deck which links up with the residential part of Barbican just beginning to the north. Make another date for the early 1970s.[37]

37. Originally the dual carriageway was intended to extend further east and west. This did not happen, the road remains bottlenecked at both ends, and the term Route Eleven has largely been dropped. The sixth glass slab (Bastion House) has now been built. The first-floor deck is also complete, and leads to the main Barbican complex (by Chamberlin, Powell & Bon, 1963–82): ramparts of flats, a colossal crescent, three slender towers, a waterside café, a conservatory, and the unfathomable warren of the arts centre. How far the residents of the Barbican are involved with the life of the City is difficult for an outsider to judge, but visually the Barbican gives the impression of a self-contained walled city, within the old City, but not really part of it.

Britannic House,[38] Finsbury Circus   142 6B
Sir Edwin Lutyens, 1924

This kind of all-out classicism is probably what Lutyens hankered for all the time. It would have been much better for English architecture if he had enjoyed enough self-knowledge to admit it and had set up frankly as a super-Blomfield. This is the best place in the City to see the end of Edwardian exuberance – eight years after the Somme, five years before the slump. The Port of London building[39] on Tower Hill comes a good second, but its designer did not have Lutyens's flair for hanging lush stone ornament up in the sky – a great drumroll of columns above the cornice – nor his spatial expertise that makes all the other members of the quadrant appear as though they didn't know what a curve was. It would probably still be the *beau idéal* of most City companies, and it is a tragedy that modern designers have been unable to suggest the qualities without reproducing the classical details. Lutyens might have known how.

38. Now Lutyens House. The name 'Britannic House' has been transferred to the thirty-three-storey B.P. building on the other side of Moorgate.
39. Now the Willis Faber building.

Sun Street Passage   142 5–6C
... Or how to walk out of the City in two hundred yards. Sun Street Passage is a yellow-brick slit between Broad Street and Liverpool Street stations, and a job to sift from the various entrances to that

bewildering pair of jokers.[40] You enter amongst the affluent flurry of the City. You leave, after just one exhilarating glance up into the frilly roofs of Liverpool Street, in the sad emptiness of south Shoreditch: warehouses, railway tracks, Hawksmoor's church peering over from the wrecked grandeur of Spitalfields. The transition is as violent as the medieval sequence through the town gate to the country outside.

40. Broad Street station has been demolished, and the Passage blocked off, as part of the vast Broadgate development.

Liverpool Street[41]   142 5-6C

Granted, from the start, that it may be no fun to catch a train here. It is the opposite of King's Cross: everything is puzzling and difficult; it is hard to get in to anyway and, when you do manage, what you want is sure to be at the other end, with a lot of steps in between: dead handy with a lot of luggage and only five minutes to spare.

But if you have the time it becomes a different place. The essential thing is to get on to the high-level walk-way and stay there. What was formerly exasperating waywardness becomes a delightful meander, in tune with your mood, as the foot-way threads its way from one side to the other. The station life unrolls beneath you, in all its unplanned variety – so organic that you always expect there to be an extra platform or two newly sprouted since the last visit. Whimsy, maybe, but everything encourages it, from the fragile roofs of the train sheds to the fey convolutions of the plan. Alice in Wonderland, acted out in E.C.2, and all done by that high-level path. The old Euston, which had a similarly disjointed layout, was just a nuisance.

41. Liverpool Street is currently (1987) surrounded by, and becoming part of, what is reputed to be the biggest building site in Europe. The eastern train shed, adjoining Bishopsgate, has been demolished; the days of the old high-level walk-way are numbered. The western train shed – architecturally the most impressive part of the station – is to stay, and there will be a new concourse and walk-ways.

Turkish Baths, Bishopsgate Churchyard   142 7C
Harold Elphick, 1895

Bishopsgate Churchyard runs through to Old Broad Street, along the side of St Botolph's. If you run through also, you may be brought up short by the Building. Green and brown glazed tiles all over, small and very Moorish, done by some roaring boy to disturb the minds of businessmen – yet sensitive as well. It used to be a Turkish bath, and the baths still stretch underground for fifty yards; it was lately used as storage space by a bank.[42] It must stay, to enlighten a city which is losing its true nonconformities in direct proportion to the rate at which false nonconformity multiplies. One might think that the City contains enough expense-account lunchers to make Turkish baths a paying proposition. The visual effect is exactly that: you shed pounds of preoccupation in sheer surprise.

42. It is now – appropriately or, perhaps, ironically – an expensive Turkish restaurant.

2 Westminster

140, 145, 146
You name it, Westminster has it: a rag-bag of palaces, parliaments, abbeys, civil servants and, in the last ten years, an explosion of offices without the benefit of City traditions. Parliament Square is the bit everybody knows, the seat of government but nothing like the heart of London: austere, muddled, and unreal. Reality inheres much more in the sequence of parks – Nash-designed or Nash-contrived – which stretches away north-west as far as Notting Hill, and also in the frank theatricality of Buckingham Palace and the Mall. St James's, north of it, hangs on to sanity by the skin of its teeth, though it flowers as soon as the pressure is off, at week-ends or in the evenings. Mayfair, north again, has been a desert these seventy years, ever since the Victorians descended on it with terracotta and terrifying self-confidence. The commercial West End, along Oxford Street and down Regent Street to Leicester Square, is indestructible, the most international part of London; north-east of it Soho's brilliant and wicked grid of streets is indestructible too, as long as Westminster City Council can be dissuaded from picking at the property. Finally, the forgotten segment of Central London, Westminster-behind-the-Abbey: the well-built, dull, regular streets of Pimlico, where after five years' residence you may still not be able to find your way home. Embedded in this mish-mash there are marvels, but they never cohere: London's inchoateness is epitomized here.

WESTMINSTER ABBEY AND THE HOUSES OF PARLIAMENT
Westminster view
146 6B
St Paul's can be reached in a hundred ways: this approach to Westminster needs to be calculated to the foot. Take an eleven or seventy-six bus from Victoria and get off at the stop called Great Smith Street or 'the Abbey'.[1] Walk on twelve paces from the bus stop and what meets you is a set of four verticals, evenly spaced like a great major chord: Big Ben, St Margaret's tower, the Crimea Memorial, and the north-west tower of the Abbey [6]. In terms of distance, they fire 1–2–4–3, rather like a car engine, folding the sequence in. As Gordon Cullen once said: 'View? It is more like organ music!'

Ignore the foreground (a crass lampstandard) and the background (a crass large building, name of Shell).[2] They have nothing to do with this real world, though they are unfortunately part of the visible one. Alternatively, go on to a traffic island at the lights and look from there. Now that the new and decent building has been set back on the south side of Victoria Street this view could be made more permanent by bending the road and building a pavilion: the simplest great opportunity in London.[3]

1. Now an 11, 24, 29, or 70 to Great Smith Street.
2. Mercifully hidden by trees in summer.
3. It has not been taken.

St Margaret, Westminster   146 5C
1504–23

St Margaret's is not a great building, but it is the best one in London to give an idea of the cold yet subtle imagination which seized the country at the beginning of the sixteenth century. This was a court building by court masons, but the spatial bareness and blankness – Protestant before its time – is as strong as in merchants' churches like St Nicholas, King's Lynn. Yet the means for achieving this economy, in details like the mouldings of the arcades, were rich and complicated.

The east window of the Crucifixion is worth far more than a glance. It is probably Flemish and was probably made for Henry VII's Chapel. It arrived here in 1758 after travelling all round Essex. Mid way between Gothic and Renaissance, the style is irrelevant beside the thick force of the composition, quite different from Flemish glass later in the century. Rouault or Sutherland might have devised these deep shadows, turbulent faces and violent attitudes, all fixed in a glaring sky of cobalt blue as vivid as a scream. A church full of such passion makes the spatial parsimony into a very different thing. The contrast[4] is as piercing as that between Skelton's simple short lines and his terrible words:

> Woefully arrayed
> My blood, man
> For thee ran
> Woefully arrayed.

4. A further contrast is now provided by the delicately coloured abstract stained glass in the south aisle windows, by John Piper.

The Abbey[5]   146 6C

That this should be Britain's official church is astonishingly just. The Abbey's architecture is the perfect governmental report on French Gothic; prepared, as it were, to see if the European style was suited to English practice. Level-headed, solving all of its problems, translating them correctly into meticulous English.

The foundation stone was laid in 1245 and the King's master mason then was Henry de Reyns (probably Reims) – either a Frenchman or an Englishman who had worked in France. He brought back a perfect compendium of the new French buildings (Reims itself, Amiens, the Sainte Chapelle) which were then new-built miraculous toys. But to them were added just a few English touches – Purbeck marble piers, a ridge rib to the vault, a cavernous galley – which all point in the same direction, towards increased richness and increased tension. This in the end is what stops the Abbey from being bland. The lasting impression is of sharpness: acutely pointed arches, taut proportions – much taller and narrower than any other English cathedral. If this is an official report, it is delivered with the incisive acerbity which only civil servants can do really well: a Buchanan building. All the detailed aesthetic problems are solved perfectly. There is none of the inane pushing and shoving of lancets that goes on in Lincoln or Salisbury, but there is none of the passion of the windblown capitals at Wells, either. It is the unexpected case of an impersonal building with a lot of personality.

The thirteenth-century abbey ended five bays up the nave, where the diapered spandrels stop. It was only completed in 1380 by Henry Yevele, the designer of Canterbury nave, and his work is one of the most astonishing performances in the whole of architecture. He continued the old system exactly, yet altered nearly all the details in tiny ways, so that you would know the correct century if you wanted to. Just as the Abbey itself is an inner compromise between French and English, not a forced marriage, so Yevele must have arrived at this compromise design by submitting totally to the existing rhythms so that they spoke through him. Once the differences are pointed out they can never be forgotten; yet they never get in the way of the effects laid down more than a century earlier.

To this austere but not inhuman shell, the royal masons added an enormous chantry chapel for Henry VII in 1503–12. The contrast is startling, most of all outside. Where the older parts with their double tiers of flying buttresses were simply stage-machinery to keep the building up, Henry VII's Chapel breaks out into an astonishing display of panelling and chunky shapes. This also, in a way, is stage-machinery for the clever spaces inside, and in a much more direct sense. For Henry VII's Chapel is one of the greatest history plays ever staged. To feel and understand it, squeeze into one of the funny-shaped recesses that make the outside so remarkable: V-shaped in the apse, semi-circular in the side chapels. Here you are outside the vault-space, which defines the stage, and from here it is a pageant, whipped up by experts at the very end of Gothic architecture to sum up three hundred years of ceremony. The main chapel is all flags and stalls and Henry VII's tomb, with the vault – a most deceitful construction, in strict Gothic terms – high above. The statues of saints and courtiers are incisive and alive, but they are acting their parts in a way that the statues of Reims or Amiens never could. This is already Shakespeare's view of the Middle Ages; it was probably built by the brothers Vertue, subtle and sophisticated men who designed Bath Abbey and St George's Chapel at Windsor. As at Bath, they did exactly what they set out to do: never has a surface been more knowingly crumpled and panelled. The join between new chapel and old ambulatory is done with a vestibule which has a transverse vault. Physically, here, the space is continuous. Spiritually, it is as opaque as the division between auditorium and stage. The same trick is repeated in the progression between the main space and the side chapels with their hanging fan vaults – a play within a play. Dreams of chivalry, everything we sum up as 'olde', are usually loaded on to straightforward buildings with disastrous effect. That trail ends in the queues at Anne Hathaway's Cottage. But here is a sophisticated invitation to dream, and at this level it is far more than a sentimental game.

Pulpitum, Newton and Stanhope tombs, and two candelabra
Pulpitum, Edward Blore, 1828
Newton and Stanhope tombs, William Kent and Rysbrack, 1731, 1733
Candelabra, Benno Elkan, 1940–3

Three styles, three dates become one thing, the gilded fantasy which takes your eye the moment you go into the Abbey. The whole is greater than any of the parts, like the buildings around a country-town market place. And a funny flavour it has too: just slightly melodramatic and stagey, something that foreigners may feel more than Englishmen. It is the gesticulations in *Macbeth*, Elgar's music, Sutherland's paintings, John Osborne's plays: what happens to the reserved Englishman when he breaks out. Through bottling up, the results come out a semitone sharp emotionally; and in some cases it makes them more lovable. The protagonists here are a Georgian screen recently re-gilded; under it, two self-consciously arranged monuments – Newton's, with a very fine face: the idea of Newton reached by the kind of act of imagination that Blake was capable of; in front, a vast pair of candelabra.

   The intellect slides all sorts of cavorting puzzles over something which is visually quite easy to understand. The screen looks old Gothic repainted in the last century, and is in fact 1828 repainted recently. The monuments are Baroque and try to be Roman, the candlesticks look Art Nouveau and were put up in the last war.

Monuments: nave and transept, north
North aisle

Eighth bay from crossing. William Morgan (d. 1683) and *Thomas Mansel* (d. 1684). Among all the posturing and inflated sentiments, this small unsigned monument is a breath of fresh air. No putti, no bloated busts: simple medallion inscriptions in a crisp frame of barley-sugar columns and an open pediment with the ends scrolled. It must, I think, belong to a City of London mason who knew exactly what he had to do. It feels like Herrick after a surfeit of Southey: unforced, apt, knowing but innocent.

Third bay from crossing. (1). *Temple West*, erected in 1761 by Wilton. A straightforward plinth, but a bust on top whose extrovert power compels from yards away. This is true power made visible – force tempered by judgement. Wilton, like most other Abbey sculptors, went on to increase his reputation and betray his promise.

(2) *William Wilberforce*. This monument of 1840 by Samuel Joseph takes the whole business into another dimension and one where it will find few companions. Here the expression and the form are quite indivisible and the result is to render Wilberforce's whole being. The genial penetrating face, the posture, the chair itself, the fingernails are all reflecting the central mystery of what made this Wilberforce different from all the other Wilberforces and from the sum of his physical parts. This immediacy, the feeling of life at the same time that you know it is marble, is supernatural.

Second bay from crossing. Philip de Sausmarez (d. 1747), by Sir Henry Cheere. Cheere was a brilliant Rococo designer, and this monument is just that: a felicitous set of balanced asymmetries moving diagonally downwards, ending on the plinth with a needle-sharp relief of a naval engagement. Emotional depth and technique are exactly balanced.

North transept

The worst place of all for emptiness. The Newcastle monument (1723) in the fourth bay next to the door is a recall to sanity – not in the bleak carving by Francis Bird but in the superb design of the architectural frame. This is by James Gibbs, newly back from Italy, and it has all the Italian brilliance in movement and composition combined with a native sense of solidity and power. The huge pediment is open, broken and curved forward, yet not for a moment does it throw away its energy. That Gibbs later chose or had to conform with Palladian rules is a real tragedy.

East aisle, north transept

Nightingale Monument (1761), by Louis François Roubiliac. A famous apparition, without any parallel in mid-eighteenth-century Europe. Mrs Nightingale was frightened by lightning, miscarried and died of it. She is collapsed in her husband's arms; he has an expression of utter terror and is pushing something off. And the something is Death itself, coiling smoothly up out of the bowels of the monument, armed with a lance (which has been broken and replaced by a piece of wood as roughly cut as a cricket stump). The funny thing is that it is Death which seems natural, whilst the humans look as if they are play-acting. The sombre grey surround acts as a proscenium arch: we are the audience – and the actors, sooner or later. This is 'All the world's a stage' with a vengeance. Death is incredibly personal, its bony parts carved almost lovingly; someone to be known every day in a familiar way. Wesley saw what he was trying to do: 'here indeed the marble seems to speak'.

St John the Baptist's Chapel

Hunsdon Monument (Lord Hunsdon, d. 1596). This is the tallest monument in the Abbey, which is some achievement. Three tiers of inexhaustible fancy ending up near the vault with a pelican on top of an octagonal cupola. Corinthian columns occur in three sizes, obelisks in four. Each time they are combined in a different way and each time to a different scale relative to their surroundings. This could be the recipe for a gigantic headache, yet all this multitude of parts is in proportion and in balance. It is an Elizabethan poem built up with a complex, sprawling image, yet with each jewel-studded phrase subordinated without strain to the whole. If you want an architectural equivalent to Shakespeare at his most swaggering, then here it is.

St Paul's Chapel

Lady Cottingham (d. 1632), by Hubert Le Sueur, 1635, and *Lord Cottingham* (d. 1672). This contains the whole strange history of Caroline England, implicit and explicit. The towering, sombre composition commemorates Lady Cottingham and was made in 1635, just before the Civil War. It could have been done by Alfred Gilbert in 1900 – each part perversely unorthodox, each part with some huge inner discord. Gleaming black, heightened by the recent re-gilding of the ornamental parts and by the lady's bust, high up and fragile. Lord Cottingham was Ambassador to Spain for both Charles I and II, died at Valladolid in 1672, and was re-buried here in 1679. A stone effigy was then added to the gaunt tomb, tricky and mannered but with all the conflict gone. The inscription that goes with it talks about 'ye unhappy civill broils' and 'ye userpers prevayling' – i.e. the Commonwealth. Beside Le Sueur's degree of mannerism, the whole being riven and turned against itself, even Nicholas Stone seems shallow – his monument to Dudley Carleton is in the same chapel. But what made Le Sueur, a Frenchman, become involved so deeply that the force of his conflict reached far above his usual level?

Henry VII's Chapel

North aisle

Queen Elizabeth (d. 1603), *Princess Sophia* (d. 1606), and *Princess Mary* (d. 1607), all by Maximilian Colt. Queen Elizabeth under her canopy aims at fantasy; but what might have succeeded elsewhere fails dismally here by comparison with the miraculous fan-vaulting and curved panelled walls. Nothing could show more clearly how coarse-grained 1600 had become by comparison with 1500. This is the debit side of the Renaissance ledger. But the two infants at the end have no false pretensions and the very woodenness of Colt's carving helps the pathos. Mary is already shown dressed like a courtier, though she was only two: Sophia died when three days old, and a doll's face peers out of a hooded cradle. The recent colouring is a drawback, for Colt was skilful enough to work the alabaster itself into crochet patterns in very low relief. Before, this was enough to suspend disbelief for a second or two; now, the gilding has ostentatiously picked out all the patterns and reduced the scale of the effect from magic to artful technique.

Centre

Henry VII and Elizabeth of York, by Pietro Torrigiani (1512–18). This is the moment when the Renaissance first touched Britain: yet it is several other things as well. Torrigiani's monument is surrounded and almost smothered by a vast brass grille, put up a few years earlier, which is the epitome of late Gothic at its worst – tricky, overloaded and graceless. It could have won a first prize at the Great Exhibition. The monument is another thing, but it has to be squinted at, piecemeal. The effigies are above eye level and cannot be seen properly at all; this is sad, because they seem to have the same combination of the particular and general as *Lady Margaret Beaufort*. The tiny scenes around the sarcophagus have already set into the academic postures which the Counter-Reformation seized on and made mandatory for half of Europe; but the figures at the corners are marvellous. Half angel, half cherub, the vital fire of the Renaissance blazes out from them and purifies everything. The faces are imperious, but never for a moment do they weaken into possessiveness or petulance. The pose announces joy and translation as positively as Tiepolo's angels, but without any hint of a sculptural game. Everything is High Seriousness, which means that it is capable of being laughed at.

Lucky England, to find an artist so talented and so compassionate; we could easily have acquired an academic dead-beat like Serlio. And lucky Torrigiani, to come to a country which was sympathetic but strange, so that his preconceptions were shifted sideways and every problem provided the opportunity for new insight instead of settlement into a comfortable rut.

South apse

[*Duke of Lennox and Richmond* (d. 1624) *and his wife* (d. 1639), by Hubert Le Sueur. Striking enough, but shallow by comparison with the Cottingham monument (p. 33). This is discordant grief to order – externalized, not instinct. So gesticulation and bronze tears replace disharmony in the proportions. It fills the apse completely, and the viewer never really gets over the guffaw engendered by the four caryatids. They support a wild openwork dome, have cushions on their nappers and the wrong sort of anguished expression.]

St Edward the Confessor Chapel

Cosmati work on tombs, 1268–80. Italy never had a true Gothic style, and parts of Italy right through the Middle Ages kept the delicacy, freshness and even much of the classical detail that usually add up in people's minds to the Renaissance. Florence did and so did Rome: and this antique courtliness is an extraordinary memento to find in the middle of London. Archbishop Ware brought semi-precious materials and masons from Rome in 1268. They did a pavement (largely covered up), the base of Edward the Confessor's shrine, and the base of Henry III's tomb. The materials have mostly been looted except on the ambulatory side of Henry III's tomb, perhaps a bit too high up for casual theft. And in an odd way this reinforces the delicacy. There is no surface glitter to lead the eye away from the grave proportions and the inventiveness of the extraordinary barley-sugar columns, each one different, which sprout wherever the designers found a spare edge. What they do most of all is to slow up reactions after the riot of impressions in the rest of the Abbey, whether Gothic or Baroque. Here every single arch or pediment has to be taken in separately.

Queen Eleanor (d. 1290), by William Torel, 1291, and *Edward III* (d. 1377), perhaps by John Orchard. These two bronze effigies are superlative, among the best in England. Eighty years and a complete style (Decorated) separate them, yet it seems inconceivable that they were not man and wife, instead of grandson and grandmother, and were not done by the same sculptor. Torel also did Henry III's effigy, but this is too high on its chest to be seen properly. Queen Eleanor is near enough to touch, with a strong yet fragile face, all women and one woman at the same time, with her hair rippling down in even waves on either side. Edward I was well served, in his grief, by the Eleanor Crosses and this tomb. Characteristically, he himself has a plain marble box, with no effigy and a later inscription.

Edward III, Eleanor's astral consort, is on the other side of the retrochoir. Where Torel might have got some help from the 'spirit of the time', the uncurling leaves of Southwell and Exeter – the man who carved Edward III was a genius right out of his age. The King looks like an old Hebrew prophet, as statuesque as the portals of Chartres: the lawgiver. Yet also, like Eleanor, each part is personal, a particular king carved by a particular artist. The toes turn up, the long beard – surely the finest beard in England – flows regularly down and then turns in magisterially. On the side facing the ambulatory, six little weepers survive. Each one, also, is a particular person and a general type: Michelangelo's huge generalizations done in nine inches of bronze.

In between these two, chronologically, comes Queen Philippa, Edward's wife. She died in 1369 and has a monument by Hennequin of Liège which is utterly competent and nothing more. Immediately afterwards are Richard II and his queen, Anne of Bohemia, made in 1394: five years before Richard was hounded out to death by a crude takeover bid. Yet even here, at the high point of an eloquent reign, with the tomb-chest designed by Yevele himself, the effigies are big and bold – larger than life, in fact – but again nothing more. Eleanor and Edward link hands backwards to King John at Worcester, forwards to Henry VII a few yards away in the Abbey, as part of a nobler tradition than 'official portraiture'.

[Henry V's Chantry
Probably John of Thirsk, c. 1425–50

This is one of the most troubled, unhappy pieces of architecture in London. Either the designer was working out his own problems or he was expressing perfectly the spirit of an age which had realized the potentialities of the Perpendicular style very quickly and didn't know what to do next. The 1420s and 30s were not a very happy time politically, either. Ingenious it certainly is, with two spiral staircases running up to a bridge which spans the ambulatory. The King's effigy, too mutilated now to make much impression, is underneath. But this promising shape was loaded with the heaviest ornamental forms, and with big statues wearing wooden expressions, yet striking distorted and cranked attitudes. It is like a complicated gearbox full of gravel. The tracery patterns of the innumerable little canopies are an anthology of weary, four-centred forms. Most of them, revealingly, are looking backwards to the last century; some are so flabby that by themselves they would be called sixteenth- or seventeenth-century. There is nothing great here; yet it is a comfort to know that other ages had as many worries as we do.]

Henry VII's Chapel: south aisle

Lady Margaret Beaufort, by Pietro Torrigiani (1511–13). Lady Margaret was Henry VII's mother and this is probably Torrigiani's first work in London. The effigy has Gothic pinnacles beside it and a Gothic canopy above; but the face and hands transcend both Gothic and Renaissance. Here is the universality where style ceases to matter – a kind of Elysian Fields, where our anxieties about communication blow away in the wind. This is simply a mature, much-travelled elderly face, still strong and intelligent, still younger than its hands. But it is also every person who has been truly alive.

Ambulatory

South side. Retable (late thirteenth century). This is as tantalizing as knowing Seurat by one corner of *La Baignade*. There is enough to see that a great and individual artist is at work, not enough to feel any sense of his whole scheme. There is no point in going to see this if you want anything complete. There are only fragments: heads and knees in unison, strong and tender and brilliant all at the same time. Scholars cannot decide whether it is English or French; in either case it is liberated from early medieval conventions, the feudal system of art. Humanity blows through it as it does through Exeter Cathedral.

Monuments: nave and transept, south
South transept

Sir Thomas Robinson (d. 1777) *and his wife* (d. 1739), by John Walsh. A smallish monument by a little-known sculptor, but two busts of such intense inner energy that they compel attention again and again, even by comparison with Roubiliac's *Handel*, which is just above. They are not specially nice people, and they may not have much to do with Sir Thomas and his wife – he was amateur architect, governor of Barbados and a good many other things. But the imperious fierce faces are locked together by some doomed relationship. They look like brother and sister rather than husband and wife; and the stage is set for catastrophe, with incestuous passion only a fraction of an inch underneath the stone surface.

Poets' Corner. Apart from the simple accumulation of talent, which is astonishing enough, the interest is not so much in the sculpture as in the various attitudes taken to Important Men after the event, something which started as long ago as 1550 with the monument to Chaucer. Shakespeare himself is a perfect example, the portrait as penetrating and friendly as two such good-natured men as Kent (*invt.*) and Scheemakers (*sculpt.*) could make it. But it is still a mask,* like the others. There is one exception: the big monument to Matthew Prior, put up immediately after his death. The design is by Gibbs, flabbily carved by Rysbrack. The bust is a brilliant portrait of a real man; a person, not a literary figure, dashing and unepiscopal. And this is not Rysbrack's, but due to the famous French sculptor Coysevox, and it is superb. But reverse the situation – a monument to Louis XIV, say – and it would be Coysevox who would be wooden, Gibbs and Rysbrack who would be vivid and inventive. Self-consciousness does funny things.

Argyll Monument (1749), by Louis François Roubiliac. If in the Nightingale Monument the humans were on stage, here the whole monument is on stage. Technically it is undoubtedly brilliant; yet, for all that, here is the ancestor of the monstrous piles in St Paul's. It is a pose, though a memorable one, even down to the famous figure of Eloquence whose outstretched arm points straight out of the monument and draws you over from the other side of the Abbey like a striking woman at a party. The point is made by Chantrey's familiar, pawky bust of Sir Walter Scott, peering round the left-hand side. Even in a copy, it feels like the real thing. A tableau such as Roubiliac's might, with such superb sculptural talent, be marvellous in a complete setting, a whole palace or a park. Isolated, it is as unreal as one scene from an O'Neill play acted out cold in the middle of the afternoon.

Nave, south aisle, east end

First bay from crossing. Sir Thomas Richardson (d. 1635), by Hubert Le Sueur. A competent, ordinary bust, peering grumpily out at passers-by. But an extraordinary frame, showing, like Lady Cottingham's monument (p. 33), Le Sueur's instinctive feeling for dissonance and ill-natured strength. Black marble and bronze, with a heavy scrolled

---

* The worst of all – in terms of incomprehension, not of sculptural quality – is Epstein's recent bust of Blake.

pediment sitting over the heavy face, a heavy sarcophagus in a heavy surround. But because this was Le Sueur's particular wavelength, because this sort of heaviness is one part of the business of living, it does not weigh you down. It is the perfect partner to Van Dyck's nervous line and Charles I's weak, watery, stubborn eyes.

Third bay from crossing. Pasquale de Paoli, by John Flaxman (*c*. 1798). A magnificent bust of the patriot, who died in England in 1807, perhaps by then a little puzzled by the megalomania of his fellow-Corsican, Bonaparte. Delicate without a hint of sentimentality; a penetrating character study with enough eighteenth-century expertise to make light of things like the way the hair curls over behind the ears. Flaxman went further, in size and aspiration, and fared much worse. Here is his natural talent: stronger men than he were forced askew by the atrocious pressures of the time.

[Chapter House
c. 1250

It should be the high point of the whole cathedral, the compressed essence of that magisterial spirit which for a few years around 1250 literally tried to build the City of God on earth. Instead it is rebuffing, wall-eyed: God's city turns out to be rather like a law court. The trouble is that the illusion has to be complete, as the Sainte Chapelle is. But the wall-paintings have almost gone, the sculpture is hacked and bowdlerized, and the windows are Victorian fragments surrounded by bleak areas of plain glass. What is left, in texture and design, could easily come in fact from the Law Courts – G. E. Street's: but however much is unavoidably missing, there is a basic rigidity – lack of forgiveness, almost – which corrodes the design.]

Museum[6]

The Stuart and Georgian wax effigies are just jolly pieces of fancy dress, nothing like Madame Tussaud's. But the medieval funeral effigies, based on death masks, are another matter. This is how people were, not how we think royalty ought to be: Edward III with his mouth twisted by a stroke, Henry V's 'dear Kate' tragically strained by childbirth, with corded neck and drawn cheeks. (The caption here has the sauce to say 'the sculptor has not succeeded well in presenting normal life in accordance with ancient tradition'.) Most moving of all are the busts of Henry VII and his wife [8 and 9]: that of Henry a death mask of wisdom and experience up to the best that Renaissance Italy was producing; that of his wife having the same sculptural ability allied to an almost supernatural intensity. Elizabeth of York stares out, full-face, like a hypnotic image ready to suck you in through her eyes. Auburn hair and a fur-trimmed blue dress surround that enthrallingly steady gaze: magic is uncomfortably, irresistibly near. It is white witchcraft, but it certainly is disturbing – 'Mr Lawrence and Fredrik his mate' have wrought something beyond the comprehension of learned societies.

Little Cloister

Not much architecture, but a wonderful bit of London, the null in the heart of the vortex. Reached from the main cloister, big and dull, along one dark passage then another at right angles. A tiny space with a fountain in it, the arcading seventeenth-century, the buildings above rebuilt after bomb-damage in the Second World War. This is just one more oasis, though a pretty one, in a city of oases. What makes it splendid is that the Victoria Tower comes marauding down into this space like the heavenly host. The result is an enhanced appreciation of both. Certainly, there is nowhere else where the sheer magnificence of the Houses of Parliament can be so well enjoyed, divorced from its symbolic function.

Monuments
Nave, south aisle, west end

Fifth bay from crossing. Major André (d. 1780), by Robert Adam and P. M. Van Gelder. This is the exact point at which sentiment crept into the Abbey: the very first tear forming in the melting brown eyes. Just here, suspended, it was genuinely sweet, like the first Wedgwood figures. False emotion is a hairsbreadth away, yet somehow does not affect the sorrowful Britannia, the placid lion, all paws and no growl, and the courtly relief underneath, which could be the porcelain set-piece of a dinner service. This is a moment of elegance snatched out of inevitable processes. The tumbrils are very near; and in fact, Major André was shot as a spy in the American War of Independence. Yet it rings true.

Sixth bay from crossing. (1) *Hargrave Monument*, by Louis François Roubiliac (1757). Roubiliac's wildest fancy, with the General starting up at Judgement Day and a pyramid crashing into pieces behind. Even he cannot carry this off. But the figure of Time, sweeping up Death like so much waste paper, is prodigious. A furiously young old man, who with his gruff and apocalyptic ringlets has stridden straight out of a Baroque church, and taken on extra reality on the way. This was the kind of figure Blake was trying to create, all unreflective energy.

(2) *Earl Godolphin* (d. 1712), by Francis Bird. Simple – just a bust above a short inscription – but as good as it could be. Ringlets from the wig ripple down below the neck. Between them is a worldly-wise, cynical face: worldly in the best sense and cynical in the best sense. Everything that is shown has been put on the face by experience, not blind prejudice; and none of the experience has corroded the man's original nature. That amused downward droop of the mouth would be worth more than many people's vows of eternal friendship. Bird was sometimes lumbering in his big monuments, but he is superb here.

5. The Royal Chapels are open from Monday to Saturday, free on Wednesday evenings, closed on Sunday. This entry has been rearranged to follow the present-day visitors' route.
6. The museum displays have recently been redesigned and recaptioned. In their new setting, with no wigs or costumes, the medieval effigies are unsettling and macabre, like severed heads on poles.

Little Dean's Yard, Westminster   146 6C

Dean's Yard itself has been ruptured by a century of architectural pretension, its fate finally sealed by the horrible Church House (Sir Herbert Baker) which slobbers its way along the whole of the south side. But Little Dean's Yard is quite different.[7] It opens off the east side, surrounded by unpretentious classical buildings belonging to Westminster School, including the back of Lord Burlington's cool, patrician dormitory. On the east side, in line with the Victoria Tower, is an entrance arch leading up to the Busby Library. And suddenly, the townscape puts off aloofness and becomes as direct as in Italy. To start with, the arch itself (1734) really means business, is there because it wants to be. It is carved like an outsize schoolboy's desk with dozens of names, mostly early-nineteenth-century, all done with force and meaning in one or other of the marvellous variety of alphabets then available [10 and 11]. Man and his environment have melted, so that the arch is serving a human purpose and the names an architectural one.

7. It is part of Westminster School, and not open to the public. But the entrance arch leading to the Busby Library can be seen from the opening off Dean's Yard.

Houses of Parliament   146 5–6D
Sir Charles Barry and A. W. N. Pugin, 1835–60
and Westminster Hall
Henry Yevele and Hugh Herland, 1394–1402

Like the Gothic Revival itself, the Houses of Parliament are a vast hallucination, set down in Westminster to bewitch and enchant ... but also to perplex and maybe irritate, because they are basically literary, concerned with the idea of Parliament rather than Parliament itself. Stage scenery which takes itself seriously; superb, but as unreal as proceedings in the High Court. The British Museum does the same thing in Classical terms; Victorian stations rarely do it, and Victorian pubs never do.

Certainly there was enough excuse, for the style seems simply to have been taken over from Henry VII's Chapel across the road. An immense classical shape, encrusted with so many towers and pinnacles that the conjuring trick comes off [12 and 13]: from Westminster Bridge in any light the result is magical, something that fixes London for any visitor. Only the Vickers Towers deflates the experience. Yet in a funny way it is Vickers, which is the natural, commercial London, and the Houses of Parliament which have strayed up from Glyndebourne. A dream in stone must have a dream landscape around it.

The inside works out the same hard destiny. As long as the unremitting pressure of gilding and feverish translation from the Gothic is kept up, then it is marvellous – truly marvellous, with no holds barred: you surrender as you do to the atmosphere of Covent Garden. The whole sequence of the tour from the visitors' entrance[8] (every Saturday, unpublicized, but one of the most exciting experiences in London) is like this: from the underside of the Victoria Tower through the Robing Room and Royal Gallery to the House of Lords. Pugin never did better, and under the spell you would happily assent to his Gothic puddings. There are many ways to heaven, and this is one of them, an illusion so fine that it floats upwards in a bubble.

After this, the bubble bursts. Perhaps it always did, or perhaps the war-time damage broke the chain of enchantment. At any rate, the rest is an anti-climax, through the central hall to Sir Giles Gilbert Scott's creepy new House of Commons (1950), which takes the old Gothic forms and stretches and twists them to become reality again, but in a neurotic, self-torturing agony. Either present parliaments richly deserve their chamber, or the chamber has made its own creatures as M.P.s. Whichever way, this shifty, look-over-your-shoulder room is richly expressive of governmental processes in the fifties and sixties.

After this, the public sequence through Westminster Hall is a breath of fresh air: simple outside, equipped with instinctive rather than applied richness inside. The hammer-beam part of the roof, when you get there, is the least of it. What matters are the basic bows and the patterns of lacework vertical struts – as it were a map of a whole personality, where even the House of Lords could only gild over a stereotype.

8. It can be undertaken at present only on application to a Member of Parliament: one of the less publicized consequences of modern urban terrorism.

SOUTH FROM THE ABBEY: VICTORIA AND PIMLICO

Barton Street – Cowley Street – Lord North Street   146 6–7C

M.P.s' deepest Westminster: secluded, near the division bell, never likely to be touched by that compulsory purchase which is distributed so liberally over the constituencies. Still, in spite of that, a very nice place: a narrow dog-leg with all the views closed, a cosy Georgian coverlet to roll up around you. The original bits start at 1722, early enough to have some chunkiness to them. The twentieth century has added so discreetly that I would not like to swear to the date of any particular stretch of brick. Around the last corner, Lord North Street is later and plainer, leading straight to Archer's extraordinary church of St John, Smith Square [14]. Blitzed since 1940 and shortly to be rebuilt,[9] extraordinary is a fair mark – violence and vehemence without conviction.* The inner poetry of Hawksmoor's ruin at St George-in-the-East is quite missing. But anyway, a wonderful object to have lying around in the townscape. A look back down Lord North Street will show that, against the odds, you can focus on one third of a flashy neo-Georgian façade (Horace Field, 1905) with complete success.

9. It was rebuilt as a concert hall.

Tate Gallery   146 9C

Poor Tate! It seems to get the rough end of every stick: first of all in the pompous, confused building, then in the unlikely combination of subject (British art of any date plus all modern art), and finally in the fact that the masterpieces of both classes are apt to disappear to the National Gallery. The Impressionists, for example, have now become classical and there is only a token display down here; there are some marvellous paintings by Constable, but not Crome's *Poringland Oak* which ought to be seen with them.[10] This unhappy spirit seems to have infected the place; foreign paintings are shuffled off in the downstairs galleries when British work of far less value is displayed above; and surely no other gallery can have two cloakrooms – one for packages, and one for coats – at opposite ends of the building.[11]

After all that, what is there to see? Blake's towering imagination at its very best, from the sombre set of colour-prints of 1795 to the ineffably bulgy *Man Who Built the Pyramids*. Turner displayed on such a scale that the inevitable absentees are hardly noticed. 'Minor painters' like Landseer and Alfred Stevens[12] revealed as unexpectedly major when the Victorian muse wasn't working too hard; then the cranky, talented humanist course of British art that ran right through to the early 1950s and now seems to have stopped utterly. Beyond that there is abstraction, experiment, and artists enjoying private jokes; academic art turned inside out, with, I fear, little more real future than Alma-Tadema.

Down below, in the foreign section, there is a higher standard and more figures to span the gap: led by that arch-joker Picasso, who is splendidly if intermittently represented. Perhaps the best solution would be Foreign paintings in the National Gallery and British in the Tate. Certainly, for good or bad, this is an overpoweringly British place: an artistic London Airport.

10. Although it is here, in an adjacent room.
11. During the 1970s the northern corner of the Gallery site was filled in by a starkly functional modern extension. This enabled the modern collection to be brought up to the ground floor, although there is still not enough room for either the British or the modern collection to be displayed in anything like its entirety.
The Clore Gallery, designed by James Stirling, Michael Wilford and Associ-

* Appropriately, it glowers at political offices of various shades.

ates to house the Turner collection, opened in 1987. It can be entered from the main building, but is best approached from outside, through the gardens. That way you see first the clever, chameleon-like exterior; then the tricky, idiosyncratic entrance hall, with its unexpected touches of day-glo colour; finally the calm, thickly-carpeted galleries. Controversy over the colour of the walls on which the Turners are hung is likely to simmer for some time yet.

Further extensions to the Tate, also by Stirling and Wilford, are planned for the next decade or so.

12. Alfred Stevens's paintings are all in store at the time of writing.

Hide Tower, Hide Place, SW1   146 9A
Stillman & Eastwick-Field, 1957–60

Hide Tower is a sober, unspectacular tower block of twenty-three storeys in the scrappy hinterland of the Tate Gallery. It has no faults and at first sight it seems to have no special virtues. But then, at a closer look, the undemonstrative detail is seen to be due to deliberate austerity, not lack of feeling; and the rough-shuttered concrete work is carried out with a devoted quietness. It shows in the objects outside, like kerbs, the dished disks which surround the new trees, the mono-lithic seat which curves round into the sun. And the entrance hall, usually the worst part of a block of flats, is more like a church than most churches through sheer integrity of purpose.[13] With so much meretricious and fancy concrete work about, this is worth a special visit.

13. It is beginning to show its age.

St James the Less, Moreton Street, Pimlico   146 9A
G. E. Street, 1860

Pimlico can be dull, but this building would liven up any walk. Closely packed on to the small site, slate and dusty red brick fuming at the shabby surroundings. The corner is taken up by the parish hall, tied in to the church with fantastic iron railings, scrolly-topped [28]. Everything is taut, curled in, fighting mad – a superb performance, on the level of the best nineteenth-century romantic music, far above the best of the Pre-Raphaelites. The inside is a complete example of mid-century originality. Everything is designed afresh in this notched, polychrome museum-piece, from the huge iron canopy over the font to the offertory boxes. But what it lacks is the overwhelming spatial power that Butterfield had which could weld all these separate pieces into a great interior – in a way, the true interior space is that hot-blooded courtyard outside. But, even as a repository for fittings, it is a place to walk round with child-like astonishment, like being translated back to the Great Exhibition. The area around is being rebuilt by Westminster City Council to a competition-winning design.[14] The whole group of church hall and school must stay absolutely intact. (Entrance to the church via the school door in Thorndike Street, on the right-hand side of the tower.)

14. It has become the much-acclaimed Lillington Gardens estate (by Darbourne & Darke, completed 1971), a low-rise warren of brick and tile and intricate broken façades, a reaction to 1950s and 1960s tower and slab housing. The church sits in the heart of the estate looking curiously embarrassed. The close relationship of church and houses seems to be physical only: the church looks under-used and neglected, and is likely to become more so now that the school has closed.

Westminster Roman Catholic Cathedral
J. F. Bentley, 1894 onwards

145 7L

For me, this building shows the difference between actually being and trying-very-hard-to-be, better than any in London. For very many thousands of others, the Cathedral is a holy place and a house of God. If I offend them, I am sorry.

The architect, J. F. Bentley, was a man who never found himself. Competent, and full of feeling, he built in many styles, yet was at home in none of them. This, a kind of free Byzantine, was just one more style. From the outside, it looks as though Bentley would have been really happy building in Art Nouveau, like many more architects of the time caught in a trap of period styles. Inside, something else took over, and he built, almost accidentally, a superb religious warehouse. The great domed bays, built of yellow bricks which have gone almost black, are a true nineteenth-century equivalent to the austerity of the Cistercians. Bentley intended the whole lot to be covered with marble and mosaic. Slowly, inexorably, with much love and great expense, this is happening. In face of such devotion, how can I say that it is misplaced? Yet, in face of the spirit of the building, how can I say anything else? The material of the marble, which is glorious, can mesmerize momentarily and so can the pretty detail which, like the tower, seems to depend more on the Imperial Institute than on anything from across the Channel. But one look at one of the chapels on the south side (third from the west end) and things snap back into place. Because here, in the choir stalls and kneelers, is a real work of being, style and expression pounding together. Ernest Gimson designed them in 1912, without self-conscious doubts. He knew his style, a bit like Mackintosh without the Scottish rhetoric, and his compound of rectilinear shapes and rich inlay burns away in what seems to be – liturgically speaking – a fairly unimportant part of the building. Beside it, everything else – except the majestic brick vaults – seems like a splendid electric appliance without the current turned on.

Portland House, Stag Place
Howard, Fairbairn & Partners, 1962

145 6L

This is the tall block which overlooks the Palace, dwarfs Westminster Cathedral, adds congestion to an already congested area [15]. Not an endearing start. But to see it among its neighbours – for example,

looking down the new road beside Gorringe's[15] – is a good place to see
the difference between alive and dead modern buildings. Portland
House is no masterpiece, but it has got a spark, it is a real live idea of
a building, where the dead fish all around it are just so many square
feet of lettable office space to exist in loveless apathy until the time
comes for their demolition. The huge slab with tapered ends rises
sheer out of the ground, hoisted up bodily by a granite arcade faced
with marble. This is the best part: above there is too much fuss,
especially in the vertical strips, which are actually guides for the
cleaning cradles. But enough of someone's vision has got through.

15. Gorringe's has gone, but the reference is to the view down Bressenden
Place from Buckingham Palace Road.

Queen's Gallery, Buckingham Palace   145 5L
New, yet extraordinarily British. It is an excellent place to see that
atmosphere need not depend on age. The gallery is at the back of the
Palace, reached from Buckingham Gate up a long ramp with outward
views rigorously excluded. Electric eyes count the visitors; attendants
in royal livery gravely indicate the way round. Yet the mixture is
not incongruous and certainly not unpleasant. Instead the feeling is
somehow of getting a secret look at a private treasure, with everyone
conspiring to keep it dark. You expect to be given a furtive plate of
muffins, with the whispered comment 'pass it on'. It gives more
understanding of the royal family than a dozen state occasions. The
gallery itself, with its translucent ceiling, is technically as good as it
can be. It is small, and everything there is worth looking at. The
displays are changed regularly so that detailed description is useless.

Westminster Congregational Chapel,[16] Buckingham Gate
W. F. Poulton, 1864   145 6M
The outside looks merely cranky, with its polychrome brickwork and
a later tower which manages to say 'shan't' in about three different
ways at once. But the inside is magnificent, a real oratorio hall; huge
and elliptical, with two tiers of galleries. The upper tier is split into
two and returns into the walls with a splendid shake of its bulbous
ironwork front. The lower runs right round the church, with the
ground floor appearing as an oval hole in the middle. From it, the pews
are formed up with parade-ground precision. The whole place is made
for massed choirs and a massed faith; and in spite of all the talents of the
Gothic Revival, this is the true religious architecture of the nineteenth
century, all of a piece with the warehouses and the pubs – as Baroque
and Gothic were before it. It is very well kept up, sympathetically
decorated in grey and royal blue. (The entrance is down the passage
on the left-hand side.)

16. Now just Westminster Chapel.

St Ermin's Hotel, Broadway, entrance hall   146 6A
E. T. Hall, 1887

Don't bother to visit southern Europe; come here and suspend belief
utterly, as you should inside all Grand Hotels. Once inside, beyond
the cavernous bricky entrance next to Caxton Hall, this humdrum part
of Westminster is far away. The hall is an ornate Florentine confection,
twenty feet high, recently decorated to be the acme of elegance in
cream, peach and grey. Around it writhes a balcony, the undulating
balustrade twice the scale of everything else, as though this were Lower
Austria. You are carried away with the scoops and scallops, thrown
back with a delicious shock on the prickly froth of ornament around.
Urgent and intoxicating; it would be marvellous to get wed here instead
of next door.

Queen Anne, Queen Anne's Gate   146 5A
Probably Francis Bird, c. 1705

Queen Anne's Gate itself is overrated: it is a complete eighteenth-
century street with some jolly porches, but nothing more, except an
oasis in a pretty grinding part of Westminster. Queen Anne herself,
however, on a pedestal next to No. 13,* is a perfect official statue, full
of generalized queenly virtues yet still a recognizable and attractive
person, stepping out into life with just enough English straight-
forwardness. Grotesque faces on either side – keystones of one of the
houses – complement these high sentiments perfectly. For the last
time, the whole of society could be seen straight. The top of society
withered early (nobody dared portray the Georges as they actually
were), the rest kept intact until 1914. Now, it's sculptural catch-as-
catch-can. The artist is not known, but was surely Francis Bird,
because this is a twin of his statue originally in front of St Paul's.

WHITEHALL AND ST JAMES'S
Scotland Yard[17]   146 5D
Norman Shaw, 1888 and 1912

Norman Shaw's attempt at Vanbrughian grandeur has fallen flat,
doomed from the start by his beefy heartlessness. The one great thing
about it is almost accidental: the way the two blocks, linked only by a
bridge, set each other off in an exciting, asymmetric way. But the
smaller south block was an afterthought, which Shaw disliked, and it
is itself incomplete. What looks like syncopated calculation (the relative
proportions are 3:5 in the dormers, 5:8 in the main windows) is in fact
syncopated accident. The final irony is that this balanced asymmetry
is the sort of thing Shaw did very well in his youth and turned his back
on in old age. And now the policemen are moving out anyway.[18]

---

* It was originally on a wall in the middle of the road, and the Gate was originally
Queen Square.

17. Now the Norman Shaw Building, housing government offices. Best seen from the Embankment.

18. They have gone to the new New Scotland Yard offices in Victoria Street.

Dover House, Whitehall (Scottish Office), entrance screen and rotunda 146 3C
Henry Holland, 1787

A low frontispiece to an earlier building by Paine, very elegant and very cold-hearted. The spatial sequence could hardly be bettered: steps, then the rotunda with its impassive columns, then a flight of steps which starts in the middle of the rotunda so that the spaces interlock and there is no awkward transition. The front to Whitehall is just as expert, with its suave balance of centre and wings and the exquisite nicety of its detached columns. Yet there is no spark; it is still all on the drawing-board and it bears no real relation to the house behind it. It makes a penetrating contrast with Adam's Admiralty screen, which is just as elegant yet has a warm heart and a feeling for its surroundings as well. (Sometimes open for exhibitions: keep a lookout.)[19]

19. Open only to civil servants of the Scottish Office.

Banqueting House, Whitehall 146 3C
Inigo Jones, 1619–25

Opposite the Horse Guards, and in the same Renaissance style, but with a huge difference in feeling. Inigo Jones was a phenomenon unequalled in Europe: a true genius of the Italian *cinquecento*, born a hundred years later and a thousand miles away. This is no copy but the real thing: every attached column, every window surround, as telling and direct as Bramante or Sangallo might have made it: part of a complete design yet at the same time intensely itself. The frieze at the top, swags and faces calcined into sooty grandeur,[20] is one of the noblest things in London. This is one stage beyond style, where the effect of each part of the building is immediate: not merely one Italian Renaissance window, but *window*. The Palladians never understood this part of classical design; the neo-Baroque of the nineteenth century, easily seen by flicking the eye across the road to the War Office, understood nothing at all. We are still trying to pick up the pieces.

20. They were cleaned, but are slowly sooting up again.

Horse Guards 146 3C
William Kent, 1745–55

Kent could have been the greatest decorator of his century. Lord Burlington, who made him eminent, at the same time killed his chances of being truly great with his rules and regulations. So the Horse Guards becomes just an echo of the staccato Baroque design it should have

been, each creaking pavilion as anachronistic and over-articulated as
the Guards who stomp back and forwards – two – three – four. Unlike
many of London's traditional ceremonies, this is a blatant tourist-trap
neither better nor worse than a Soho strip-tease club. Changing the
guard at Buckingham Palace means something; changing the guard
here is an exercise as academic as a Palladian pattern-book, designed
only for the clicking of camera shutters. The backsides of the sentry
boxes, with their perpetual dribble of horse-piss, are fair comment.
There is a parish boundary mark exactly half way through the main
arch, another fair comment: this place is so inorganic that it splits into
a dozen pieces.

Admiralty Screen   146 3C
Robert Adam, 1759

The Admiralty is a galumphing building of 1722 by a galumphing
architect, Thomas Ripley. The eighteenth century realized this, and
stretched a screen in front, thirty years later, by the young Robert
Adam: as it were, a delicious aperitif to a large main course that you
have doubts about. This was exactly Adam's *métier*, and his screen
blows you weightlessly from wing to wing of the doughy big building.
Without weight, but not without solidity: one of the very few things
in London which would benefit from being kept sparkling fresh,
perpetually clean.

Admiralty Arch – The Mall – Buckingham Palace   146 2B
Aston Webb, 1911–13
The Mall originally laid out c. 1660

Separately, and considered in the abstract: an overloaded arch, a
pleasant straight avenue, and Brock's Benefit of Edwardian pomp and
circumstance at the other end. Together, and endowed with knowledge
of their function – rightly endowed, because the spaces and buildings
express it anyway – they become a great formal gesture. Forget the
fact that it is all designed in that unfashionable classicism of 1910: here
is an axis of exactly the right length, with a circumstantial entry from
the bustle of Trafalgar Square, and with the royal palace at the other
end – still an inaccessible home and not a museum, its bulk and gravity
just enough to control the lavish stone explosion of fountains and gate-
piers in front, yet not enough to overshadow it. In the end the whole
thing is dominated by the four-fold line of planes in The Mall: nature
on top, as it should be in a symbolic compression of England. The
Champs-Élysées, and other academic layouts, come miles down the
list compared with this reasonable yet dramatic gesture. The particular
Recessional flavour, an Indian summer of Empire fanned up briefly to
be hotter than mid July, is very poignant now; not a museum-piece
but a living exposition of 1910, calling to the Edwardian hidden in
every person's character.

The Citadel   146 3B
W. A. Forsyth, 1940

Whilst the loud-hailed masterpieces of the thirties are peeling and
chipping, this ugly duckling has settled into the affectionate line of
London's jokes. It is a shelter for Top People, with the same datum
as an iceberg. What appears is a cubist essay in brown concrete,
composing by accident or design into the kind of effects that architectural photographers then strove for. It has a hilarious effect on the
blimpish Admiralty extension next door; there is creeper up the wall
and grass on the roof, as you can see from the top of New Zealand
House. A wonderful personality, amongst all the overdressed emptiness around.

St James's Park   146 4A, etc.
John Nash, 1828

Londoners are so used to the genius of John Nash and the public spirit
of the Crown that it takes a visitor to exclaim at the royal parks. Hyde
Park and Regent's Park could – just – be public open spaces. St James's
Park can never be anything but a regal gift. It is the Palace's front
garden (the utterly private back gardens are in the same style), landscaped to get the maximum effect from the minimum space: and
landscaped by a man to whom picturesque, intricate design was not
just a fashion but a faith. No meander but leads somewhere, no
accidental-seeming vista but is deliberate. The long narrow strip, not
much more than the central reservation on the Mickleham By-pass,
has a lake running down it,* and a bridge running across the lake. The
views from it are the high point of the whole layout. To the west, the
block of Buckingham Palace, usually in deep shadow; to the east the
most romantic view in London, an epitome of all the stories about
Englishmen with staid exteriors who burn with passion underneath.
Nash wriggled the lake and split it around an island. Beyond, the Horse
Guards skyline, solid but with a twinkle in its eye. Behind and above,
now, the domes of the War Office and the turrets of Whitehall Court.
Xanadu; and as unexpected yet natural as Coleridge's poem in an
anthology of subdued nature poets.

Carlton House Terrace   146 3A–2B
John Nash, 1827–9

The stucco peels, the brickwork underneath is shoddy, the design was
thrown together. But it was thrown together by a genius, and this
impressionist sweep of columns is one of the traveller's firmest friends
in London [16]. It will see him through a grey February day, or sparkle
in the first illusory sunshine at the end of March, or loll languidly in
August. Every bit can be faulted in the mind, every bit succeeds in the

---

* It was drained in the First World War, and had a hutted camp on the site. Nash
could doubtless have turned this to advantage too.

heart. It needs to be kept in tip-top order, whatever the cost, as a tribute to illusion become something more than reality. Some of the money misapplied to wiping the face of experience from Portland stone buildings might well be diverted here.[21]

21. It has been restored to sparkling condition.

Duke of York's Steps   146 3B
John Nash, 1828–33

Steps, splitting Carlton House Terrace, going up from the park to Regent Street across the site of Carlton House, the Prince Regent's palace that was originally the end-point of the whole great composition. Steps splitting around Benjamin Wyatt's Duke of York's Column, the granite a good foil to Nash's yellow stucco, better still in the crystalline sootiness of a few years ago. Just steps? Well, no. These are in their more direct way the London equivalent of the Spanish Steps, the tension built up by a backwards and forwards motion instead of by spirals. There are three flights, with two intermediate landings. To begin with, there is a skyline on the approach, a hint of Regent Street, which disappears at the foot of the steps themselves, reappears up the first flight, and slips away again on the first landing. The second flight establishes the street at the end all right, but now it has no floor. For Regent Street is slightly concave, and the landing slopes upwards very slightly: the combination means that buses seem to float without their wheels, buildings disappear into what seems to be a canal. The whole truth doesn't appear until the last few feet. Look backwards, and there is one of central London's best views, all fantasy: the Westminster towers amongst trees, with Vickers well out of the way to one side.

Carlton Mews   146 2B
John Nash, c. 1830

By the time this book appears, Carlton Mews may well have been mutilated or obliterated for the sake of a few extra bedrooms in a clubhouse.[22] In that case, this is an obituary for Nash's gentlest gift to London, the sort which shows his true mettle, because there is no top dressing. This is why his big schemes succeeded – because they were based on an exceptional and very humane understanding of space. Carlton Mews is best seen from the back of Carlton House Terrace. Between Nos. 22 and 23, there is a three-bay stucco house with what seems to be an extra front door. This (NOT dedicated to the public, etc. . . .) leads through to a light-well, then to the magic mews itself, a courtyard with stables below, houses above, a big tree peering over the wall at the end. All empty now, one of the saddest sights in London. Under another arch, past the grass-grown ramp, and out skew on to a Trafalgar Square that has turned into a squad of squint-eyed men: one portico of Canada House going one way, another at an obtuse angle,

Nelson himself stepping out in a different direction altogether. Normal rectilinear space has somehow slipped on a banana skin.

22. It was swept away in 1970 for the new building on the north side of Carlton House Terrace, now occupied by the British Council.

Pall Mall
146 2–3A

A straight, gloomy, reserved street, the epitome of nineteenth-century closed doors compared with the wider, jollier, eighteenth-century St James's Street. They are the last streets that ought to have to accommodate through traffic and our traffic engineers have run a one-way system through both. But it will need more than a few buses to prise open this clam – a character perfectly matched in the mannered vagaries of No. 100, on the site of the Carlton Club, by Donald Mac-Morran, 1958. The interest, apart from Schomberg House, is in four buildings at the east end, just beyond No. 100. The two on either side of Waterloo Place (United Services[23] and Athenaeum) are part of the stucco scenery of Regent Street. The two farther west aim higher (not higher than the total effect of Regent Street, but higher in themselves). Both are by Barry, both were designed before he became lost in the labyrinth of the Houses of Parliament, with Pugin's unbalance for an Ariadne. The Travellers' in stucco, the Reform in stone, both correct, nobly disciplined, gravely assured, with every relationship of window to wall justly calculated. But neither has any of the inner excitement of their Renaissance models. Here, in these truly handsome clothes, is the first indication of the blindness which led to the military catastrophes of 1916 and the architectural catastrophes of the 1920s – Earl Haig and Sir Herbert Baker both. What Barry really enjoyed most can be seen by walking up Waterloo Place and looking at the back elevation of the Travellers' [17]. Chic round-headed arches jostle each other: the clubman had naughty pictures hidden in the bottom drawer. But the top drawer, within its limits, is as good as it can be, and what more can you ask?

23. Now the Institute of Directors.

Schomberg House, Pall Mall
145 3M

A jolly, beery town house of 1698, the only one of its type left in Central London. It was built for a Dutchman, and the cornice with its florid consoles is very Dutch indeed; as far as I know it has no parallel in Britain. But the really remarkable thing is that the three bays on the left-hand side were missing for a hundred years. The reinstatement was done by C. H. Elsom, the designer of Eastbourne Terrace, Paddington, and the join is absolutely imperceptible. (South side of Pall Mall, near the west end.)

St James's Palace   145 3M

Like many other places in London, you have to play this by ear [18].
The eye won't help you much in an organized, Hampton-Court sense.
The courtyards are ordinary, deliberately casual: the red tunics and
bearskins are no less military than at the Palace but seem here to be
just doing a job, semi-casually. Tourists come in accidentally, perhaps
sidetracked from the Palace and The Mall by the thought of a cuppa.
No hope of that this side of Piccadilly – this is the underside of a
monarchy, an equivalent to the garden side of Buckingham Palace
which no ordinary person can ever see. And not only of a monarchy:
we would have been a republic long ago if this passion for discreet
authority, understatement and privacy were not part of the essence of
most Englishmen. It is not so much one note in the English scale as a
key signature.

26 St James's Place and Spencer House   145 3L
26 St James's Place, Denys Lasdun, 1959
Spencer House, John Vardy, 1752–4

One of the best juxtapositions of old and new in London. The two
palaces, 1750 and 1960, stare out at the park, totally dissimilar, yet
now as inseparable as Guinness and oysters. On the face of it, there is
no resemblance between the fussy stone Palladian front and Lasdun's
much taller and bolder block with its fierce, jutting balconies, marble
fronted, and its purple bricks. Yet this is no shock success; the new
design has responded to the old with deep sympathy so that each
classical feature finds a complement or a contrary. All marriages of
dissimilars should work out like this.[24]

24. Additional modern flats to the north have, ironically, slightly diminished
the force of No. 26.

TRAFALFAR SQUARE TO SOHO
National Gallery   146 1B

As a building (William Wilkins, 1832–8) the National Gallery is a set
of good porticoes and bad domes, badly arranged. As a place to visit,
it is two quite different things. Outside, the main portico is one of the
few real meeting-places in Central London, as thousands of foreign
visitors have realized. It is a place in itself, thanks to Wilkins's talent
with individual units, and it looks out on a place: Trafalgar Square,
but with the view arranged for once so that the shape matches the
meaning. Instead of the familiar falling away, there is a set of horizontals – the upper balustrade, the plinth of Nelson's Column – backing
up, throwing the space in again. Traffic is neither here nor there
because you are looking down at the roofs of double-decker buses.
Farther parts, like Big Ben, beckon at the ends of the views. London

in the palm of your hand; member of the vortex at Piccadilly Circus, detached and clinically observant on top of New Zealand House [21]; both detached and engaged, down here. Between the three of them, the essence of Europe's biggest city is plotted.

The inside is a job to summarize, even without the need for a detailed description, and even in a guide already devoted to superlatives. If the National Gallery could only be performed a few times a year, as we perform *Hamlet* or *King Lear*, then perhaps it would not be taken for granted. For here is one of the best, and perhaps the best single picture gallery in the world. Every painting is worth looking at, perhaps three or four in each gallery are masterpieces, and there is no specialization. If you want Van Eyck, there he is with the Arnolfinis, as super-real as a Van Gogh chair; if you want Seurat, then there he is also with the *Baignade at Asnières*, placing his irregular mauve dots with an inimitable French flourish. In between, there is no sag. El Greco speaks as violently as he does in the Prado, and Rubens provides an epigrammatic summary of what is waiting for the traveller in Brussels and Antwerp. Here also, a little ironically, are the Gainsboroughs and Turners which ought to be set-piece decoration at the Tate. And all the time, the whole glorious ten-century agglomeration is celebrating man and what made him, rather than social-economic circumstances, art history, and the abstract value of pure colour. (This needs to be forcibly asserted if you are within earshot of some of the lecturers.) The Mond room, full of Rembrandts, is the most spectacular set-piece of all, dead in line with the main entrance:[25] and down to the last fleck of white paint on dark brown background it says: here we are, mortal; but we can be something else as well.

25. The Rembrandts are now in rooms 26 and 27 in the new rear extension.

Suffolk Street and Suffolk Place   146 1–2B
John Nash, G. Ledwell Taylor, Edward Cresy,
Lewis Wyatt, 1820–30

A yellow stucco resting place just round the corner from Pall Mall and Trafalgar Square; and the best place in London to see how fluent and how adaptable Nash's language was. Here is a formal effect without any formal design, just gentlemen's agreement: regularity without any loss of individuality. Part of this harmony of difference is the enchanting back elevation to Nash's Haymarket Theatre, with oval windows stretched across the top like a repeated wink. Another, round the corner in Suffolk Place, is the way in which his swaggering Doric ground-floor columns rest – as one looks down into the basement – on nothing more than a corbel. This is so transparently naughty that it offends nobody; and neither does it affect the townscape effect of the

Doric columns. The building at the end of Suffolk Street (No. 15)[26] by Lewis Wyatt, which ties the rest together, was reinstated after war damage. Thank goodness.

26. Now No. 16.

New Zealand House, Haymarket   146 2A
Robert Matthew, Johnson-Marshall & Partners, 1960–62

Full of small virtues, of the accommodating kind for which one will willingly forgo a grand gesture. The eighteen-storey block does not spoil any London views; the careful projecting profile of the floor slabs [19] provides an anchor for the perspective views along Pall Mall instead of the facelessness of a glass wall. Nash's Royal Opera Arcade, on the west side, has not only been preserved but doubled in effect, with an extra row of shops. And the view from the roof terrace [21] is superb:[27] the site is as near the hub of London as could be – rather like peering out from inside Big Ben – and all the expected London monuments come up in turn. But many of them wear unexpected faces: the Admiralty Citadel turns out to have grass on top, Tower Bridge is seen wildly romantic amongst a forest of cranes. In spite of all the bricks and mortar, the biggest thing in the westward view is London's precious band of green running from St James's Park through Green Park away to Kensington. This is the central equivalent of the view from Primrose Hill [37]. If that might begin a London visit, this might well be the culmination. It would be worth spending all of one day here, identifying the landmarks, feeling the flux of London's traffic by road and river, watching the rush-hour jams and the couples in the park with Olympian detachment: and then going back down into them.

27. Now open only to New Zealanders.

St Martin-in-the-Fields   146 1C
James Gibbs, 1722–6

That the British have a genius for compromise may be a commonplace. But to have a genius for anything is very special, and this particular brand is exactly what Gibbs had. Compromise, not as a deadening average but as a positive thing, a balance of tensions, runs all through St Martin's. Italian licence and native sobriety are exactly matched, not mechanically or intellectually but out of the nature of the man. Each stage of the steeple is a natural balance.* Resting it on the roof

* Another kind of balance, very Anglican, is between Church and State. The royal arms appear outside on the pediment, with a splendidly cut inscription beneath them. They appear inside in plaster on the coving above the chancel arch. In both cases they hold a key position in the composition: but nothing is forced and nothing overbearing.

of the temple to combine it with a portico is another kind of compromise between intellect and display. Whether it is architecturally correct is irrelevant; it *works*. Inside, the balance has been taken a stage deeper. It is one unified space, yet it is exactly half way between Wren at St James Piccadilly and a full-blown Baroque church. The key is in the curved quadrant walls which take up the difference in width between nave and chancel. On the first floor they have panelled rooms (royal pews, originally) open to the east as well as to the church. So space comes rocking in diagonally as well as through the sober east window. In just the same way an Italianate orchestral figure by Handel would come swooping down across a four-square melody. That the architect came from Aberdeen and the composer from Saxony does not in the end affect the quintessential Englishness of the gesture. And, to say it just once more, at this level it is as worth while as the most inspired outspokenness.

Great buildings don't always get the owners they deserve. Dogma imposed on this wise and generous-hearted building would be unbearable. So it is very just that this of all the London churches should be a byword for tolerance, and for charity without strings. If you have nowhere else, you can use the crypt for a kip. No wonder Londoners have taken it to their hearts, along with the pigeons outside and the pillar-box red of the buses.

St Martin's National School, Adelaide Street   146 IC
George Ledwell Taylor, 1830

This poignant stucco façade at the back of St Martin's announces one of London's loveliest buildings. In mist or rain it will never let you down; and the glint of sunshine on the pilasters puts a dagger straight into your guts. This is the kernel of London, an epitome of what makes cockneys homesick. It was built in 1830, as it announces in splendid lettering on the entablature. The architect was George Ledwell Taylor, an astonishing man responsible for masterpieces as diverse as Sheerness Docks and the crazy steeple at Hadlow Castle in Kent. The style is Nash's, but the glitter is quite individual. It used to be painted cream, and is now lime green – a slight pity, because this *stretto* masterpiece needs no cosmetic aids at all. (Apparently it will become empty in 1966. Advance warning: this building is as important to London as the Tower.)[28]

28. It has survived, and is painted cream again.

National Portrait Gallery, Charing Cross Road   146 IB

Tucked away at the back of the National Gallery is an oddly chaste classical building by Ewan Christian, who was usually pretty cross-grained. Not a place for claustrophobes: room after room crammed with stuffed full-faces, three deep. It is unfair to treat it as an art gallery, because it is not trying to be; but all the same, England does seem to have been incapable of producing official portraits with much depth to them. Reynolds and Lawrence come out with their integrity unbreached; but Kneller's Kit-Kat portraits and almost all of the twentieth-century stuff is really terrible.[29] The best straight portraits, conveying some of the real personality of the sitter, are probably the pair by Millais of Gladstone and Disraeli. The treasure trove is amongst the pictures which were done for their own sakes, not for commemoration: a coloured bust of Colley Cibber by Roubiliac (did it come from Vauxhall?) and a self-portrait by Isaac Fuller which is one of the few things in seventeenth-century British art to come anywhere near Rembrandt. And tucked away in a side gallery is a delightfully dandified army officer by Tissot, his air of humorous foppishness completely at odds with the heroic details of his career recorded underneath.[30]

29. The twentieth-century collection is constantly changing and enlarging, and a generalization is no longer possible. Among recent royal portraits, Bryan Organ's studies of the Prince and Princess of Wales stand out as original and penetrating.
30. Captain Frederick Burnaby; now in the main Victorian gallery.

The Salisbury, St Martin's Lane   140 9C
Architect unknown, c. 1900

Real West End glitter, with all the stops out. In the middle of theatre-land, just about the perfect theatre bar, with as much sparkle as a brandy-and-soda [22]. Cut-glass mirrors, brass-topped tables, Art Nouveau lamps, and lincrusta ceiling beautifully kept up and recently beautifully re-decorated by John and Sylvia Reid. The locals are nearly all stage people, which helps to keep the froth afloat, too. A small square back bar is treated with the utmost of rich simplicity: plain mirrors and red plush seats all round the walls. A pint in here is like drinking in one of Inigo Jones's cubes.[31]

31. A little of the sparkle has gone with the replacement of the red plush by light brown.

Goodwins Court   140 9C
A tiny alley off St Martin's Lane opposite the Salisbury. The view is just blocked by a projecting door, and then steps into a contrast as unexpected as anything in London. Hey presto, a Georgian street, bow windows and all; the Castle Museum at York ... except that it is not a museum. Eight identical Georgian shop-fronts step up the lane without turning a hair (not quite what they seem, I guess. They look as though they were done about 1900: could anybody tell me?)[32] At one end, half a dozen theatres. At the other, the grim Peabody blocks in Bedfordbury.[33] The combination makes up London.

32. Pevsner accepts them at face value as late eighteenth century.
33. Partly replaced.

Globe Theatre, Shaftesbury Avenue 140 9A

Most of London's theatres have a fluffy Edwardian bounce to them, as suitable to an evening's drama as the Victorian pub is to an evening's drinking. This one gives the gilt a special twist and it is also more or less visible from the street – most theatres are, naturally enough, more or less inaccessible to casual sightseers. Like many inspired architectural ideas, this is very simple. The pretty foyer has an oval hole cut in the roof. Above, there is a gallery bar for the circle, wrought round with more nice snippets. Two floors tied into a knot, and your theatre-going made just that bit more memorable.

Tower of St Anne Soho, Wardour Street 140 9A
S. P. Cockerell, 1802–6

Nothing could represent the seamier side of Soho better than this louche presence, its bottle-green top winking invitations to an astral strip-tease, the louvres and obscene, bulgy columns hiding god knows what perversions in the belfry. Pure, too, in the sense that a person can be pure evil. Architecturally, it has no ancestors; the nominal architect's other buildings are placid except for Sezincote, the Moorish country house in Gloucestershire. The body of the church was blitzed and is to be rebuilt; the tower must always remain, as an emblem of deeper pressures than mere beauty or ugliness.

Soho 139 8–9M and 140 8–9A

The clearest identity in London. North of Leicester Square, east of Regent Street, south of Oxford Street, west of Charing Cross Road, with all of the boundaries commercial meeting-places, so that the area links hands with its neighbours.

That's for the maps. Inside this square rule, you can get the best and worst of almost anything. It is the free port that every city must have. Because of it, rebuilt Hamburg is splendid; for lack of it rebuilt Rotterdam is dismal. Whatever you want of it will be there. If you want the wickedest place in Britain, you can find it; if you want a cosmopolitan village in the city, with village shops and pubs, it is there also. Not any one thing but every kind of thing. For five bob you can have a bad caff meal or some of the cheapest good food in London. The tarts are off the streets now. Instead there are traffic wardens, taking up the same kind of stance but not looking nearly so inviting. If you want a lady, ring on doorbells marked Marie or Sabrina; and good luck. But also, if you want, for example, genuine Italian food served by genuine Italians who are not trying to impress anyone, come here also. Something for everybody.

Soho itself splits up the middle, east and west of Wardour Street. East is High Soho, a chequerboard of streets (Dean, Frith, Greek) which are hard to tell apart, as formal as a minuet though far less innocent. Here the grid works far better than an intricate pattern would do, because the area stands or falls purely on the interest of its shopfronts. Something here for every purse and temperament, a world of serial astonishment.

West of Wardour Street, Low Soho is cosier, shabbier, more winding and more mixed up – council flats and old-established businesses amongst the *trattorie* and nude bookshops. Here Westminster City Council has put up one tall block of flats and is about to build another: decent buildings in themselves, but a hopeless pattern for this teeming jungle whose essence is lack of uniformity. Architects and administrators need much more feeling for life than they usually display before they start tampering with a place like this. Life wins, of course; beside the first tall block in Berwick Street is the best street market of Central London, road and pavements completely solid with stalls and shoppers. But why couldn't the architecture have helped instead of hindering?

This is not the place to seek out points of detail. As well make delicate assessments of texture in the stomach of a whale. Two which are worth a look are Meard Street (a short link between Wardour and Dean Streets), which is still untouched early Georgian, and a Victorian-Jacobean café, No. 75 Beak Street, designed with real spirit. Until a few years ago it had a curly gabled top which made it one of the best view-stoppers in London, seen down Great Pulteney Street. Now only the lower storeys are left, a great pity. Because it was the wrong period, and no exalted name was responsible, nobody bothered to preserve it – yet it was worth ten of those inorganic fragments in the Home Counties for which people fight so furiously.[34]

34. For a time in the 1970s the seamier side of Soho threatened to swamp everything else. The area is now being cleaned up with a good deal of determination, and the remaining clip-joints and peep-shows are unenticingly sleazy. Meard Street survives, but very much run down. The café in Beak Street has become a very ordinary sandwich bar. In addition to High and Low Soho it is now possible to distinguish a richly colourful third segment: Chinese Soho, centred on Gerrard Street.

PICCADILLY AND THE WEST END

Piccadilly Circus   146 1A
Statue of Eros: Alfred Gilbert, 1892

This really is the centre of London. But why? What makes it the focus of everyone's night out; why, when you stand under Eros, with the traffic swirling endlessly round, does it suddenly feel as though the whole enormous city is in the palm of your hand? What happens, I think, is a mixture of Nash and accident. Every important line of force in the West End goes through here: not only Nash's axis of Regent Street dividing Mayfair and Soho, which now leads directly to the Victoria Tower of the Houses of Parliament in one of London's great views. Piccadilly comes in, looking utterly respectable and club-like. Coventry Street slips in short and lewd from Leicester Square. Shaftesbury Avenue creeps out as though it knew that it led nowhere. And behind the bland façades on the north side, a dozen alleys slip away into Soho and sin. Long may they stay sinful. Every scale and temperament of London is represented somewhere, nowhere more than in the contrast between east and west sides of the Circus. Swan & Edgar's has all the circumstance that Norman Shaw could give it, and also pomp rather than pomposity, which is quite a rare thing. The buildings opposite on the east side are small, cramped, and covered with illuminated signs which are one of the best, least self-conscious displays of popular art anywhere in London. (The rooms behind them are quite windowless.) And all this fits together. Piccadilly Circus is not one or another, but the mixture. The east side will be rebuilt soon, and the architects of Britain will find themselves stretched not to put the dreary finger of good taste on it. This is a bit of real life, not an academic design problem, and if the circus is reconstructed the traffic must stay visible and circulating, for it is an essential part of the hub-of-the-world feeling. At the very centre, the hub of the hub, is Eros. Pellucid and innocent, quite free of Alfred Gilbert's neurotic manoeuvres, and utterly right. This is T. S. Eliot's 'voice ... in the stillness between two waves of the sea'. And it all depends on traffic.[35]

35. The Circus's decline into the neon-lit slum of the 1970s is nearing its end; redevelopment and renovation are happening on all sides. But the swirl of circulating traffic was lost some years ago when the Circus became a one-way funnel, west to east, and the process was completed when the newly restored Eros, with the best of intentions, was moved nearer to the Criterion to be within easier reach of pedestrians.

Ward's Irish House,[36] Piccadilly Circus 146 IA

This is a basement under the angle between Shaftesbury Avenue and Coventry Street. It is not trying to be Irish; it just is. A big, bare room with a central zinc-topped bar; no concession to comfort, but on the other hand some of the best draught Guinness in London. More private spaces wind off it, reached under curly ironwork inscribed *Ulster, Leinster, Munster* and *Connaught*. It seems hardly credible, only a few feet from the edgy, metropolitan roundhouse of Piccadilly Underground. Like many places in Ireland, what you see is just the top of the iceberg. The rest is atmosphere, here as tangible as bricks and mortar. It has surely got the fairies on it, though mentioning fairies in this rough, shabby, real place you might get some strange looks. If it ever feels the need to rise in the world, may it shoot straight from a pint of porter to the elegance of Gaelic coffee.

36. It was part of the London Pavilion building, and is disappearing in the redevelopment scheme.

The Quadrant, Regent Street   145 IM
Norman Shaw, 1905–8
Sir Reginald Blomfield, 1920–30

Most of Regent Street, rebuilt in the twenties and thirties, is a disaster.
But Nash's plan was so good that it survives any amount of meddling:
Regent Street as a place or an entity is still intact, and the Quadrant,
leading out of Piccadilly Circus, is a fair exchange for Nash, especially
as his colonnades were removed in the 1850s (nasty things went on
inside 'em). It began with Norman Shaw, in Swan & Edgar's[37] and the
Piccadilly Hotel, beating the Baroque drum in a frenzied way. Sir
Reginald Blomfield, who carried on with the rest of the curve and the
whole of the north side, did better by getting rid of the histrionics yet
keeping the ponderous strength. For him, certainly, the Classical
Revival was a living thing. The County Fire Office, 1924, carried out
by W. G. Newton, deflects Nash's axis from Lower to Upper Regent
Street as effectively as the old building did; and the Quadrant itself is
inexhaustible, a real layer-cake of sensations at every level. At one end,
there is the wonderful play between the rooflines on the convex and
concave sides. According to where you stand, always, one is a smooth
sweep and the other is knobbly with alternating dormers. At the other
is a Pissarro-like haze of a majestic tube of space filled with red buses
and the glitter of the circus at the end. Where Air Street intersects the
Quadrant there are openings portentous with rustication and columns
[24]. The views through them are marvellous: from Piccadilly the
arches frame the small-scale hubbub of Soho; from Soho, the Piccadilly
frontage looks like an outdoor room. And in between, borne sublimely,
the tube of space which is still Nash's, dividing Soho from the West
End smoothly, firmly and with complete understanding.

37. Their former premises are occupied by Tower Records and other shops
and offices.

St James, Piccadilly   145 IM
Sir Christopher Wren, 1676–84

Wren's favourite church, and no wonder. This is as far as the Wren
virtues can take you, as good of its kind as it could be. Lucid, sane,
balanced, not unfeeling; not much depth but immense breadth. A great
lucid barrel vault to the nave, transverse barrel vaults above galleries
which have the grammatical problems of pier and column worked out
once and for all. White and gold, with clear glass: all part of the
restoration by Sir Albert Richardson after severe war damage [3]. Alas,
the inexplicably insensitive light fittings are his too, sticking up like
totem poles into Wren's clean English-Miss space. In other hands the
placidity easily becomes quite empty, but Wren's evenness was always
positive. Each dispassionate arch in this building has tremendous
power, like an unemotional, fairminded judge. This is the true language
of the intellect, a piece of calculus in plaster and wood, and it is

extraordinarily impressive. Inside it, originally, rich and full-blooded carving would have struck a more human balance – a parallel to Inigo Jones's idea of plain exteriors and rich interiors. Now, all that is left is the superabundant fecundity of Grinling Gibbons's carving around the reredos. Like a Chardin still-life, this fruit is more fruity than the real thing. (The font, which is also by Gibbons, is another matter entirely.)

Red Lion, Duke of York Street   145 2M

If I could keep only one pub out of the whole London galaxy, this would be my choice. It is not especially comfortable or especially atmospheric, but it strikes deeper than any other. All around the walls are magnificent cut-glass mirrors, the best in London, recently renovated so that they gleam as sharply as they ever did. And, as the bar space is roughly square, wall after wall after wall is reflected in the real walls, a process which oddly enough reinforces the solidity. Nothing is fuzzy, but everything has incredible depth and compassion combined with brilliance. It is the spirit exactly of Manet's *Bar at the Folies Bergère*.* It sees and feels everything, yet you are thrown back on your own resources, enriched. This is the opposite thing to the gentle, sentimental pub where you can wash your troubles into oblivion. If you had a problem, the Red Lion could not ease *it*, however much you drank; instead it would strengthen *you*. It is a place to walk out of ramrod-straight, reinforced by those proud, sparkling arabesques.

4 St James's Square   146 2A
Probably Edward Shepherd, after 1725

This is one of the few London town houses that is usually accessible – it is the headquarters of the Arts Council and exhibitions are held there regularly.[38] The designer was almost certainly Edward Shepherd, and it has a country twin at Boreham in Essex. It is a reassuring example of how the new rules could have all the strictness taken out of them by a cheerful builder. There is nothing here Lord Burlington's men would have quailed at, yet everything is done with an insouciant swagger that is the last thing they intended. The staircase is a giant Baroque thing with the details gone inexplicably pure, and the flow of space around the rooms is easy and informal. Complete, even to a tiny garden with a coachman's house at the bottom.

38. No longer accessible; the Arts Council has moved to Piccadilly.

Paxton & Whitfield, 93 Jermyn Street   145 2M

It may seem invidious to put in just one London shop, but this one is a quintessence of what metropolitan choice should stand for. It sells

* See p. 97.

several things, but its first love is cheese: great roundels of it in the window, along with a list of more cheeses than you are likely to have heard of. If the proprietor finds a piece that he likes the look of, he is quite likely to give you a slice to nibble. Long may it stay humble and dedicated. Amongst all of London's West End tinsel, this is a bit of real gold.

Piccadilly Arcade   145 2L

Across Piccadilly from the Burlington Arcade, and far more interesting. It is one of those weird places which has one element to a much bigger scale than anything else. Here, it is the curved glass windows. Everything else is a normal, cosy shopping scale, but the bows are fifteen or twenty feet high, uninterrupted – a wonderful piece of glass-making, apart from anything else – with top cornices to match. They ripple down the slope from Piccadilly like the sides of a Greek temple all done in glass. Above them, rooms with balconies are squashed under a pretty Regency roof with two domes in it. Some of the shops are subdivided, but most keep their extraordinary proportions inside, almost taller than they are wide.[39] So would I, in their place: for despite all the apparent inconvenience, this is the sort of shop that you remember. The effect is exciting and unnerving, as though it is not the shopfronts that are too big but yourself that is too small. All the time you expect a giant paw patting you on the head.

39. Most of them have now resorted to false ceilings.

Royal Academy and Albany   145 1L–M

The nineteenth century has seen to it that the courtyard of the Academy is an indigestible lump of classical pudding, and the original decoration in the public rooms is not much fun either. But the atmosphere of the place, on all but the busiest exhibition days, is extraordinary. Through the fussy archway from Piccadilly there are placid galleries, a place to park your car and a bar which at lunch-time can be one of the quietest spots in the West End.[40] The same feeling exactly is provided by Albany, a few yards farther east. The main building is made up of private chambers and is very select indeed; the forecourt is public, and you can step straight out of the bustle into an aloof quietness, matched exactly by Chambers's patrician, close-fisted façade. Neither place is much fun to look at, but the experience of calm among hubbub is very near the centre of London's personality. So, too, is the deliberate lack of surface charm. Sometimes in England it implies lack of any other charm also, but finding out can be fun.

40. Closed; the only bar is a very small one in the restaurant.

Westminster Bank, Piccadilly and Albemarle Street   145 2L
W. Curtis-Green, 1927

Food for thought here, in the slot between Mayfair and St James's. This is one of the very few buildings that belongs to the twenties and can be proud of it. Only the very end of the classical re-revival could have produced such a fluid juggling of motifs. Lutyens was good at it, as a party trick, but this is a serious thing, the classical members treated with real feeling as they were by Alberti and Bramante. The columns keeping up the fragile attic have real weight, the arches framing the two middle storeys are there from conviction. Opposite, the Royal Insurance[41] by Belcher (or rather his partner, Joass), 1907 has original detail that makes it a suitable subject for research, but no conviction at all. And the building next to it was done by the same architect as the Westminster Bank (or rather, the same firm) without any spark at all. The golden thread leads you a funny dance sometimes.

41. Now the Bradford and Bingley Building Society.

The 'Economist' Building, 23–7 St James's Street   145 2M
Alison & Peter Smithson, 1964

The buildings on this site may interest only the 1960s, for this is where the angriest of Britain's young architects were finally given their chance:[42] it was ten years in coming, and the time-lag shows. But the space between the buildings is a permanent gain. At last, an architect has suggested and a client allowed that a highly valuable slice of W.1. be treated imaginatively as part of London (those who flat-pave part of the site and put up a thumping slab on the rest are doing no better than the bad old cover-it-all boys). The L-shaped area contains three hexagonal towers, one medium and two small. In the angle of the L is a showy eighteenth-century club (Boodles); the rest of the space is open to the public – and it is not just 'open space': the levels enable you to squint out at a sloping St James's Street, lord it over the side streets from under a colonnade, or just sit down on a stone bench. This is only the starting point for what could happen, like Whittle's first jet, and nothing much will come of this particular example unless some activity can be attracted or allowed into the central space; but the idea has an enormous potential. Here is a kind of Saint-Denis, no more accommodating and no less pregnant than that other prototype.

42. The buildings look remarkably even-tempered, compared with some that have appeared in London since.

The Ritz   145 2L
Mewès & Davis, 1906

The overwhelming thing about the Ritz is not ostentation or even luxury but a deep quiet. Through the swing doors is another world from Piccadilly. The tempo gently winds down; the long corridor, the space and the unhurried waiters seem to have come out of a dream. Money here does not buy a multiplication of gadgets but deep wedges of privacy. At the Ritz they are enclosed by decoration in eighteenth-century French style of the utmost delicacy and discretion, done from conviction and not fashion. The outside is just the same: polite and respectful but never obsequious. Mewès was French and elderly, Davis was English and young, and they made admirable partners.

37 Dover Street   145 2L
Sir Robert Taylor, 1772

Worth a special visit to see what a man who really knew his business could make of three ordinary storeys and three ordinary bays in an ordinary Georgian street. Originally the town house of the Bishop of Ely, it achieves memorable tautness and urbanity without straying outside a strict vocabulary. Every inch of plain wall has the right weight, every ornament is precisely spaced. It is almost the only truly West End façade in the West End apart from Barry's clubs, which have the same noble setting growing out of the social contract between house and street. A look at No. 39 will show what we can achieve in this direction today. You may then need a double brandy: Shelley's is the place, in near-by Albemarle Street.[43]

43. No. 39 has recently been replaced; probably no longer warrants a double brandy, but Shelley's is still handy, in case.

44 Berkeley Square   145 1J
William Kent, 1742–4

This is now beautifully done up as a gambling club,[44] after lying empty for a long time. Inside, Kent provided the most spectacular staircase in the whole of London, a swinging masterpiece which really will stand comparison with the best that Germany or Austria can do. It is probably worth a flutter to see it. If you don't want to go in, it is still worth comparing the outside with 37 Dover Street which is not far away. Kent wasn't really interested in correct design – his front is trying to swing in and out; Taylor was. From each according to his deepest wishes is not a bad recipe for artistic excellence.

44. Now private, and open to members only.

Hill Street and Chesterfield Hill   145 2J

An oasis in the fussy, addled streets of Mayfair, the only place in the West End where the patrician calmness of Georgian London still holds: and only just. Wide streets, tall houses and an air of justifiable formality and frostiness: justifiable because completely appropriate. It is when you find these qualities applied to a civic centre or to Alderman Bloggs's flats that they look so bloody silly. And as always in Georgian

England, the formality is set off with mews, alleys and cosiness. There is a perfect example in Waverton Street, where the Red Lion, still effectively a village pub, faces a large and cheerfully informal elevation which is weatherboard from head to foot.

Shepherd Market, W1 145 2–3J

Of all London's villages this is the most determined and most unexpected. In the angle between Piccadilly and Park Lane, where any reasonable freehold would fetch £25,000, this is a tangle of lanes and alleys, and also of boutiques and general stores. It is still rough; or rather, rough and very smooth at the same time. The two seem to get on. But you do not escape from the city's bustle; you have it made personal. The true feeling of a big city – that every next person may be a saint or a rogue – is screwed to a pitch here. The whole pack of humanity is dealt to you, knaves and jokers included. Anything can happen to you, but it is your own choice: there are no alleys that it is unsafe to walk down.

Wellington Museum, Apsley House 145 4H

Benjamin Wyatt, 1828–30, incorporating Robert Adam, 1771–8

Wellington was one of the most Ulster of all Englishmen, and to really understand or apprehend him will do more good than reading a dozen social histories. Apsley House was his house from 1817 until his death in 1852. Here he faced the mobs of the 1832 Reform Bill, and from here in his eighties he used to go across almost daily to the Great Exhibition. The house contains very few personal souvenirs, which is a pity, but as an official record of the years after Waterloo it would be hard to beat. And it has one superb, Wellingtonian gesture, one of the funniest things in London. The Prince Regent had presented him with a huge nude figure of Napoleon, fifteen feet high,[45] carved by Canova with all the blind academic talent of which he was capable at his worst. The Iron Duke thumped it down in his stair-well, where it dwarfs everything else and where he must have passed it several times a day. *C'est magnifique.* The house itself was originally an Adam building, and for this the Duke must have been the worst possible owner. Two refurnished rooms survive, and the headlong clash of temperaments, masculine and feminine, is still tangible. The outside was refaced and the inside redecorated by Benjamin Dean Wyatt (or probably by his assistant John Harper), in the most regal manner possible, Victorian before its time. Wyatt's imagination was lush but not inspired: Nash would have been the man and Wilkie's preposterous portrait of George IV in a kilt[46] would be more at home in the Brighton Pavilion. The Waterloo Gallery has enough atmosphere to smudge the details into a haze of gilt and red damask, and the chandelier in it is a miracle of exact brilliance (look at the other chandeliers, themselves good, to see the difference). For me the Striped Drawing Room contains the best objects: portraits of some of Wellington's generals by Jan Pieneman,

1821, where real people look out at you (though the guide stiffly says that they 'show the sitters wearing inaccurately rendered uniforms'), and two superb posthumous busts by Nollekens, of the Younger Pitt and Spencer Perceval. On the first-floor landing a painting by Wilkie (the Chelsea Pensioners receiving the news of Waterloo) is shown next to the original sketch, and all the folly of the nineteenth century peers out: the attitudinizing and artificial story-telling.[47] In the sketch, a soldier is leaning back calling for another pint. In the painting he is regaling an enfeebled pensioner with the Great News. That is why we now have action painting.

The house, itself literally on Hyde Park Corner, has become known as 'Number One, London'. The recent alterations have left it on an island, and the old address is more than ever true. Buses, park, Palace, Mayfair, Belgravia: all meet just here. Outside and in, it is one of those few places where you have the spirit of London in the palm of your hand, as fragile as an eggshell.

45. It is actually eleven feet four inches.
46. In the Dining Room.
47. The painting is now in the Piccadilly Drawing Room; the sketch is no longer on display.

Hyde Park Corner
Screen, Decimus Burton, 1825

145 4H

Hyde Park Corner is a maelstrom of useless motion – useless because the roundabout here, unlike Piccadilly Circus, does not mean anything to London. The real meaning – a tiny strip of green joining the royal parks diagonally – is lost in a welter of underpasses with dreary new mosaic walls, where the pedestrian is made to feel like a frightened rabbit. But Decimus Burton's screen on the north side is a really fine thing. It must be taken for granted more often than any other building in London, perpetually glimpsed out of buses, never looked at properly. Even when you do, the limpid tenor voice is self-effacing, and you need to have seen a lot of neo-classical stodge to appreciate just how easily and deftly Burton has handled his three triumphal arches and the Ionic columns between them. Most designers would have made a static monument. This is a genuine screen, inviting motion, saying *Come on in*, and the trees behind are a really important part of it. It should be a high point in a great pedestrian walk (Westminster to Notting Hill) instead of a perilous sandwich between whizzing cars.

The park behind serves millions of Londoners, and is loved because of it. Of itself, as a personality, it is not quite strong enough; and the remarkable character that some of its inhabitants used to give has been gone these six years since the Act.[48] Now there are only lots of dogs and people keeping fit, in a space that is too nearly flat, not thickly enough planted to keep out the built-up sides. St James's Park succeeds better with a much more difficult problem.

48. The Street Offences Act, 1959. Made it illegal for prostitutes to solicit in the street or in public places.

Hungerford Lane, Charing Cross   146 2C–D

A very fine passage called The Arches runs underneath Charing Cross station from Villiers Street to Craven Street. The steps at the western end announce a different world as magisterially as God might wish to at the Last Judgement.* But under this runs another way, Hungerford Lane; and this is like meeting a person five hundred years old. It starts by the Wimpy Bar in Villiers Street, and ends opposite the Strand Corner House.[49] In between there are Piranesian brick vaults tunnelled into the foundations of the station, and a crevasse running uphill to the Strand, embroidered with wine vaults and tiers of fire escapes. Where it passes under The Arches, there is just one grating – linking the underworld with an overworld which is itself under the bustle of the trains to suburban Kent. Once experienced, this threefold relationship is the kind of thing that nails you to a place. Newcastle has this multiple recognition, and so has Gloucester; but the New Towns will never have it in a thousand years.

49. It now starts from Ponti's snack bar in Villiers Street and ends opposite Corner House Street (the Corner House has gone).

Adelphi   146 ID
Adam Brothers, 1772 onwards

The Adelphi was an (unsuccessful) speculation by the Adam Brothers, those Cottons and Clores of the 1760s; too slick and shallow to be great, but ten times better than what replaced it before the war. All that is left is the *Lancet* office, in Adam Street, and mysterious underground fragments. For the Adelphi, two hundred years ago, employed that now fashionable thing 'multi-level circulation'. Each of the streets, named after the brothers, had its lower counterpart. The end of one can be seen from the Strand, running under the drastically restored Royal Society of Arts building and now blocked. But one of them is still complete and public. Lower Robert Street runs from York Buildings down to the level of the Embankment, now curving and burrowing amongst concrete supports, and none the worse for that. At the Embankment end there are a few pathetic fragments – a string-course and some stock-brick walls – to show that the Adam inventiveness created this. Two hundred years ago, and where is the second

* What they actually announce is the Ship and Shovel.

example? Well, the Ministry of Transport turned down a similar scheme at the Elephant and Castle a few years ago. What a way to run a civilization!

Peter Robinson,[50] Strand   146 1D
Denys Lasdun, 1957–9

Utterly unlike Lasdun's other buildings in London. Around the side, in Adam Street, he has gone in for some more typical playfulness, and this is in fact the least effective part of the design. It is the street front which is really mature and metropolitan. Ground floor (glass) and first sales floor (blank stone), differentiated from the three bronze-faced office floors above. Logical, disciplined and elegant, the model of what a West End building should be. It is the only new shop in London to match up to the promise of Peter Jones and the performance of the best Continental stores. The first floor, incidentally, makes a splendid background for advertising displays which can be as exuberant as they like yet become part of the rhythm of the building – and naturally too: contained, not constrained.[51]

50. Now New South Wales House.
51. I cannot recall that it has ever actually been used for this purpose.

Lazenby Court   140 9C

There are some bits of townscape that throw the book at you in a few yards. This one takes thirty-one paces – a by-law distance for a sub-urban road. It is a tiny passage between Rose Street and Floral Street, in the indeterminate bit of London where Covent Garden has subsided but Soho has not begun. Start from Floral Street: into a slit three feet wide and three storeys high, the end of the world. A few feet down, a bend has a gas lamp guttering above an evil stretch of dark brick. You hardly dare turn the corner. And then, as suddenly as the switch in *The Winter's Tale* from tragedy to comedy, the second half unrolls: a jolly passage with a comforting street at the end and a more than comforting pub (the Lamb and Flag) at one side. After the moment of terror it is too good to be true that the whole of one side is weather-boarded (the only bit between Mayfair and the East End) and that a chubby lintel brushes your head. Whew! – a near thing: have a half.

St Paul, Covent Garden   140 9D
Inigo Jones, 1631–8

This is Inigo Jones's 'handsomest barn in England'. It was burnt in 1795, and the replica (by Thomas Hardwick) has taken away the thrilling liveness of the detail, something which can be checked at the Banqueting House or Greenwich. The inside now is just a box, instead of one of Inigo's intense cubes. Yet, even at half-voltage, the grasp of fundamentals comes through in the great eaves and the great door, with the windows shrinking away into the brickwork. This is a box with a lid on it; but 'box' and 'lid' never mean quite the same again. Mini-Minors park close to the west door, Covent Garden lorries back up to the false portico on the other side. Like a Neapolitan church, this building is really needed.

Covent Garden   140 9D

The thing that matters here is bound to disappear eventually, and that is the head-on collision between market and opera house. Architectural contrast between classical surroundings and the anarchic life of vegetables, filling the original market building and overflowing all round the neighbouring streets. At one point, accident is more telling than any design, and the piled-up fruit boxes echo the rustications of the original *piazza* (a replica, but the same shape and size). Nothing in the Garden is quite the same after this. Life is greater than art, and you are swept away, like a discarded bunch of bananas, on a tide of human contacts. And if you go around meditating in this fashion, a few of the contacts will be personal and pungent. These are the hardest-headed and most cantankerous cockneys in London, and they give no quarter. It is the Guards Barracks or public school inverted: sloppy drill in one becomes a bad bit of reversing – in the worst conditions in London – in another. All the time it feels like sharp London versus the dozy provinces. If you can stay the pace, there's nothing like it, and amongst all this ribald tension there is the umbilical cord of all this fruit and veg – being unloaded, being pushed around by grandfathers, just lying around in London's offhand backslang equivalent of a cornucopia. London can't do without buying it, and the counties can't do without selling it.

When the market goes, as it will some time in the next ten years, ballerina is likely to meet office clerk: one kind of unreality meeting another. Common humanity has got to hold them in balance: there must be some common-and-garden use of this knot in London's trunk. Meanwhile, see it while you can.[52]

52. The market buildings have been preserved, and all credit to everybody involved. To some extent this has still resulted in one kind of unreality meeting another: as it has turned out, the ballerina meets health shops, herb shops, and chi-chi boutiques. Your reaction to the new Garden may depend a lot on when you catch it. On some days it will feel warm, human, and exciting; on others, like a big, profitable tourist sideshow. Nevertheless, all in all a notable achievement so far.

The shops and boutiques occupy the central market building of 1828–30. The former Flower Market houses the London Transport Museum, an evocative exhibition of venerable trams, buses, and other L.T. memorabilia, once part of the collection at Clapham (p. 172); the disappointing new Theatre Museum is in a basement underneath. It is a pity that the mid-Victorian Floral Hall, which actually abuts the opera house, is still derelict and unsightly. Its future is under discussion as we go to press; it is likely to become an annexe to the opera house.

Drury Lane   140 8E
Benjamin Wyatt, 1810

Another catchy tune to add to your harvest from *My Fair Lady*, which ran here for so long. A rotunda with a coffered dome, slung between two square-rigged staircases, with a hole in the floor to watch the lower orders going into the pit.[53] It is the only piece of Georgian theatre design left in London, and, ironically, it should have been built later. It is obtuse, and needs the protective camouflage of thick stucco mouldings: an enchanting idea without a heart. None of this applies to the vibrant colonnade along Russell Street, added in 1831 by Charles Beazley; this is theatre at its best, urgent and purged of unessentials, the curly lamp-bracket on exactly the same wavelength as the Ionic columns themselves. If you do not believe that a strict Ionic order can have personality, then take a trip up Kingsway to the British Museum, which has a great many, and see the difference.

53. This is the inner foyer; it can be glimpsed from the outer foyer if you are not going into the theatre.

The Wellington (corner of Strand and Aldwych)   140 9E
Extraordinary-ordinary; comfortable and quietly elegant and what every pub or street should be and isn't. The amazing thing is that this has happened in the last few years. A recent redecoration has realized potentialities which have been lying fallow for half a century. Two bars have been thrown into one: usually a fatal step, here essential to give an over-all shape. The distinction between the bars is still made by a couple of steps; everything else is made really new, but quietly, so that you can register the difference without noticing it. Good stuff behind the bar (a Free House), spirited Irish girls to serve it; more truly up to date than the most trumpeted pub rebuilding.[54]

54. Still as described, but twenty years older of course. And the spirited girls seem to have gone back to Ireland.

Savoy Chapel   146 1E
The implications of this are as disturbing as Einstein's second law of relativity. The Savoy Chapel is a quiet little late Gothic building, almost as black as it would be in Newcastle.[55] Rearing above it is the glazed white backside of the Savoy Hotel. Neither part is memorable but the tension between them is. And the tension not only comes by accident, but depends on it. Only a sadist would design this kind of affront, yet the affront is the essence of the place: and the final effect is not disgust but compassion for the tired old animal down below.

55. Now scrubbed clean to natural stone colour.

CHARING CROSS TO FLEET STREET 71

Somerset House
140 9E–F

Sir William Chambers, 1776 onwards

Sir William Chambers was a natural academic, with an academic's enjoyment of secret licence such as the Pagoda at Kew. So it is a minor tragedy that Somerset House should be the one public building in London to be completed as its creator intended and then preserved from alteration. Soane's unmutilated Bank of England would have been worth six of this. There are exquisite bits, but they never go to make much more, even down on the Embankment where gaping arches originally opened directly on to the river. From the Strand there is an exquisite three-part loggia; in the vast courtyard [25] there are exquisite units like the cupolas on the sides and the individual grooves on the rusticated walls. But there is nothing like greatness or inevitability. The one extraordinary thing about the courtyard is that the whole thing is two storeys above ground. Peer over the railings at any point and there is an immense slot. Plenty of stairways lead down to it, and once amongst the maze of rough stone arches the polite civilities up above become a monstrous kind of joke: perhaps Chambers enjoyed this too. The western part facing Waterloo Bridge approach was done by Pennethorne in 1856; the eastern part, which houses King's College, by Smirke in 1829. The difference between them even on a duplicating job like this is astonishing: Pennethorne deeply in the spirit of the original, and more effective than Chambers himself; Smirke bumbling along in his bloodless way, free from praise or blame.

St Mary-le-Strand
140 9E–F

James Gibbs, 1714–17

This is something much more than a clever young Scot's marriage of Wren and the Italian Baroque. It is a perpetual British plea for sunlight and movement, a kind of poem to Italy which has been part of our life for four centuries, unaltered by temporary misalignments such as the recent war. Gibbs never designed a better thing than this magical, flickering exterior, calling up St Paul's in one bay and the newly built Roman churches in the next [29]. And just as the sun – when it comes – strikes sharper, so this goes deeper than anything of the date in Rome. Nothing is weary; the alternating pediments rock along the roof-line, the English cherubs gurgle above the long festoons of fruit and flowers. The Portland stone, half gleam and half soot, has a fantastic range of textures, and to clean it would be like making over the face of a beautiful mature woman.[56]

The inside, after this, is a puzzle; tall and aisleless, with everything going on up at roof level. It almost needs to be split into two storeys, a theatre without galleries or audience. In 1750 Bonnie Prince Charlie was received into the Church of England here, on a secret visit, an unlikely sequel to Culloden. His faithful followers were given less opportunity to discriminate.

The final flourish at St Mary's is the way in which the back of Bush House curves round to hold it carefully in place on its island site – deference without obsequiousness. Bush House was designed by Americans at what will eventually be recognized as one of the high points of American civilization, the golden years of the early 1900s before the New World went soft. Between the two buildings a crescent of London planes has grown up. America to London, London to Italy: a thin chain of pure civilization and mutual respect, an island site which is a symbol of Britain's own island site.

56. It has been cleaned nevertheless.

St Clement Dane's   140 8F
Sir Christopher Wren, 1680–82, rebuilt by W. A. S. Lloyd, 1955–8

Blitzed Wren; the only rebuilding to realize that his interiors demanded dark woodwork instead of genteel staining. The squadron badges you tread on in the wide central space are a real commemoration, not fulsome mouthing. It will grow back into London again, and the defects of space and tension – for it is not a great building – are due to Wren, not the restorer.

Law Courts, Strand   140 8F and 141 8G
G. E. Street, 1868–92

Just as the Houses of Parliament killed Barry, so the Law Courts put an end to G. E. Street. There was never enough feeling to go round, and it was concentrated into one stupendous room. The rest of his practice – all the outside, all the country churches of the 1870s – was clever, heartless hack-work. Nothing but duty would entice you through the main entrance, yet inside it is all different. The Great Hall is a superb room, useless only by those legal definitions of architectural function which recognize merely the visible part of the iceberg. It seems as though Street has knocked it back into the thirteenth century through sheer will, the kind of endurance that confounds medical prediction: 'he shouldn't have lasted the night out'. And there it is, magisterial in all the good senses of the word: ordered, compassionate, direct and to a huge scale. It is a funny way to get to greatness – Beethoven's way in the Ninth Symphony, and in human terms the hardest, most meritorious way of all. Every word of this is wrung out against my own inclinations, for I hate what Street did by pretending to himself that he was sensitive and understanding: so this may be the truest entry in the book.

There is a good deal more in the Law Courts, including a bar, the unlikeliest local of all,[57] and the courts themselves – stuffy Dickensian rooms where lawyers argue endlessly through civil actions whilst their principals are miles away.

57. Gone.

The Temple   141 8G

One plus one makes six; a set of courtyards which adds up to something
far more than the individual spaces. This oasis, which most cities
would give their eyes for, runs along half of Fleet Street; tight at the
northern end, shaking out into isolated wings and gardens beside
the river – a view perpetually compromised by the roaring traffic along
the Embankment. So it is best to hug the top, parallel to Fleet Street,
and to travel from west to east. The place to start is at the corner
of Devereux Court off Essex Street, opposite the Devereux pub, which
goes very legal in the evenings and then closes early.[58] First New
Court, with the river just far enough away, behind trees; and then the
marvellous sequence: Essex-and-Brick Courts, one space unhappily
full of cars, but then Pump Court, quiet and car-free, approached
through an arch and left through an open arcaded ground floor (the
Cloisters) to a four-storey building [26]. Stop underneath in the middle
of the Cloisters and pivot; you can hold the whole of this extraordinary
equation in the palm of your hand. Forwards to the formal centre of
the Temple: church facing Inner Temple Hall across undisturbed
paving. Back through the courts you have just crossed. North through
an archway to the hurly burly of Fleet Street, south not to the river,
but to the unexpectedness of a ragstone wall amongst all this brick,
part of the original refectory. The way through here slips sideways
past it into Elm Court.

There are plenty of variations, but this is the basic pattern, as
memorable as anything in Oxford or Cambridge. And more than half
of it is post-war, reinstatement of what went in the blitz. So, ironically,
the best new townscape in London is neo-Georgian. No need to
fear that the atmosphere will be spoilt by the inhabitants. For every
hectoring or choleric lawyer, luckily, there have to be several hard-
working and unaffected solicitors' clerks; and that is mostly what you
see.

58. It now stays open until 11 p.m.

Temple Church   141 8G

This little building, despite heavy restoration and the blitz, is still
London's Notre Dame and Sainte Chapelle rolled into one. Notre
Dame – the rotunda – was built by the Templars about 1170. Circular,
to commemorate the church of the Holy Sepulchre in Jerusalem, but
completely up to date with its magisterial foliage capitals and pointed
arches. It is the earliest Gothic in London, still nursing its ornament
but completely sure of its spaces. The west portal is an extraordinary
mixture, almost a style of its own. Ostensibly all ornate Romanesque,
yet with the ornament welling up from inside with newly acquired
energy. The choir, finished in 1240, is as complete an expression of
English mid-thirteenth-century energy as the Sainte Chapelle is in
France. A hall church, broad and low, with everything worked out in

terms of triple lancets. Already, this points to 1688, whereas the overwhelming pride of the Sainte Chapelle foreshadows 1789. Only the east end runs into difficulties; the rest is a blend of correctness and humanity which appropriately enough is a model for legal behaviour.

The Templars are laid out on the floor of the nave, battered and burnt. Only two still read as people, one in the 'aisle', the other nearest to it under the rotunda. Both late enough to have relaxed their pose (i.e. late thirteenth century), and perfect types of two kinds of warrior: one robust and the other sensitive.

229–30 Strand (Wig & Pen Club) 141 8G
1625

This is what all London was like before designers started flinging architectural styles at the public like so many different varieties of spaghetti. Two tall, narrow, seventeenth-century town houses compounded into one, their beams mercifully covered up, their surface a wise old mixture of dark wood and yellow plaster. Different shape, different floor heights but a community of being. This is true coexistence, and how twentieth-century London needs to learn about it.

114 Chancery Lane (Law Fire Insurance Office) 141 8G
Thomas Bellamy, c. 1850

This little building shows what happens when a style is revived by someone with true taste and discrimination. This is the Florentine Renaissance given just enough of an English square-cut to stamp it as the nineteenth century. The building on one side is grossly commercial, the building on the other is grossly academic (Greek Revival, by Vulliamy, 1831). In between, this sets down proportion and detail with delicate refinement; a high, cultured English tenor threading its way surefootedly between the port and the brandy.

Public Record Office, Chancery Lane 141 7G
Sir James Pennethorne, 1857–66

Pennethorne was one of the tragedies of the nineteenth century – a great classical designer forced to build Gothic whims. The Public Record Office is basically a grand neo-classical palace as Dance might have done it, equipped at the top with scornful crockets borrowed from King's College Chapel. Here, underneath, is the true Victorian architecture, but the effect is only that of a dour man, the size of Hawksmoor, kicking against the pricks, watching the clever and the shallow climb on the bandwagon. Inside, the museum (open Tuesdays to Fridays, 1 to 4 p.m.) is a fine place to get a sense of English history.[59] Here is Domesday Book, Wellington reporting Waterloo and Marlborough reporting Blenheim, and an anonymous threatening letter from the Welsh Rebecca Riots. And also, taken over from the Rolls Chapel which used to be on the site, the monument to Dr Yonge,

Master of the Rolls, who died in 1516. It must surely be by Torrigiani; the wrinkled face has all the serenity of Lady Margaret Beaufort at the Abbey. The faces above, of Christ and two cherubs, have something more, which perhaps only the Italian Renaissance could do: an intense face which is completely symbolic and completely personal at the same time. These faces are prototypes for a stream of sentimental piety, yet remain quite untouched by it (where Raphael, for example, does not). The difference between original and imitation is a thrilling example of the boundary of art's mysterious kingdom: an intangibility more real than any solid.

59. It is due to reopen in 1988, to display Domesday Book and a selection of documents from English history, 10 a.m. to 5 p.m., Monday to Friday.

St Dunstan-in-the-West, Fleet Street   141 8G
John Shaw the Elder, 1829–33

Gothic architecture in the early nineteenth century was largely a matter of playing about – saying 'pretty please'. This was one of the consequences of Horace Walpole and his like. But within the limits, it can be well or badly done. St Dunstan says its please so prettily that it is a much loved bit of London, its octagonal lantern – the design borrowed from York – beckoning you round the curve of Fleet Street from the Strand to Ludgate Circus. In a tolerant London way it has collected older bits around it – Queen Elizabeth from Ludgate Circus, and a seventeenth-century ornamental clock from the old St Dunstan's which wandered up to Regent's Park and only came back in 1935. It would take a sour sub-editor to dislike it. The inside is an octagon too, and so child-like, and transparent, that it regains the integrity which should be every building's birthright. So this is one of the most religious interiors in Central London; give it a froth of stucco and St Dunstan's could be in Bavaria.[60] Something of this must have been felt when it was built: John Shaw died twelve days after the outer walls were finished, and the parishioners commemorated him with a naive, touching tablet over the west door.[61] Not many clients would do that for their architect today.

60. One corner of it could be in Rumania, since the acquisition of an icon screen from a monastery in Bucharest.
61. The entrance door: liturgically west, geographically south.

3   The Northern Ring: Paddington to Finsbury

138–141

The New Road was cut in 1756, the world's first by-pass. Now Marylebone Road–Euston Road–Pentonville Road–City Road is sluggish and diesel-clogged, but the whole of the northern edge of Central London keeps a basic classical unity. Marylebone itself is a decorous late Georgian grid with points of real elegance and the delicious sequence of Regent's Park opening off to the north. Holborn, farther east, is older and cosier, and fragments of it feel like a city-village. Bloomsbury is later and grander, made noble by a sensitive builder* and now just about wrecked by an insensitive university. The self-respecting early-nineteenth-century formality carries on east into Finsbury and finally loses itself, east of City Road, in the smaller scale of the East End.

At the other end of the chain, Bayswater was built last (about 1850) and has worn worst, the only part of the sequence where the surface architecture became more important than the layout or quality of life. But, altogether, it is a very noble achievement.

PADDINGTON

Connaught Square, Bayswater   139 8D–E
S. P. Cockerell or George Gutch, 1828

The square is late Georgian brick, plain and unremarkable. But what is remarkable is the complete change in tempo and scale within fifty yards of the Edgware Road and two hundred of Marble Arch. The contrast is pure London, and the way that the back of one of the Edgware Road's monsters edges into one corner accentuates the effect rather than spoiling it. Another exit looks straight on to Hyde Park, only a few yards away. It is one of the places where topography stops being something on a map and starts to live. You feel how the Edgware Road is and how the park is. But how long will it last?

The Victoria, Strathearn Place, Bayswater   138 9C

The saloon downstairs is itself one of the best London pub rooms, dark and plushy and glowing. The Gaiety Bar upstairs [23], easily missed, is super-plush, up to the real traditions of Bayswater. And no wonder, because it contains the gilt gallery front, painted ceiling (from the foyer ?), and seats from Norman Shaw's old Gaiety Theatre at the end of the Strand. They have been fitted in to the wedge-shaped room with extreme skill; the feeling of drinking here floats in a delicious lacuna mid way between a theatre bar, a club, and a Baroque library.

* Cubitt.

Paddington Station   138 7A
I. K. Brunel and Matthew Digby Wyatt, 1850 onwards

The moment you go in through the tacked-on arrival platforms with
their funny skew roof, bulging over the side like a corpulent businessman, you feel that this is no ordinary station, even in the noble company
of Victorian train sheds. It is subtle, unexpectedly allusive, where St
Pancras and King's Cross are grand and straightforward. The plan,
with its double transepts, belongs to a cathedral, not a railway station:
the Gothic ornament added by Sir Matthew Digby Wyatt belongs to
the eighteenth century, not the nineteenth. The colours are a copy of
the original scheme, and are just as suavely unexpected: brick-red,
cream and grey. It has the same kind of lyric poetry as the best rooms
in the Soane Museum; so the result has to be taken all at once and
can't be broken down into constituents. It makes the other lines look
slightly uncultured and obvious, and by all accounts this was exactly
the effect of the pre-war G.W.R. Buy this Keats sonnet for the price
of a platform ticket or see it from the high-level footbridge up at the
far end, which takes you almost up into the roof.

Eastbourne Terrace   60 6A
C. H. Elsom, 1958

This gaunt bit of plain speaking takes up two blocks opposite the long
flanks of Paddington station. Low and high parts lock together to give
something as unified as the stucco swagger of Westbourne Terrace,
backing on to it.* But not an imposed discipline; noble right down to
the individual bay unit, glass and yellow brick in a grey concrete frame.
The grime from the railway is merely filling out the volumes, giving it
an indelible London stamp. It is as independent of clichés as Telford's
warehouses in St Katharine Dock.

MARYLEBONE

All Saints, Margaret Street   139 7L
William Butterfield, 1849–59

To describe a church as an orgasm is bound to offend someone;
yet this building can only be understood in terms of compelling,
overwhelming passion. Why boggle, when there are a hundred ways
of reaching God? Here is the force of *Wuthering Heights* translated
into dusky red and black bricks, put down in a mundane Marylebone
street to rivet you, pluck you into the courtyard with its harsh welcoming wings and quivering steeple [27]. Outer and inner doorways
show you in, within a few inches of each other; both flowing over with
ornament – nothing was too much trouble for the beloved. Inside,

* The inspiration was to put the tallest block parallel to the street, not end-on, and
recess it only a few inches. Easy – once it has been done.

Butterfield had to rely for decoration on other men's intensity of
feeling, so it is pointless to look closely at the walls; but the proportions
and transfigured gilded violence of this unexpected Heathcliff burn
through any artificiality. The violent selfless love carries you up with
it, just as the serenity of Bevis Marks lifts another part of you to the
same end.

Butterfield never repeated this – how could he? – and his passion set
iron-hard, unapproachable, altering his pupils' drawings in ink so that
they had to do them all again. Perhaps he met too many portly bishops;
perhaps there is no way but death to discharge an experience as violent
as this.

Welsh Baptist Church, Eastcastle Street   139 7L
Owen Lewis, 1889

'*Capel Bedyddwr Cymreig*' is what this says to the startled visitor, and
the building itself is just as much of a surprise. It does to the fussy
metropolitan *hôtel* of the 1880s what the best Welsh chapels did for
the pedimented Nonconformist box. Everything is shaken up until it
rattles. The top is timid enough, but below that the whole front is cut
away. Columns *in antis* screen a pair of outside staircases and a grand
lamp. All the detail is still mechanical, but it doesn't matter, because
the imagination behind is working overtime.

All Souls, Langham Place   139 6K
John Nash, 1822–4

The circular steeple has earned the thanks of millions, for the way it
insouciantly frisks Regent Street around a corner to become Portland
Place. One of the most difficult of all jobs is made to seem dead easy.
(The spire used to stand up clear against the sky, seen from Oxford
Circus, but this has been ruined by the B.B.C. extension.) This was
Nash's special genius; what is more surprising is the success of the
interior. Nash has frankly accepted a box and frankly, operatically,
inscribed a colonnade inside it. Doubled columns at east and west ends
are just enough, like the easygoing arch over the painted altarpiece.
Because it is utterly honest and true to its time (in its theatricality,
also – a kind of Rossini church) it succeeds as a place of worship too.
Whatever happened on the surface, Nash never lost his deep integrity
to the total act of living, and it always shows. Brilliantly restored after
war damage by H. S. Goodhart-Rendel with scagliola columns and
green walls.[1]

1. The walls are now pale grey.

Chandos House, Chandos Street   139 6K
Robert Adam, 1771

It is hardly worth notice at first, from Cavendish Square, just a plain
end to a short street. Then it catches alight like a slow fire, and by the

time you are in front of it the great stillness is shouting down all surrounding blether, old and new – and the new blether around here takes some shouting down. It is simply four bays and three storeys of severe brown stone. But it was designed by Robert Adam, and when his immense talent could discipline itself to eschew snippets, as it did in Edinburgh, the result is unforgettable. Sheer proportion, the silence that speaks volumes. The inside (inaccessible) is quite different, and rightly; the back elevation to Duchess Street is full of snippets, which makes good sense if this were originally a kind of mews elevation, canny Robert undoing his fly-buttons. Now, in plain gaze, it looks petty after the true nobility of the front.

46–8 Portland Place   139 5K
James Adam, 1774

A bitter irony has put the headquarters of the R.I.B.A. in Portland Place. For of all the streets in London it is the one which has been most stupidly and selfishly and blindly ruined by twentieth-century R.I.B.A. members – velly professional, velly respected, oh yes. Only one block of the Adam composition can bear a look now, on the east side between New Cavendish Street and Weymouth Street. The rest is as chopped up as a body after it has been on the dissecting table. The centrepiece is still intact, and the double doorway (Nos. 46 and 48) shows the Adams' pliant facility perfectly [30]. The entrance arch is stretched and segmental, and to make more space the doorways themselves are part of a circular niche, with beautiful big fanlights and parallel vestibules running away behind. Curve against curve: polite, elegant, convenient and witty. No wonder they were successful; yet this was just a small accent in a speculative scheme.

Wimpole Street – Harley Street   139 5J, etc.
Nothing spectacular, but full of atmosphere – a kind of anatomy of English reserve. The richest physicians in London practise here, though you wouldn't think so; here is the icy understatement that is still at the top of every British ladder. You may never meet it in a lifetime, normally; but here it has become attached to a professional code and attached also to an equally understated formal plan. This is a grid plan, but you never really know it (though at the same time, you always know that it hasn't the organic eloquence of Regent's Park near by). Views are blocked, not endless; sometimes by buildings, sometimes – looking up Harley Street, for example – by the green slope of the park. The original buildings were plain Georgian, and most of them still are: after a few years of extrovert dash in the 1890s and 1900s, rebuilding has settled down again to unostentatious luxury (e.g. No. 37 Wimpole Street, by Sir Hugh Casson for the General Dental Council). Meanwhile, up the middle of every block run the mewses, cottage terraces gone up in the world: pretty, almost unaffected by the kind of arty renovation that has cankered Chelsea, and

damned expensive. For most readers, as for me, it is how the other half live: yet it is never thrown in your face – not even in the local pubs like the Dover Castle in Weymouth Mews or the Devonshire Arms in Devonshire Street. There could be worse prescriptions for the way to spend money.

York Gate   139 4G–H
John Nash, c. 1825

This is Nash gone *pomposo*, but with a twinkle in his eye. Rather than force an axis on Regent's Park, he sought out buildings on the perimeter which he could use to create an effect. Marylebone parish church, newly finished: what better? So he ran up deft stucco blocks, with Ionic orders beautifully controlled *in antis*. The church, imposing but nowhere near greatness, looks up with a frightened look, 'unaccustomed as I am to public speaking', and then performs very creditably. The extra humanity and more-than-architectural relation between the blocks makes this short street into something special.

Madame Tussaud's   139 4G

You may need to have had one or two before going in; not because the illusions are inadequate, but to release your inhibitions about meeting them. This is one of London's traditional amusements that is really worth a visit: never less than interesting, and in the Grand Hall something much more. Here, the topical tableaux are created with a good deal of insight, hardly ever with the truly waxen blankness of an official portrait or photograph (the Queen, alas, is an exception).[2] And those disturbing glances see more in effigy than they seem to in real life. Are our various bosses any better than waxworks? Are we ourselves, when we come out with conditioned remarks at the touch of a button, whether the subject is the weather or love and hate? After this, a visit to the Planetarium puts this impatient disgust into a cosmic perspective, and oddly enough sharpens it. Unreal nonsense under the eye of a personal deity at least stands some chance of eventual redress; unreal nonsense in the immense emptiness of the solar system is there forever. Best to dive into the Bakerloo before these speculations become really serious.

2. Some of the recent likenesses are a bit approximate; the Queen is now one of the better ones. But the presentation is always imaginative and sometimes dramatic, with sophisticated modern techniques of lighting and sound.

St Cyprian, Clarence Gate, Glentworth Street   138 4F
Sir Ninian Comper, 1903

Quiet and reserved, outside; but the most joyful church interior in London. Tall white arcades, clear glass to let the light stream in across the polished wood floor, uncluttered by pews, to Comper's lacy gilded rood-screen. Religion singing and dancing, as it does in Bavaria, light and space bounced about from wall to wall. This is Soane's 'poetry of architecture' again, with artistic form and religious content quite indivisible. The intangible, here, is as solid as the walls; the central mystery of life, open free from 7 a.m. to 9 p.m.

Castrol House: doors to Martins Bank[3]   138 5E
Geoffrey Clarke, 1959

Castrol House itself is only remarkable if you have not seen the best skyscrapers in Germany or New York. But the main doors to Martins Bank are something special: a jagged screen of metal slats designed by Geoffrey Clarke. It suggests the bank's solidity and security without any of the meretricious correspondences of 'banker's Georgian', and it is also a bit of abstract sculpture used as part of the city instead of being isolated in a gallery or on a pedestal, purchased out of a sculpture fund. So natural, once it has been done; yet the double shock of art and use at the same time never fails.

3. Castrol House is now called Marathon House. The sculptured doors are still there (left as you face the main entrance) but no longer lead to Martins Bank.

Barley Mow, Dorset Street   139 6G

Just off Baker Street; a real pub, a proper local, with a Public on the street and the most sober of Saloons as a back bar. The really remarkable thing is the pair of mini-bars on the way to the saloon.[4] Tiny cubicles with high walls and two chairs, places for romantic indiscretion or flogging atomic secrets. And they are open to the bar, without the claustrophobic effect of the cabins in Irish pubs. Here is a permanent deflation of the idea of average man. There are big bars and small bars, with different users and needs. That's all, and it is more than enough.

4. The back bar is now a disused space, but the two little box bars are still intact.

Wallace Collection, Manchester Square   139 7G–H

A poor third to the National Gallery and the Tate. It is an overwhelming, suffocating display of expensive nineteenth-century taste. With all the gilded clocks and boiseries it feels exactly like a provincial French museum. The impression is heightened by the fact that all of the exhibits seem to be speaking French – for here, perversely, is one of the best places in the world to see Watteau's delicate, disturbing miniatures. Only he and Fragonard come out of the fulsome welter with their self-respect intact: Watteau by a personality which comes out more often in the backgrounds (e.g. of *La Toilette*) than in the figures, Fragonard by a natural prettiness which meant that he could fit into the artificial conventions without compromise. *The Swing* and *The Souvenir*, both here, are far more than confections.

For the other painters, the surfeit of furniture, the crowding together, and the atrocious lighting mean that only the strongest can survive: Velazquez, with *Don Balthasar Carlos at the Riding School*, and Rembrandt's heartrending head of his son Titus, which draws you in as though you were going to end up inside the boy's skull. But when you get close, all you can see in the cruel reflecting glass is your own silly face.[5] Amongst a welter of indifferent but well-authenticated paintings are some of Reynolds's honest value for money and one of his very best, *Nelly O'Brien*, which has all of the Jane Austen virtues. Well may she sit forward and stare levelly at mediocrity, sober but not prim. Also, the *Laughing Cavalier*.

5. The collection is unchanged, but the lighting is good, and there is no longer glass on the pictures. All the paintings mentioned here are in galleries 19 and 21 upstairs.

Gloucester Place   138 5–8F

Just a very long, dead straight street of plain Georgian brick houses, yet it sticks in the memory when many more elaborate effects have faded away. It runs straight out of the West End, heading north for the open spaces. When the sun glows on the old yellow bricks and a translucent blue sky outlines the Regent's Park trees and the Hampstead church at the end of the view, the impossible seems easy. The country is only a mile away from Oxford Street, after all. And the illusion, the piercing cadence, soft and sharp, that is pure London, is stronger than any reality. Look north, and Wood Green doesn't exist: only those polite, wise bricks close to and the trees at the far end. Now that Gower Street is compromised, this is the last of its kind in London. The yellow tube of space and the view at the end needs to be preserved: the buildings need not be.[6]

6. The buildings have been preserved; the view at the end has been invaded by Burnham Tower, a horrific block of flats in Adelaide Road, north of the Park.

Selfridge's   139 8G–H
Daniel Burnham (consultant), 1908 onwards

That ninety per cent of pre-war big stores look horrible is no reason to ignore the others. Here, the brash grandiloquence is carried through with such force and sincerity that it succeeds where a thousand others have failed. Selfridge's is a person or point of view which is not doing anything at you and is not malicious: an opening bid for understanding by anyone's rules. The actual designer was probably the Chicago architect Daniel Burnham, the man who killed Louis Sullivan's career in the 1893 Chicago Exposition. Here he is Henry James's antiphon, at his best around the preposterous lovable clock over the main entrance –

ugmented, most years, by a preposterous and lovable Christmas display. If the detail puts you off, then see the same qualities running on much more respectable lines in the Mount Royal Hotel,* a bit farther west. The vital difference is in the voltage: and this makes the Mount Royal worth a glance only if you happen to be there, whilst Selfridge's is worth a trip up from the country.

2 Dunraven Street, Park Lane 138 9F
Architect unknown, c. 1820

This should be numbered as 132 Park Lane, because that is where its face is.[7] It is part of the block between Green Street and Marble Arch, which is almost all that is left of the original buildings, bow-fronted and seasidy, treating Hyde Park as though it were the briny.† All of the group are jolly, and this is something more, done in a crisp witty Soanic style. The segmental arches and the incised ornament on the second floor give a wonderful springing rhythm, fresh and clear and resonant. The area around, deadened by half a century of clichés, certainly needs it. This is a perilous site, 'ripe for development', as the vultures say: I only hope that the freehold is in the hands of splendidly benighted men, so that the building can continue to delight.[8]

7. The relevant part now *is* 132 Park Lane.
8. It can, and does, and is in the safe hands of the Allied Arab Bank Ltd.

AROUND REGENT'S PARK

Regent's Park 60–61
John Nash, 1812–26

Before anything else, Regent's Park is a unity, trees and terraces together, a great animal stretched out on the northern edge of Central London. Compared with this, the details are almost unimportant; and it is this rather than Nash's wonderful stage scenery that keeps the park alive and well-loved. The achievement is – alas – unique: for once neither formal nor informal, neither leafy nor urban, but all the elements acting together to create consciously the kind of living tissue that we sigh for in primitive or medieval villages and fumble at with such crassness in the latest phase of modern architecture. Man managed to emulate nature not as Rousseau thought by going native but by using all his talents. And also by designing for a complete social order: the scheme originally flowed eastwards over Albany Street into an enchanting pair of working-class squares (Munster and Clarence) and a canal basin: all gone, now, and replaced by new flats; the latest and best of them, by Armstrong & MacManus, making a brave but too highly-strung attempt to live up to the master of relaxed design.

* By Francis Lorne, 1932.
† Gordon Cullen's idea, originally, like very many other things.

Nash began at the south end, that is, at the top of Portland Place: the edge of town – which it still is – and a place for quiet formality. Hence Park Crescent (1812), now complete again after having to be rebuilt in replica – smooth curve and colonnade leading the eye away on either side, overcoming the barrier of the foliage in front which was needed to close the axis. Also, getting you into the park off centre, hence more ready to explore it – the opposite of the Versailles method. Beyond, on either side, Park Square East and West (1823–5), grand and strict Ionic. Thereafter the sides split, the green centre develops as an entity but always in the bigger entity of the whole park. Thanks to Nash's sensitivity, the park always implies Greater London around it. It is a green forum, not a barrier like Hyde Park. The decline from this order of unity to the almost exactly comparable Central Park in New York and hence to most of our present day public open spaces is enormous. One view can sum up the whole of the green space. Opposite Hanover Gate, a path strikes off towards the Inner Circle. It crosses one arm of the lake and approaches another. Just before the second bridge, the right-hand view orders itself into one of the loveliest set-pieces in London: a plate straight from a Regency edition of Gentlemen's Seats. With the lake as a foreground, ordinary trees and weeping willows half conceal one of Decimus Burton's smoothest and mellowest stucco villas, The Holme [31]. In summer it sways and melts into a green masterpiece: Nature used and controlled, but not disciplined, allowed to be itself. Here is man really justifying his existence, engaging his whole being to make a contract with Nature. If you want a definition of western civilization in a single view, then here it is.

On the east side, after Park Square there is Denys Lasdun's College of Physicians which has the same flair for fitting in whilst looking as completely different as his flats in St James's. North again is Cambridge Terrace, half-blitzed, and then the two grandiose set-pieces, Chester Terrace (1825), and Cumberland Terrace (1826).[9] Chester is the best design, Cumberland is the best stage scenery, but both are unfor-gettable: Chester [32] taut and crisp, its columns held well in to its stomach, a wonderful sight in perspective through the triumphal arches at the ends, best of all in mist or winter sunshine. Cumberland is strung out grandiloquently, a fat man's rich embroidered waistcoat, porticoes all round and a pediment which is so patently and un-justifiably a backcloth for the Coade stone figures that the eye doesn't mind at all. As well tell a giraffe in the Zoo that its neck is much too long for London. See it from the park, i.e. in bits, peeping through the trees, when the sculpture is completely convincing. Best of all, improbably lovely, at night in the two back squares on either side of the centrepiece, announced by triumphal arches with a twinkle in their eye. After dark, the houses at the end are lit indirectly by the derided sodium lighting in Albany Street;[10] and the artificial orange completes the stage-set to make a superb outdoor illusion. With ramps running conveniently downhill on either side, they are ready made for actual performances.

9. Cambridge Terrace has been rebuilt; the others look new and glowing from restoration.

10. The lighting is now mercury vapour.

Park Village West
John Nash, 1824 onwards

61 2F

Nash built two Park Villages, or miniature suburbs, as part of his great scheme. The eastern village was soon cut into by the railway and is only a fragment. But Park Village West [33], off Albany Street, is almost complete, a perfect example of *rus-in-urbe*. In a few yards, you are plunged entirely into the leafy oasis: serpentine road and copious trees and the counterchange of crocket and bracket perform the conjuring trick. Though obviously not in the country, you are a hundred miles from London. Tower House, the prettiest of all, is at the time of writing lived in by a prominent M.P. on the right wing of the Labour Party.[11] This somehow gives more of a key to British politics than several months of *Hansard*.

11. He has moved house, and been made a life peer.

The Zoo

60 1–2 D–E

Everything is happening all at once, like a film projector gone crazy. There are not only all the different animals; the architecture is just as much of a bizarre jumble. Neo-Georgian pavilions, utilitarian galleries, cosy kiosks, the colossal mock rocks of the Mappin Terraces, and the witty *jeu d'esprit* of the Penguin Pool [36]. All sorts of new shapes are now going up, equally diverse, from Sir Hugh Casson's concrete elephant house to Lord Snowdon's aviary, which turns out to be far more robust than it looked in the model. It would be a pity if the Zoo ever became too uniform, because it makes such a good match for Nature's craziness. The whole thing could float off down the Thames as Noah's Ark and the Tower of Babel combined. Some of the oddest effects occur from outside the Zoo, in Regent's Park itself. By day, a mountain goat high up on the terraces where you least expect it. At night, a terrifying set of squeals and snuffles to liven up a walk home to Swiss Cottage.[12]

It may be a silly thing to say, but the Zoo is one of the most under-used amenities in London. It seems to be regarded as a place to bring the kids and not much more. In fact it would be a good place to get to know someone, to talk over all but the most hard-headed business, or simply to drown one's indignation at human imbecility in the antics of the rest of nature's jokers. After all, it costs no more than the price of a scotch and soda,[13] which is a more usual remedy. And if the baboons and sea-lions don't work, you can always have the scotch and soda anyway, in the Zoo's bar. London offers unlimited opportunities for pleasure, but so many of them drive you slap up against man's pettiness – a fashionable play, for example, or a meal in the King's Road. It is good to have a place which takes the mickey out of architecture, the animal world, and its human visitors simultaneously.

12. The Zoo is rather depleted at present – no bears, for example – while plans are completed for another period of major rebuilding. Notable among the areas for redevelopment are the Mappin Terraces, largely to be replaced by new terraces and an aquarium. A number of Victorian and Edwardian animal houses will go at the same time.

13. Rather more now, alas: £3.60 for an adult in 1987.

Primrose Hill   60 1D

A very few feet above Regent's Park, beyond the Zoo; but the only place to get a close panoramic view of London from ground level [37]. A London tour could well begin here – every important big building is in the view, from the City of Westminster and beyond as far as Crystal Palace. Many unimportant ones also, and this is a real and very recent tragedy. Ten years ago, all of the interruptions in the view meant something; now, half of them are gauche packing-cases. Only the slabs along Route Eleven have any meaning at all, symbolizing the City. The view is still exciting, as any city view is, but there is now nothing especially London about it. It could be Birmingham or Manchester instead of Britain's capital: and all for a collection of inessential buildings.[14]

14. The proportion of inessential buildings is now even higher – so many, in fact, that the slabs in South Barbican are impossible to distinguish. The three most prominent landmarks are the National Westminster Tower, the Euston Tower, and the Telecom Tower. Of these, the last is the most distinctive and popular. In 1967 Ian Nairn described it as 'London's tallest tall story ... a guffaw which adds point to the crazy barbarisms dumped down on the London skyline within the last ten years'.

Hanover Gate   60 3C
John Nash, c. 1825

A sparkling toy at the north-western exit from Regent's Park [39]. Cars roar by on either side of this scrolly octagon, unaffected Baroque a hundred years after the Baroque style was supposed to have ended. Long may it stay to defy the traffic flow and cheer the passer-by, a superb gesture among so much milk and water.[15]

15. It now has an improbable neighbour: the London Central Mosque. Of the two it is the octagonal lodge which appears substantial and permanent, while the mosque looks as if it might all be carted away by scene-shifters at any moment.

Lodge Road Power Station 60 3C
Sir Charles Reilly, 1904

Adding art to industrial structures is usually a bad thing. But there's always an exception, and this is it. The power station itself is splendid, with its angular wooden cooling towers, stretched out along the rail tracks parallel to Lisson Grove like a bizarre animal. The turbine shed butts on Lodge Road, and here the art was added by the young C. H. Reilly, later to become famous as a critic and the head of the Liverpool School of Architecture. The classical dress is as noble as Behrens's turbine factory, and as logical: hefty pilasters marking the centre and sides, and coming down to the ground on great feet [44]: singing swags and garlands in between. Singing with the building too; plenty of plain yellow brick, all the ornament florid and curling over, everything saying that this is a bloody great shed.[16]

16. Demolished, except for the lowest courses of some of the outside walls, on which the great feet of the pilasters are still visible, but meaningless.

Lord's Tavern 60 3B

Sandwiched between the backs of grandstands on a windy road just north of Regent's Park. A thick Victorian building with 'Lord's' on top, and bars in the bottom, not putting itself out for anybody. And then, inside, like the pearl in the oyster, the tiny oval of green, the heart of all cricket, on view for the price of a Guinness. It is one of the most poetic, most unexpected and most English of transformations – the sudden line of Herrick which bowls you over, the English girl who turns out to be so much more than she seems. When matches are being played the pub is split and you can only reach the back bar through the cricket ground; but otherwise there is no hindrance. If the pub is rebuilt then this relationship must be kept; but why mess about with it at all?[17]

17. Why indeed, but they went ahead and did it. The relationship has gone, and the unpleasant new Lord's Tavern is outside the ground entirely.

[St John's Wood 60 1A, etc.

This is now one of London's ghosts. There a few disconnected leafy streets with Victorian villas behind the trees – Clifton Hill is about the best of them. But there is no connected place, no especially piquant villa: and even taking into account the disastrous attrition of the last fifty years, there can never have been more than jolly houses in pleasant streets.]

12 Langford Place 60 2A

Sheer horror: a Francis Bacon shriek in these affluent, uncomplicated surroundings at the end of Abbey Road. It looks like a normal St

John's Wood villa pickled in embalming fluid by some mad doctor. Two very pinched gables, and a bay window like the carapace of a science-fiction insect. There is something far beyond architectural wildness here, even Victorian wildness. The design radiates malevolence as unforgettably as Iago.

Waltham House and Dale House, Boundary Road   60 1A
Armstrong & MacManus, 1954 and 1956

Plain dealing: an outstanding and far too rare example in London of what honest design and professional self-respect can do with the leanest of programmes. Just four-storey flats [67] and maisonettes, respectively; just yellow brick, just long-stepped terraces with some planting in front. But all the simple things have been cared for, not fussed over and not made into 'features', but treated as straightforwardly as the nineteenth-century dock and warehouse men would have. Plain dealing.

AROUND ST PANCRAS
[St Pancras Church   140 2B
W. & H. W. Inwood, 1819–22

Athens come to the Euston Road; the Tower of the Winds repeated in two lean diminishing stages to make a steeple, caryatids stepping two by two around the east end supporting tribunes, *anglice* vestries. It is not on, of course, even when the detail is as superbly executed as it is here. The Inwoods' cheap editions, in Regent Square and Camden Street, are far better, with some creative spark to them. The inside shows painfully what happens when the precedents run out. Heartless elegance is all that is left, and the pulpit displays this to perfection.]

St Pancras Station   140 1C
Shed, W. H. Barlow, 1868
Fancy work, Sir George Gilbert Scott, 1874

St Pancras is the most Continental of London train sheds. By comparison, the others are put together additively, like an English cathedral; this is one huge all-embracing sweep of the same family as Hamburg or Cologne. A vast throbbing hangar; the phrase needs to be repeated sixteen times to make enough weight in the book and convey the overwhelming solid force of this beginning or end to journeys. It is painted light as some kind of campaign to 'brighten the image of British Rail', but its only true colour is jet black.

Gasholders loom up at the far end of the platform. They are worth a closer look, and to get there turn right out of the station. The concoction in front of the shed is by Sir George Gilbert Scott, incredibly clever in composition and incredibly heartless. No Victorian quaintness here, in this competent reckoning up of fees-per-crocket.*

Right again, and you are in Midland Road. You might as well be round the backside of New Street at Birmingham or London Road at Leicester. It is one of the most astonishing transformations in London, a jump of a hundred miles in a few yards, achieved with the unemphatic red brick and hypnotic arcading of the Goods Station. London for a moment – and just for a moment – seems fussy and flurried, using two words where one will do. Anyone whose heart was lost to bricky Leicestershire would find this place unbearably nostalgic.[18]

Up Midland Road to the traffic lights, turn right under the railway bridges; then, in Goods Way, the gasholders come back, a cascade of intersecting circles, a shout of sheer joy from the most unlikely place. All of them come to the party equipped with classical columns, simple Doric and a kind of gasholder Composite. The nineteenth-century equivalent of a Baroque angel is not a Victorian angel but a Baroque gasworks.

The whole of this place at the back of St Pancras is incredibly moving: tunnels, perspectives, trains on the skyline, roads going all ways. If you get nothing from it at first, stay there until something happens: it is really worth the effort.

18. The Goods Station and the whole west side of Midland Road have been demolished to make way for the new British Library.

King's Cross Station
Lewis Cubitt, 1851–2

140 1C–D

Overwhelming honesty, taken to the point where it is something far more than a component virtue. The shape is the building, a point made straight away by comparison with the clever fribble on the front of St Pancras, next door. The defects are the building, like a drawback in someone's character which flows inevitably from their good qualities. Cubitt provided two identical train sheds side by side and scorned any of the deceptions which the nineteenth century would gladly have provided to disguise the fact. Nothing but yellow brick, grand proportions, and in the last few years the eerie other-worldly whinny of big diesels. Outside, two sheds, hence two huge brick arches. A clock, hence a turret perched in the valley between them, spoiling the composition in an academic sense, yet right on a deeper level. Cubitt wanted a brick tower here, which would have satisfied both. It was cut out of the budget, and he scorned subterfuge. The railway reorganizers need their noses rubbing in this quality until they feel it as impossible for the station to go (it is due to be replaced in the 1970s[19]) as it would be for the Church of England to demolish St Paul's.

19. It has not been replaced, a reprieve for which the addition of a low spreading foyer is a small price to pay.
* Perhaps not true of the inside, which I haven't seen.

Holy Cross, Cromer Street
140 2D
Joseph Peacock, 1888

The outside is cheap and shrugged off; there are a hundred like it in London's suburbs. Inside it is as honest and selfless as King's Cross station, which is only a few yards away. Nothing unnecessary, and nothing put on for form's sake as the big boys would have done. Narrow aisles, tall clerestory, high reaching-out east end. The church itself is worshipping, something much deeper than Pearson's tinselly wish to 'bring people to their knees'. Five eastern lancets, backed up mightily now by a rood beam with three German-looking figures on it, designed by Sir Charles Nicholson. All the other modern fittings have the rightness which you might strain after for half a century and never get to.

St Peter, Regent Square
140 2D
W. & H. W. Inwood, 1824

Only the Grecian portico and steeple are left,[20] since the war. But that fragment is better than the whole overblown sepulchre of St Pancras parish church. Less money, less opportunity for academic expertise, more chance for the Inwoods' own qualities to come out. The Bath stone makes the Grecian detail sing, and London soot and London sunshine make the Bath stone sing. On a winter day, the crisp cylinders and bare branches of the trees in the square against a light blue sky make one of the most evocative places in London.

It has a near relative a mile to the north in All Saints, Camden Street, built in 1822. This is now a Greek Orthodox church, and a wedding here is something to see.

20. Gone; replaced by flats.

HOLBORN AND BLOOMSBURY
'Daily Mirror' Building, Holborn Circus
141 6H
Sir Owen Williams & Partners,
with Anderson, Forster & Wilcox, 1957–60

Good in two things. One is the way in which the glass wall is stretched over the long sides to endow it with the same kind of dignity as a nineteenth-century warehouse. There are no tricks; this is a big building housing a lot of people with a good deal of air-conditioning above. The full blues and reds of the spandrels are in the same mode, which goes far deeper than mere functionalism. (Who injected this very personal rectitude into what could have been an impersonal design? Cecil King?) The same understanding in the other, smaller thing, which is the roof of the delivery bay in New Fetter Lane. Here the trunking of the building is all exposed, each service painted a bright, deep colour – blues and greens and reds. It makes functional sense; but it is also an invitation to delight.

Westminster Bank, Southampton Buildings 141 6G
T. E. Knightley, 1895

The outside looks like something that was left behind when the seas
receded, all green and brown barnacles, a bit of good Victorian fun.
But there is more to it than that. Inside, this is a noble and up-to-date
sequence of spaces (up-to-any-date). To reach it you need to start at
the corner of Southampton Buildings. White majolica for the key
signature, one vestibule square with niches, then another octagonal,
trailing *fin-de-siècle* clouds of glory. But then, instead of a transcription
of the Baths of Caracalla, there is a narrow light-well full of staircase
and four storeys of galleries. This sudden injection of commercial
purpose explains what has gone before and endorses what comes after –
the banking hall itself, a rotunda apparently as big as the Reading
Room at the British Museum, glazed white tiles and glittering mosaic
to the very top. Banking seems for a moment what the adverts try to
make it. A mighty passage winds round it back to Holborn; but 'Action
will be taken against persons using it solely for this purpose'. So be
legal goodies, and come to observe the late Victorian architecture. Now
that the Coal Exchange has been demolished for an extra few inches
of roadway, this is the best accessible Victorian office in London.

(Written in 1964. The bank was closed in January 1965 and then
demolished. Nobly done. This is the kind of thing that makes me not
too proud of being British.)

Long Bar, Henekey's,[21] **High Holborn** 141 6G

Any long bar implies serious drinking, but this has a sense of dedication
that is far beyond mere commerce. Perhaps because of this it is often
cram-full: it is more of an experience to be uncomfortable here than
to relax amongst a farrago of clichés. It does not depend on Victorian
ornament either. The effect is due to the long, tall proportions, the
dark woodwork and especially to the scale of the huge oval barrels
behind the bar, as concise as an airliner's skin. A walkway high up
connects rooms tucked under the roof and you expect to see acolytes
coming out on it to perform some liturgy of alcohol. Cabins all round
the walls, as a souvenir of Belfast or Dublin; but this place needs no
stage props. They sell spiced buns.[22]

21. Now the Cittie of Yorke (*sic*). The Long Bar is on the ground floor at the
back.
22. No longer; but good lunches and Samuel Smith's beers.

'Meridian', in courtyard of State House, High Holborn 140 6F
Barbara Hepworth, 1959

In the long run, abstract art depends on only one thing: internal energy.
Shorn of any props, the task is not easier than it was a century ago,
but immensely more difficult. Many think themselves called and few
are chosen; this sculpture is one of the few. Set back from the street,

Meridian is energy made visible, each involuted curve reinforcing the total shape. It is, roughly speaking, part of a spiral turned in on itself by running some of the rings together. The energy short-circuits between them and builds up so that you expect a shock if you touch it. At the same time sexless and vital, it says serenely, excitingly: hands off. A machine of this order could make you believe in a mechanical universe.

Lincoln's Inn   140 6–7F
Stone Buildings, Sir Robert Taylor, 1774

Much of the Inn is too demonstratively picturesque to be memorable; the visitor reels from all the diapered brickwork and grossly pointed windows. The best part is the north-east corner, near Chancery Lane, where Robert Taylor's Stone Buildings of 1774 look across a long court to a later block in Mylne's style though still apparently done by Sir Robert's firm. Taylor at his best was a true Roman and set out his attached columns with real gusto and exquisite masonry technique – he began as a sculptor. There is an exit from the north-east corner of the court through a narrow arch into Chancery Lane, and this in reverse is one of the most delicious bits of Georgian London. It begins as an unprepossessing passage beside 76a Chancery Lane which leads to the back of the arch, set on the diagonal and giving just a glimpse of the courtyard beyond. Above it the Stone Buildings have a grandiose pedimented elevation to welcome you in, like finding a tiara under a factory girl's headscarf. The base and the arch itself are rusticated, and the channelling on the stonework is some of the best in London. The textures and shapes are countercharged with a verve which in another country would have led to a crop of putti. This is the English stiff upper lip ingested, and paying a splendid dividend in controlled power.

Soane Museum   140 7E
Sir John Soane, 1812 onwards

Extreme greatness in art has two faces. One takes the usage of the time and transfigures it with humanity and intensity. The other leaps forward not only in style but into what appears to be a higher organization of humanity altogether. Rubens *v.* Rembrandt, Handel *v.* Bach – and Wren *v.* Soane. The Soane Museum is as deep as St Paul's dome is wide; an experience to be had in London and nowhere else, worth travelling across a continent to see in the same way as the Sistine Chapel or the Isenheim altarpiece. Soane as a man was proud and cantankerous, but his architectural imagination was superhuman or saintly. The museum was his house, and he altered it to contain his collections in a series of meditations on space which go as deep as any more orthodox mystical experience. After a visit here, four walls and a ceiling can never look quite the same. The outside is idiosyncratic enough, but like many of Soane's buildings is no more than the fly-leaf of the book. Inside you get every trick of mirrors, proportion and shock juxtaposition of scale; but it is not thrown at you, never done primarily for an illusionistic effect, always a by-product of an ever deeper burrowing into the nature of space – Soane splitting the spatial atom – and also into the personality of space. Soane was after what he called 'the poetry of architecture', and so his rooms are never just exercises. His library on the ground floor with its hanging ceiling is a 'mood' room, meant to be lived in; the stylized details, which are certainly odd, are quite subservient to this. Soane's imitators could only copy the details; the only true match is in Nash's interiors for the Brighton Pavilion. (As might be imagined, Soane hated Nash and Nash held Soane in amused contempt.) His imagination was always truly original, rather than conventionally original: half way up the stairs there is a recess devoted to Shakespeare. It has plaster cherubs on the ceiling, arranged neither with symmetry nor with artful asymmetry. They just seem to have arrived at random – literally, flown in from the treetops outside; and so you can believe in them. Because of this, the crustiest of Soane's archaeological confrontations seem credible, and his Monk's Parlour has the authentic *frisson* that Fuseli could only grope for. And along with all the plaster casts and weathered fragments from the Palace of Westminster, there are two of Hogarth's best-known moral sequences: *The Rake's Progress* and *The Election*.

All these are really sidelines to Soane's primary purpose, the meta-physical inner exploration of space which had to wait a century and a half for its physical counterpart, astronautics. On the first floor there are twin drawing-rooms, sober and spacious and at all times suitable for their worldly purpose (Soane here was several up on most mystics). The front room has a flat ceiling with panels cut in it, into which separate little segmental roofs have been fitted. Easy; yet somehow the whole business of what ceilings are for has been looked at afresh. In the back room the roles are reversed; a big segmental ceiling contains a coffered central square recess. The drawing-room talk is not self-consciously different, but not quite the same either.

And God knows what the breakfasts must have been like. The Breakfast Room is downstairs, behind the staircase. One of Soane's hanging ceilings fits over it (and over you) like a floppy hat, elegantly top lit. But it is embroidered with tiny convex mirrors which show up the room with you in it, in miniature – a microcosm. On two sides of the ceiling, great bleary light comes streaming down from outside – macrocosm. The third side is a bookcase (inner life), the fourth side is the outside world (outer life). It is all the bathroom mirrors anybody ever looked into rolled into one. And it is also probably the deepest penetration of space and of man's position in space, and hence in the world, that any architect has ever created. You might infer the second part from Soane's other buildings, but the first part, the human under-standing of the nature of eating breakfast, can only be caught here. If man does not blow himself up, he might in the end act at all times and on all levels with the complete understanding of this room.

57–8 and 59–60 Lincoln's Inn Fields   140 7E

A funny business here. The right-hand house, Nos. 59–60, was built in 1640 by someone who accepted Inigo Jones's style but was not able to match his quality. Ninety years later, Henry Joynes – Vanbrugh's clerk of works, turned Palladian – put up a deliberate match, smoother, stricter and better. Soane at the end of the eighteenth century added a silky double porch to make it semi-detached (Nos. 59–60 had this done to it in the eighteenth century too, but much more crudely), and the result is one of the most polished town houses in London. For once, a copy is better than the original, intellectual refinement is better than natural force, a hybrid is better than a complete design. That's life.

Millman Street   140 4E

This is part of a long Georgian ribbon[23] which runs up from High Holborn half way to King's Cross. Where Great James Street becomes Millman Street, the roadway takes a sideways jump: only by the width of a house, but enough to block the views down both streets, and make the join into a place with a definite shape instead of one more intersection [41]. On the other corner, by a stroke of luck, there is a proper cheerful neighbourhood pub – the Rugby – so that this is one of London's best remaining villages. Long may it stay, unaffected by sweeping demolition or Chelsea cosiness.

23. The Georgian east side of the street was demolished in 1971, after some years of dilatoriness and neglect, and replaced by modern terraced housing. But the corner – now paved – by the Rugby Tavern has survived.

The Lamb, Lamb's Conduit Street   140 4E

A very near miss: but the margin between success and failure here is so small and the reason for it so relevant to the purpose of this guide that the pub is worth including. The people here would pull it back over the line anyway: half cockney, half doctors, students and actors: the result is one of the few places in London where an intellectual top-dressing is not the kiss of death to the real atmosphere. The Lamb is a good Victorian pub, low, dark and intimate. It was redone in 1960 by Duncan Thomson with great care – yet somehow the wrong sort of care, the kind of thing that takes an ordinary cottage, treats it lovingly yet removes its essence. Everything is now just a bit too suave, the colours just a bit too subtle; a Victorian pub looking over its shoulder and become Victoriana. Before and after photographs on the walls show what has happened: the full straight sparkle has gone. Only just, perhaps only by one per cent: but here it is that vital difference between ninety-nine and a hundred.

Passage by St George, Bloomsbury 140 6C
Church by Nicholas Hawksmoor, 1720–31

St George is for once a church where Hawksmoor's prodigious invention ran away with him and produced such disparate elements that he
simply could not call them to heel. But on the west side of it there is
a narrow passage which distils that great man's imagination in a more
personal and direct way than any of his better buildings. Start in
Bloomsbury Way and follow signs around the left-hand side of the
portico to St George's Hall. The gap between church and neighbouring
buildings narrows to a few feet, so that you are thrust against the
prodigious keystones, actually touch the wonderful time-worn scales
on the Portland stone. Then the way dives down: a Hawksmoorean
turn even though it is provided by accident. It turns a corner by going
down and then up again. Seven steps down, a ninety-degree bend, six
steps up. It sounds simple but in fact has the drama of a full symphonic
movement, charged up by the stupendous classical detail that bores a
hole in your right flank. Once upstairs again, you have a new character –
quiet, not busy; a new street (Little Russell Street) and, bless me,
when you turn round there's a new building – the rear elevation of St
George's, completely different from the rest: the best part of the
church. One huge pediment over five bays, thickly columned, the
perspective artificially enhanced by that old wizard so that the ground
floor is hugely overscale whilst the top cornice is delicate. Back again,
if you wish, and the whole thing unwinds in a completely different
sequence.

British Museum 140 6C
Sir Robert Smirke, 1823–47
Reading Room, Sydney Smirke, 1854–7

The outside is a prime illustration of the difference between a real
design and honest application. Smirke was under the impression that
architecture could be created by wrapping a great number of Ionic
columns around a big E-shaped mass. It is putting together a building
from the outside, instead of designing it from a central idea, and it
never comes alive for a moment. Inside, the King's Library is a fine
room, but Smirke has contributed almost nothing: the dimensions
guarantee success on their own. This leaden-footedness seems to have
got into the displays too. There is marvellous stuff, but it is hard to
reach, embedded in a great deal of mediocrity. Everything seems
designed to instruct, not to delight – the opposite of the seductive and
selective galleries at the Victoria and Albert. A large room filled entirely
with Greek vases, for example, is far too much of a good thing. My
own favourite, by far, is the Ethnographical Gallery, above the King's
Library. The decorous surroundings contain enough emblems of evil
and pure magic to translate everyone in the Museum into rabbits.
They make a wonderful contrast to the lumbering Greek and Roman
theology on the other side of the building.[24]

The Reading Room is, strictly speaking, inaccessible. But you can peep in through the door, or obtain a day ticket.[25] It is as sure-footed and live as the rest of the museum is embalmed. An intense, odd world, inside, rather like an aquarium.

24. The presentation has been modernized in many areas, but the museum is still enough to induce total panic in a non-specialist. The Ethnography Department has moved to the Museum of Mankind, 6 Burlington Gardens, off Regent Street. Only a selection of its exhibits is on display at any one time.
25. You can now see it by joining one of the silent, disciplined groups that are shepherded in for a few minutes' glimpse every hour on the hour from 11 to 4, Mondays to Saturdays.

[Bedford Square   140 6B
c. 1780

With so many London squares neglected or unknown, this one is over-praised. It consists of pretty Adamesque elevations with especially pretty pedimented centres, fitted uniformly round a big circular garden. But it has nowhere near the sense of enclosure or entity of places like Trinity Church Square in Southwark. The sides are not positive enough to contain the middle, and tail away into the plain brick streets around. Everything is hopelessly underpowered.]

Bloomsbury   140 3–6 A–C

As anything more than an area on a map, Bloomsbury is dead. Town planners and London University have killed it between them – a notable academic victory. The splendid plane trees are still there to soothe when the strain of looking at buildings becomes too great. But instead of their gay yet discreet stock-brick surroundings, there are doughy intrusions like the droppings of an elephant. The original was built as a decent speculation, to make a profit and be an enjoyable part of London as well. The replacements are designed from God knows what backwater of the intellect. If this is progress, then I am a total abstainer. Pick up the old and honourable in Bedford Place (late-eighteenth-century) and then in pathetic fragments of Burton and Cubitt's noble scheme farther north, in the mutilated squares: Woburn, Gordon and Tavistock.[26]

26. The university has continued to advance, Georgian Bloomsbury to retreat. Bedford Way and another part of Woburn Square have been demolished in the process. The recent university buildings, notably Denys Lasdun's sweeping, assertive Institute of Education, have risen above the doughiness of their predecessors, but take no more account than they did of Bloomsbury's old residential character.

Courtauld Gallery[27] (entrance in Woburn Square)   140 4B

Ignore the outside, which is the late work of a man (Charles Holden) who deserved better of old age than this – it replaced probably the most elegant part of old Bloomsbury. Galleries can be simply collections of pictures or a complete experience, just as a town can be a collection of buildings, like Philadelphia, or a complete unit, like Venice. This is the only public gallery in London to be something more than the exhibits inside. The rooms progress chronologically, and also from simple attitudes to complex ones – from Sienese gilding to Toulouse-Lautrec. There are always English inflections to remind you that this is not just an international gallery: two full-length gentlemen by Tilly Kettle who achieved by straightforward honest feeling what Goya broke into in a lifetime of struggle, and *The Allegory of Sir John Luttrell*, whose soft Spenserian fantasy could only have come out of Britain even though the artist was Flemish. The collection builds up to the Impressionists – a roomful of pictures so familiar from reproductions that it is almost a *déjà vu* – and hinges on Manet's *Bar at the Folies Bergère*, one of the half dozen best paintings in London. Here is the real human condition, set down as Rembrandt did, so that there is no end of looking into the reflections and the eyes of the barmaid, disillusioned but still open to everything. (England has a justifiable stake in this picture, apart from the accident of ownership; there are two bottles of Red Label Bass on the counter.)

After that, a quieter room, taking the same humane preoccupation into the twentieth century, and then finally, a room of drawings done by artists when the art dealer wasn't looking, as it were. Rodin, Matisse, Epstein, Picasso, all with the same burrowing into the mystery of the human body, muck and marvel at the same time; and all delivering the same message to today's artistic fashions – put up or shut up. The whole gallery has the same message: that life and death are bigger than any abstract assemblage of colours and lines, but also that those colours and lines can sometimes reveal life and death more vividly than anything else.

27. The present gallery is large enough to show only one-third of the Institute's collections, so plans are in hand to move to Somerset House. Meanwhile many of the paintings have been moved into the vaults to make room for the recently acquired Princes Gate Collection, dominated by Tiepolo and Rubens. Of the paintings described here, only Manet's *Bar at the Folies Bergère* is at present on view.

4 South Bank

Brothels and theatres in the Middle Ages, an untidy compound of commerce and culture today. Here is the key to London and it has never been fully realized. The Georgians, notably Dance, almost succeeded by laying out a set of boulevards in the only part of the city which could take them, but their efforts have been frittered away – though, even now, the scale of Kennington Road is a fine thing to see. Topographically, this is the centre of London. From Vauxhall to Tower Bridge via the Elephant and Castle is three miles and St George's Circus is the only point in London equidistant from the City, Fleet Street and Westminster. Here is the place for huge gestures, away from what is left of the famous skyline. Yet, apart from the half-finished and mediocre work at the Elephant, the area is in a chaotic muddle.[1]

1. POSTSCRIPT 1987. The Elephant is finished, but the area is still in a muddle. The arts complex has given it a public image but no real centre, and sometimes feels like a bridgehead from the West End. Outside this oasis, at least until one gets to the populous cheerfulness of Rotherhithe and the redeveloped docklands, the impression is of a forgotten district, with too few people on the streets, and traffic hurrying through on the way to somewhere else.

Courtenay Square, Courtenay Street, Kennington 78 5A
Adshead & Ramsey, 1913

This is the best Georgian square in London [42]. It is neither here nor there that it was built just before the First World War for the Duchy of Cornwall, and that the delicate classical ornaments are cast in concrete and can be seen to be. An astonishing throwback has produced this dolls' forum, apparently fragile compared with the robust streets around, yet tough and compact. Alone among London squares, it has really accepted what is meant by a formal space: all the detail is directed towards the whole space, and the centre is not a lawn or a folly of flower-beds, but regular trees on gravel, kept down around your ears by deliberate, directed pruning. Constructed formality, when it really works, can be marvellous: a knowing contact with life to suspend some methods of behaviour and stress others. This dainty old lady could walk anywhere without harm: whilst the near-by Cleaver Square, which is genuine Georgian gone up in the world, seems to have an uneasy concordat with the spirit of South London, always risking a bust in the mouth.

Imperial War Museum, Lambeth Road 147 7H
The building itself was the second home of Bedlam (Bethlehem Hospital), and is, aptly enough, a bad-tempered piece of late Georgian

utilitarian design, with the ornamental bits – the dome and portico – added by Sydney Smirke in 1844. But as part of its work it contains a gallery of paintings by official artists in both wars. The job sorted out the sheep from the goats: the bad painters became worse under stress, but the good ones were pushed into a depth of feeling which they sometimes were unable to match when painting for themselves. Nevinson is outstanding from the First World War – *Road from Arras to Bapaume*, a white streak across a landscape grey from foreground to sky, is as telling as the most gruesome trench photographs. Paul Nash, with *Existence*, and Epstein, with a devastating bust of Admiral Fisher, both thrust their art further into life than it normally penetrated and brought it out enriched. In the Second, Graham Sutherland's paintings of industry and bomb damage have the creative urgency which is missing from his skilful portraits just across the river in the Tate. The oddest thing here is a head of Mussolini by 'Bertelli, R.A.', in which the Duce is represented as an object like the porcelain top of an electric transformer. The lighting does the rest and reproduces his facial features in a futurist conjuring trick as witty as Severini's running dog.[2]

2. The museum is painfully cramped at present, and most of the works of art listed here are in store. A major expansion is planned over the next few years.

County Hall, Addington Street Extension[3]
146 5F
L.C.C. Architect's Department, Special Works Division, 1960

Good straight stuff. Four storeys of office space, given the kind of detail that the early engineers were good at, rich and simple at the same time. Purple bricks, and a curtain wall with deep blue panels: tough and resilient in an area plagued with faceless buildings. Two of these are that pompous titled ass, the original L.C.C. building (by Ralph Knott, 1911), and the fawning, curry-favour extensions at the back done by the L.C.C. after the war.

3. The building has become an I.L.E.A. annexe, on the edge of a huge traffic roundabout, facing a pyramidal office block. It has not worn well, and the deep blue panels are now faded magenta.

[Royal Festival Hall
146 2–3F
L.C.C. Architect's Department, Special Works Division, 1948–50 and 1963–4

The new façades will be complete by the time this book appears, and so the unsuspected tragedy has come full circle. The old elevations were an honest muddle – the new ones are a faceless smoothing over of dissension: the difference between the political climate of the forties and that of the sixties. Why the muddle, and why the smoothing-over? Because this is the most terrifying example in London of the difference between statistical and artistic reality. The Festival Hall, inside, is acoustically perfect and musically dead, an epitome of all the occasions when a pattern of human behaviour has been given precedence over humanity itself. The Albert Hall is fallible and understandable, a vehicle for compassion. This in its icy blind perfection is unforgivable, and nothing will ever change it. Fiddle around with the front while London burns, if you like. But it won't do any good.][4]

4. Downriver are the grey crags, block-houses, and uncouth angles of the Queen Elizabeth Hall/Hayward Gallery building, a brusque, assertive repudiation of any hint of gilt cherubs or red plush, designed for people who like their art in the raw. Beyond is Sir Denys Lasdun's National Theatre: inside, an ingenious and complicated machine which dovetails together three auditoria with their attendant foyers, staircases and galleries; outside, a bleached desert landscape of white mesas, sills and ledges, with strata formed by rough-shuttered concrete. Against all this the Festival Hall looks almost classical.

Waterloo Bridge   146 IE–2F
Sir Giles Gilbert Scott, 1940–5

One of those structures which make the whole complicated process of designing look absurdly easy. It is effortless, making its small slam without a qualm. Yet it comes from the middle of the equivocal thirties, and was designed at least nominally by an academic architect: things should have gone abysmally wrong. Five tense, shallow arches leap the Thames [43], drawing extra spring from hunched abutments, exactly right for the kind of bridge – the opposite of the even flow from end to end over London Bridge. The rhythm is syncopated further because the arches don't run the full width of the bridge: there is a deep channel between them, which gives a breathtaking view from directly underneath, on the Embankment, looking down what seems to be a majestic colonnade. And syncopated yet again by outlining the arches with brown concrete aggregate, against the gleaming Portland stone of the rest. The arch of Rennie's original bridge is built into the southern approach, near the National Film Theatre, and the bridge itself is the best place to feel how London bends around the river, equidistant from Westminster and St Paul's. Six no trumps; it just misses the seventh because it is too self-absorbed.

Whittlesey Street, SE1   147 3H
1820–30

Real cockney, still in good condition, still where cockneys ought to be, embedded in Central London. Here is true architectural purity, and not a Calvinist's idea of it, nothing but yellow London brick and unselfconscious self-respect. Whittlesey Street is on tiptoe with self-respect, two storeys made into three with a blind attic window concealing a monopitch roof of pantiles [48]. But the opposite of a sham; it was in its nature to be as tall as this. At the end, Theed Street at first seems to stub out the view, then takes you round at an angle:

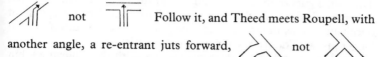 not 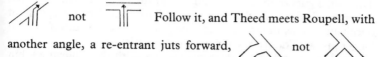 Follow it, and Theed meets Roupell, with

another angle, a re-entrant juts forward, not

Roupell answers with a wavy parapet: the gables transverse, not along the street. On one level, there is no finer architectural effect in London; on another there is no better sense of place in London. And the whole lot is truly humble and all screwed in to the big city. Behind Roupell Street are the offhand platforms of the other Waterloo, on the way out from Charing Cross; the reverse view up Whittlesey Street has the Georgian steeple of St John, Waterloo Road, overtopped by the Shell Building.

Bankside   147 1J–149 4L

This is the longest and most exciting connected walk in London.[5] Apart from a first flying visit it can do more to interpret the city than anything else, a real skeleton key. London is bent around the Thames; however much the north bank might wish to forget it, the south holds the centre of gravity. The shortest way from Pimlico to the City is via Southwark, not Charing Cross. London's signature is a moving and dramatic dissonance, exactly like those odd geometrical figures which have their centroid outside their circumference. North = outsider's London, south = cockney London. But also, north-east = City = business outsider; north-west = Westminster = international outsider; north central = Oxford Street and theatreland = provincial English outsider.

After all this generalization, something concrete is needed. The mood is set perfectly by walking over Blackfriars Bridge and bolting down a truly Stygian passage, property of the Southern Railway, open from eight a.m. to five p.m. The stock bricks have got you, and they won't let go until Rotherhithe. At the end, the river is on the left; but first turn right a few yards to see the Hopton almshouses. By car, turn left over Blackfriars Bridge and then left again down Hopton Street to the same point. The almshouses are simple brick cottages with a chapel in the middle, built in 1732. The surroundings have grown up around, but the humble buildings are more needed today than ever. Fun for the old people, with action all day and quietness in the evening; fun for Bankside, with a relief to the carefully zoned industrial area. London used to be full of such contrasts; now they have to be picked out in books like this.

Back to the riverside, and after a few yards the river itself. Here, there is no need for any guide. Look on to the dirty water slapping around the bows of barges, and the grand unselfconscious row of warehouses on the City side, with St Paul's suspended above at just the right height [45]. If it doesn't move you then nothing else will.

This is the guts of the thing – and part of the guts is the sliced-bread wrapping floating on the Thames, and the weird counterpoint of dockhand versus the too-sophisticated visitor. You, yourself, are no longer just a guide-user, but part of the equation.

If you wish, inflect the downstream flow with the following – but don't come for any specific place. Surrender to the general, and the particular takes its place naturally.

(1) Cardinal Cap Alley. Up from the river, a vision of how South Bank alleys could be: stock-brick walls between a big tree and a back garden, leading from public to private world. Turn round, and the tube of space is focused exactly on the west tower of St Paul's [46]. An accident, but the kind of accident that fate tends to bestow if you design well in the first place.

(2) The Anchor. A good pub, endowed with associations (Doctor Johnson and that), but with far too many people looking-at (like you) and not nearly enough living-around.

Beyond the Anchor, the warehouses take over. Clink Street – from the Clink, the original of the slang name – gives a foretaste of Shad Thames, tall and narrow, with bridges high up. It leads to Winchester Square, which is a near-mystical re-use of the exact shape of the medieval courtyard of Winchester House. Somewhere among the storage space is a 'gorgeous rose window', bricked up, one of life's perennial possibilities. Beyond that, Cathedral Street comes suddenly on an arm of the river and just as suddenly slap up against the west front of Southwark Cathedral. If a church means anything, it is this: head on to the work-places like a charging bull.

If you can, slip under London Bridge approach through Hay's Wharf. But it is a private road, closed at week-ends, and the legal way is to make one's way up to the front of the station and down again along Tooley Street. Plenty of roads run down to the river, but a connected walk is impossible until Tower Bridge. Steps on the down-stream side of the abutments lead directly down to Shad Thames, the grandest part remaining of the docks. Six-storey warehouses tower above the old right of way, with repeated high-level bridges. You are not so much looking at part of London as walking about inside it. Shad Thames is beginning to be cursed with setbacks and demolitions, and unless these are forced by sheer commercial necessity (which I doubt, because they reduce the floor area) then they are criminally stupid. This Thames-side ribbon is worth maintaining at least as much as Belgravia or Chelsea.

All this applies with more force to the sections farther east. Shad Thames returns to the main road, and other old thoroughfares take over, all much impaired even from what they were ten years ago. Bermondsey Wall was in some ways the oddest of all, because it had repeated right-angle bends just when you thought the whole thing was going to peter out; but everything is being smoothed away or not thought about at all. This is one of the great places of London, and all that architects and planners have done – private, borough or L.C.C. – is to dump down old and new clichés irrespective of the site. The only exceptions are some of the warehouse buildings, and I guess that nobody bothered to employ an architect for them. But try and follow the golden thread, however thin, because it is the city's real lifeline. Farther east it thickens up again, and the bit around Rotherhithe church is still a real place although the municipal flat-builders have tried to do their worst. The church is decent plain Georgian (and is usually kept open, something which is rare enough here to be worth noticing specially). Opposite is a good, unspoilt pub, the Mayflower. This has a verandah, reached through the Saloon, which is the quintessence of Thames-side London. It juts out into a muddy river between muddy buildings. Barges crowd up to it, the even skyline and sombre palette seep in until it has as strong a hold as the silhouette of Manhattan. It is the kind of belvedere which should be repeated by the dozen between Blackfriars and Greenwich, the basis of remaking the docks into a living place instead of a background for union disputes and lackadaisical rehousing. Long may it remain truly boaty and unsophisticated, not one more place for the unspeakable to come and see how the other half lives.

5. The walk is now fragmented and best visited piecemeal. Many of the specific places mentioned here survive: the general spirit has gone with the movement of most of the river-based industry down to Tilbury and beyond. East of London Bridge rebuilding is going on at a furious rate, faster than any guide-book can keep up with. Some of the best warehouse buildings have been renovated and converted; this is happening to Shad Thames. But they are interspersed with modern blocks of every size, colour, texture, and variety. The same fate has overtaken the north bank; seen from Bankside, St Paul's rises, not above warehouses, but above an uncoordinated ragbag of waterfront offices.

Other survivors include the Hopton almshouses, Cardinal Cap Alley, the Anchor, Rotherhithe church, and the Mayflower. On the positive credit side, the foundations and part of the walls of Winchester House have been uncovered (east end of Clink Street) and the rose window has been unbricked for all to see.

Southwark Cathedral

148 2A

Choir, c. 1240

A proper working cathedral, squeezed on one side by the high-level railway approach to London Bridge, crowded out almost by inches on the other side by the stock-brick backs of riverside warehouses.[6] This unsentimental throwing-together is its essence and should never be exchanged for a pious open approach from the river. Opening-out would only accentuate the architectural defects: Southwark is a large friendly lump of a building but no more. The east parts are thirteenth-century, the nave a mechanical copy of 1890. But even allowing for restoration the design is crowded and heartless: French lack of feeling done in an English way. The low retrochoir behind is no better; official architecture – or the official temperament – has been with us for a long time. The most memorable thing about the building is the intangible contribution of a friendly unsanctimonious atmosphere, just what a cockney cathedral ought to be.

The best part of the fittings is the series of fifteenth-century wooden bosses at the west end of the nave. The roof itself was destroyed in 1530, and this is probably the only place in England to see a lot of these objects close to. They are as big as beer-barrels, carved with unselfconscious virility: not great but very refreshing.

Otherwise there are two jokes. Shakespeare, in the south nave aisle, is given a gelid apparition by H. V. McCarthy (1912) in some astonishing stone which looks exactly like frozen aspic or frog-spawn, very creepy. Lionel Lockyer in the north transept, on the other hand, was provided with an effigy whose texture is more like papiermâché or melted golf balls. He was a renowned quack doctor who died in 1672: there is an uproarious inscription, one line of which reads: 'His virtues and his PILLS are soe well known ...'

6. Now by the yellow-brick backs of riverside offices.

Guy's Hospital Chapel   148 4B

Merely a door on the right-hand side of the entrance courtyard. It leads to a pretty eighteenth-century building, which is a pleasant enough surprise; but what is worth a special visit, even in London, is John Bacon's monument to Thomas Guy, set up in 1779. The figure of Guy leading a sick man into his hospital is all compassion without the least taint of moralizing or the horrible smugness of Victorian charity. It is like the tender parts of the Messiah – 'Come unto me, all ye that are heavy laden' – with the same sweetness: sentiment without sentimentality. Bacon was thirty-nine when he did this, and afterwards did more than anyone to sink the true feeling of eighteenth-century sculpture in a welter of empty gestures. Perhaps it was inevitable, and these few years of the 1770s (with Adam's best interiors and Wyatt's Pantheon) caught the tide just on the turn. But the nobility of that grave, concerned face is universal, and in a way we are more than ever in need of it now. Every autocratic hospital matron and bureaucratic Ministry of Health official should be exposed to this for an hour a day, as to a heat lamp, until the humility and true concern sinks in.

Tower Bridge   148 2–3E

In daylight, the romantic aspirations never get off the ground: this detail was meant to be taken seriously, like Wagner. But at night it is magnificent. Intermittently lit, tremendously bulky, the pompous trimmings concealed and the huge suspending cables emphasized: one of those high points which lose nothing through being frankly melodramatic. Best to see it from below on the south side, in Shad Thames, where the apparition is framed by cranes and warehouses.[7]

7. Still a good angle of view, but there are no cranes to frame it.

Trinity Church Square, Southwark   147 6M

One of the best squares in London, and all the better for being early
Victorian rather than Georgian. The Italianate trim to the windows
on the first floor is just enough to stiffen the shape. The roads are
sensibly managed, too. Great Suffolk Street runs down one side, and
the only other opening is in the middle of the opposite side; so there
are two solid corners, and the space does not leak away. In the centre,
too big for its surroundings, is Bedford's graceless classical Church of
the Holy Trinity (1822) which is dilapidated now.[8] There is also a
large statue of a king, supposed to be a companion piece to the set in
Westminster Hall. But the effect is all due to the crispness of the
houses, which make the Islington squares look flaccid.

8. It has been converted into an orchestra rehearsal hall.

Lawson Estate, Great Dover Street (between   148 7A
Spurgeon Street and Bartholomew Street)
Sir John Burnet, Tait & Partners, 1953

A bit of modern Denmark, transplanted to the top end of the Old Kent
Road. If you have seen the outskirts of Copenhagen, the similarity is
unnerving: the same angular polygonal blocks, the same beautifully
cut yellow bricks, and the same feeling for people first and architectural
expression second. After twelve years it is growing into a lovable place
where most London estates are set to be the next generation's slums.
The paths under the flats are firm to walk on, not a statutory desolation,
the tiny gardens to the stepped terraces of cottages are real flower-
bowls, not a social duty.

This style seems just to have been one person's whim – the result
of a summer holiday, maybe. The tall slab of flats that was added later
(Nashe House) is half way back to fumbling brutishness: the standard
L.C.C. concrete slab a little farther south is all the way. Lawson will
outlast them all.

Surrey Docks[9]   80 3A–B, etc.

Mostly a terrible disappointment, with the dock buildings low and
mean, and the horrible pre-war flats along Rotherhithe Street meaner
still. But just once the conglomeration of utilities cracks into poetry,
and it takes a bit of finding. In Gulliver Street, off Redriff Road, is a
pub called the Ship and Whale. Beside it, a walled alley leads south.
Walls give way to wooden slats with intermittent views of barges – if
you run fast enough they coalesce like a movie strip. The slats in turn
lead to a swing bridge, just a few feet higher than the rest, and the
whole place suddenly unfolds. This is the main entrance to the dock,
the Thames is only a few feet away, and the view all round the clock
is water and ships, with the domes of Greenwich inflecting the horizon.

9. The docks were closed in 1969. The area is being developed – not without
local opposition – by the London Docklands Development Corporation as, in

effect, a New Town within the metropolis, with groups of pitched-roofed housing. The Ship and Whale and its side passage have survived, but at the time of writing the passage leads only to building sites around the mouth of the dock. It should be a lot more interesting by the early 1990s.

5 Kensington-and-Chelsea

75, 76, 144, 145
The Royal Borough and London's artists' quarter are now in a forced
Greater London marriage. It may be their salvation, because each
desperately needs the qualities of the other. Chelsea is an overrated
and overpriced collection of cottages, Kensington a monolithic parade
of Victorian terraces which sometimes conceals tremendous vitality
(e.g. the itinerant Dominions population around Earls Court) but
rarely expresses it. The only thing which is truly expressed here is
opulence – in Belgravia, which is the equivalent of pre-war Mayfair,
and in freaks like Kensington Palace Gardens, translated effortlessly
from housing nineteenth-century millionaires to doing the same for
twentieth-century ambassadors. Potentially, Kensington could be a
marvellous place when the leases fall in, and one hopeful sign is the
number of good modern buildings to be dug up in obscure streets.
Fulham, at the nether end of the King's Road, is one of the most
characterless parts of London, as firmly lowest-common-denominator
as one of the huge mining villages near Doncaster. The people are as
friendly, too.[1]

1. Kensington and Chelsea have gone from being very expensive to being
expensive beyond belief. Consequently the natives of Chelsea have started
spilling over into Fulham, complicating its social mix, even though they have
not radically changed its appearance.

BELGRAVIA AND SOUTH KENSINGTON

Belgravia   145 5–6G, etc.
Pantechnicon, Motcomb Street, W. H. Seth-Smith, 1830
The Grenadier, Wilton Row
Houses, Albert Gate, Thomas Cubitt, 1845

There is an enormous drop in voltage between Regent's Park and
Belgravia. Using the same forms, and with far more responsibility in
construction (Belgravia stays up where Regent's Park has had to be
propped up), the creative charge started lower and dropped steadily,
street by street, from Belgrave Square through Eaton Square, Chester
Square, across the railway tracks, then a canal basin, to Eccleston
Square, Warwick Square, down to the humble streets of the back end
of Pimlico – Sussex and Gloucester and Alderney. Most of it was built
and designed by the Cubitts; never shoddy, never unbearable; but
never a real spark either. What in Nash was a complete philosophy of
designing had become a good builder's responsibility to his job, and
it was not enough. What the spirit of the age would have preferred is
shown by the pair of houses which make such a brave entry to Hyde

Park at Albert Gate. They were built by Cubitt for the rogue railway magnate George Hudson, and for their self-harmony are almost the best individual thing in Belgravia. Worth a look anyway, because they are utterly symmetrical in effect, yet on a close look completely asymmetrical in detail.

Otherwise, the effect of Belgravia is the odd bits – and the continuous human oddity of extreme contrasts, smooth and rough. One pub will offer lunch at four and six, the next at fifteen bob. Some of the richest, the wickedest, the oddest of London, is to be found in the square mile between Knightsbridge and Victoria. Here is all the spirit which is so lacking in Mayfair. Two buildings which would be worth a visit anywhere happen to indicate the range very well. The Pantechnicon in Motcomb Street is a preposterous, lovable Doric temple, sitting down like a stucco elephant in a back street off Belgrave Square. The name is original, spelled out in huge letters above the cornice, and sums up both the pretensions and also the reasons why the pretensions don't offend. The Grenadier is just the opposite. To reach it you first of all find a small hole called Wilton Row, off the eastern arm of Wilton Crescent. It seems to be petering out in a nest of Rolls-Bentleys; then, round a bend, is this simple stuccoed pub, untouched by half timber, leaded light, chromium plate, or Festival of Britain lettering. It is the old servants' pub that has short-circuited to become a local for rich mews-dwellers, rich enough to appreciate the shabbiness and leave it alone.[2] As often happens in London the two ends dovetail, and it is the middle that doesn't fit. The English *ancien régime* had and still has a lot of faults; but one of its great virtues was that it was really prepared to tolerate eccentricity. You can still feel this in Belgravia; and it is somehow a cleaner air than the King's Road, Chelsea, with every-man-his-own-eccentric and nothing real any more.

2. It has been in so many guidebooks since that a significant proportion of its customers will be visitors from far away, who will be looking at you curiously and wondering if you are a genuine Belgravian mews-dweller.

St Paul, Wilton Place, off Knightsbridge 145 5G
Thomas Cundy jun., 1840–3

The outside is one more lean early-nineteenth-century church, religion on the cheap. But the inside is a kind of miracle. It is what happens if you start with one glowing ember and slowly, lovingly build up a fire. It was built in 1840 and has one huge asset, an enormous, frilly, queenpost roof. Here, amid the utilitarian provision of pew space, was a beginning; every addition has added to it. A vaulted chancel, fancifully painted, ornate chandeliers, a gilded rood and screen (by Bodley), the galleries shortened by one bay to increase the spatial tug of war. The talent has somehow been returned a hundredfold; it is a wonderful thing, especially now, to see a building in which everyone has truly understood and respected what has gone before and at the same time has not been afraid to add to it. That this should be Belgravia's parish church, i.e. a ritzy place to get married in, is another letter in London's alphabet.

Beauchamp Place   144 6D–7E

A short, straight, traffic-ridden street near Harrods which by some accident of social drift has compressed together the Mayfair feeling that is now so hard to find in Mayfair. The interest is in the shops, or rather the shop titles, a kaleidoscope of how the other tenth lives. There is[3] Susan's Beauchamp Club, and Mrs Payne (Party Specialists) Ltd, and the Dogs' Bath Club – 'Through These Portals Pass the Most Beautiful Dogs in the World'. For good measure, there is also Remake-Remodel Handbag Co. Because it is not trying to prove anything (why bother, we've arrived) it is endearing, not phoney: a genuine true-blue English eccentric.

3. In 1965. By 1987 only Susan's Beauchamp Club remained, and the street had become less eccentric and more tourist-conscious. But there were two nanny agencies representing the older tradition.

Ovington Street   144 8E
c. 1840

Ovington is a long and straight street, on its way up, near the borders of Chelsea and South Kensington. It was built late enough to go naughty in the balustrade – i.e. the 1840s – and it has an enchanting stop at the southern end. This is what looks like a former literary institute, in Milner Street; it is now a luxury house, decorated theatrically in peach and cream. Sense of the theatre is just what is needed: this is a Roman scenographic view, squared up and given a stiff collar and an old-boy accent. Earlier, people were too polite; later, they became too serious; this is a rare, extrovert vintage: Brunel or Disraeli townscape.

Michelin House, Fulham Road   144 9C
(corner of Sloane Avenue)

One of the least likely buildings of an unlikely city. There are glazed tiles all over, and motor tyres on the parapet – though no chubby rubber men – and the Michelin monogram and 'Bibendum' in thumping great letters, and all round the walls at eye level are early motoring scenes with such an air to them that the Fulham Road dissolves and you are back in the 1900s, with clouds of dust and the enraged sputtering of the motor in a deep, quiet countryside. You come to giggle at the vehicles and the titles (*Szisz sur Renault, Lautenschlager sur Mercedes*), stay entranced at the delicate, spare evocation of the different landscapes – Brittany, or the Ardennes, or the road to Spain. They are a bit like Toulouse-Lautrec posters done in tile.

Pelham Crescent and Pelham Place, South Kensington
George Basevi, c. 1840   144 9C

Basevi was a man with a rich imagination who was pushed into pomp-
ousness by the spirit of the time. But here, temperament and the job
to be done are matched exactly. Bayswater should have looked like this.
The Crescent is part of the Fulham Road, the Place runs northward out
of its centre. One side is longer than the other and is curled round to
keep the space intact [47]. It makes a perfect urban unit – formal but
not rigid, self-contained yet not sealed up. It could be plugged in to
any part of London's structure, and would be as happy off the Mile
End Road as in Belgravia.

Brompton Oratory and the sequence behind it   144 7C
Herbert Gribble, 1878

Incredibly Italian, so well done that the truly Baroque stone saints in
the nave (from Siena) fit in perfectly. On a cold day in February it can
be quite a pick-me-up. So well done, in fact, that it takes on all the
faults of its seventeenth-century prototypes. It could be a middling
Baroque church in any big Italian city: and this is not enough.

   Behind it, though, is a sequence which is really worth visiting. At
the end of a leafy avenue is the skinny white-brick Anglican church of
Holy Trinity, an astonishing contrast with the florid rump of the
Oratory. Behind that a placid big churchyard, and then all sorts of
puzzling things – a dainty mews with a noble post-and-lintel entrance,
the big modish students' hostel in Prince's Gardens, suavely Corbusian, by Richard Sheppard & Partners. It is like going out through a
secluded gate in the bottom of your garden to find yourself on someone
else's front porch. The whole sequence is potentially one of the most
surprising in London, and if it has not been fully realized, it has not
been impaired either. Yet.

Victoria and Albert   144 7 B–C

A colossal treasure-chest which does for sculpture and decorative art
what the National Gallery does for painting. It shares the job with the
British Museum, but the atmosphere is completely different, sym-
bolized by the rapid change in gallery shapes compared to those
stupefying Grecian rooms up in Bloomsbury. Everything is worth
looking at, and, mercifully, there is no automatic draw such as the
Elgin Marbles. So the visitors are evenly spread, and the immense
range of masterpieces have a chance of speaking to you unblurred. If
you want to look at something as crazily marvellous as the Eltenberg
Reliquary, then nobody will be likely to be breathing down your neck,
whether Global Tours or Kunsthistorischer.

   With the objects so various – iron, ivory, stained glass, terracotta –
things are much less formal, more like a walk through a fabulously
appointed private house. So aesthetic fatigue sets in much less easily –
there is not often the B.M.'s belligerent mood of 'if I see one more

bloody Greek bust' – and much more important, there is the chance
to see that all art is saying the same thing, though it may find a hundred
thousand ways of doing it.

Any detailed guide is impossible here; apart from anything else, I
don't know more than a twentieth of the exhibits myself. But two of
my favourites might not turn up on a casual visit. One of them, in the
middle of an interesting but not outstanding set of English period
rooms, is a collection of Nicholas Hilliard's miniatures, saying more
in a couple of inches than many famous painters say in twenty feet.
The other is that in the sub-basement on the west side, near the
entrance in Exhibition Road, there is some magnificent Baroque sculpture: the most striking of all portrayals of Charles II, by Honoré Pelle,
and Bernini's enchanting Mr Baker, frothed around like a poodle or a
man being shampooed in the barber's, foppish pretensions transformed
by an Olympian sense of humour. On the way down there is a bust of
Cassandra Sirigatti by a sixteenth-century Florentine sculptor, Ridolfo
Sirigatti. If it doesn't stop you in your tracks then I reckon you ought
to have your money back.[4]

4. The Eltenberg Reliquary is in the new Medieval Treasury. The Hilliard
miniatures are in the Henry Cole wing, fourth floor. Pelle's Charles II is on
the staircase up to the Department of Ceramics. Cassandra Sirigatti is in gallery
21 (High Renaissance). Mr Baker, prominently displayed, is still in the west
sub-basement, gallery 1c.

Albert Hall   144 5A
Captain Fowke, 1867

A poignant contrast with the Festival Hall: that, acoustically perfect
and spiritually numb; this, a mangler of anything but the loudest noises
yet a wonderful place which converts each concert or meeting into an
occasion. It is more like an opera house than a concert hall: England's
nineteenth-century La Scala, waiting for the Verdi who never
appeared. The outside is original but unimpassioned, like all of the
buildings by the remarkable band of Royal Engineers who worked
under Sir Henry Cole. The inside is splendidly impassioned. Every
seat involves you in what is going on, even if you can't hear it. The
hall becomes a collective animal (where the Festival Hall is a brilliant
icy cave). The section avoids all the separateness of balconies and their
overhangs by running three tiers of boxes straight up the walls between
two raked banks of seats. Above that, the gods, really noble, with
standing-room framed in Venetian three-part arches: display where it
is most needed. Everyone can see everyone else and is part of the whole
space. You can always change acoustics (and in fact the Albert Hall is
far better than it used to be);[5] but you can never graft a heart into a
building that was designed without room for one.

5. Better still, since the installation in the dome of the crop of acoustic mush-
rooms, whose abstract extra-terrestrial shapes provide a weirdly effective
counterpoint to the ceremonial architecture of the Hall.

[Albert Memorial   144 5A
Sir George Gilbert Scott, 1863–72

Taste has swung from for to against and back again. Taste is welcome;
this remains a very big and very Victorian emporium: rich, competent
and – like the Law Courts – completely cold-hearted. The wonderful
spark that animated some Victorian pubs and churches is just not
there, and no swing of the pendulum can kindle it. Plenty of fun to be
got, which is just about its mark, from the juxtaposition of artists of
all ages in the frieze: e.g. Rossini sandwiched between Josquin des
Prés and Monteverdi, to the amazement of all three. And the elephant
on one of the corners has a backside just like a businessman scrambling
under a restaurant table for his cheque-book.]

Royal College of Art, Kensington Gore   144 5A
H. T. Cadbury-Brown, 1961

This is a very good place to feel the husky, direct temper of young
British architects. It is the opposite of a firework; it smoulders through
to your consciousness with quiet intensity: purple brick and concrete
aggregate, humped up against the Albert Hall like a gruff egalitarian
greeting. This building is meant to be used and worn and thumbed
over and hugged, like the family's big woolly dog. Seven storeys of
classrooms, the staircase coming where it needs to: a lecture theatre
on the ground floor, and bolshie paired roof-lights on top nudging the
sky along with the Boeings and Caravelles. All of it is done with feeling
for the students (compare the glacial complacent emptiness of the new
Imperial College, a few yards farther south): all of it is troubled, asking,
questioning, scrutinizing. Perhaps it serves the wrong college; a science
department would desperately need this; the R.C.A. has, already, too
much of the feeling of God's elect.

KENSINGTON

Kensington New Town,
south of Kensington Gore, west of Gloucester Road   75 2–3K

Most of London's villages are overpraised, and you end up staring
gloomily at one tarted-up brick terrace and an old lamp-standard
whilst the traffic roars by. This one, which is a real *rus-in-urbe*, is
relatively unknown: and the traffic cannot roar by because by a happy
accident of the road pattern it is a very large cul-de-sac. It is really
big, which most of the 'villages' aren't, so that you can feel yourself to
be in the middle of it, not on the edge of something else. It is mixed
up too, with all the styles jostling each other, not crowded out with
flats like St John's Wood. The best single house, a real sophisticated
puzzle, is 19 Eldon Road. At the west end the village runs into Kensington Square (but only with local knowledge or a good map), which
has been equally undervalued. Its character lies not in the eighteenth-
century fragments, but in the fact that half of them have been demol-

ished and replaced piecemeal with a wonderful *mélange* including a
wild 1860 church front, and some strays from Cadogan Square. It is
the only London square to accept, albeit accidentally, the implications
of the thick planting in the centre and to treat the sides as united by
overall shape but nothing else. And peering over the north side with
Parisian spectacles of a generation ago is Barker's, with the uncom-
mitted bustle of High Street Kensington, more cosmopolitan and
impersonal than Oxford Street.

The whole of the New Town has the fairies on it. When you find at
the end of a cul-de-sac (South End), in the boskiest part, that one of
the doors in the wall is the London Taxi-meter Testing Station, it
seems quite natural. But afterwards, you begin to wonder . . .[6]

6. Perhaps it was always an illusion; anyway, it has gone.

Kensington Palace Orangery
Nominally Sir Christopher Wren, 1704

75 1K

The Palace is unpretentious and humdrum – which is just marvellous,
from any other point of view than that of this guide, because this self-
effacement ensured that we had an 1832 rather than a 1789. The
London Museum, housed in part of it, has caught the bug, unhappily,
and whatever comes over from the posed set-pieces is certainly not
London.[7] But the Orangery is worth going to see. It was designed at
a time when Hawksmoor was probably in charge of Wren's office. The
outside, indeed, looks like Wren: a long, plain, dignified envelope, like
Chelsea Hospital, vamped up at the ends and centre. But inside, the
new style had free rein, and though the details are meticulous and
conventional, they are stated with far more force than Wren could
normally have mustered. A long, narrow main room has what seem to
be apsed ends. When you get there, they are complete circles, hidden
by the narrowness of the opening. Impeccable entablature bends round
into an enticement.

7. Much improved, it has merged with the Guildhall Museum and moved to
new premises in the Barbican.

Kensington Palace Gardens

75 1–2K

Nothing else like this in London: a Victorian Millionaire's Row, stone
and stucco *palazzi* on either side of a leafy straight private road. It is
a motorist's short cut from Notting Hill to Kensington High Street –
if you can outface the formidable guardians at either end. Yesterday's
money-power has given way to today's much more sinister political-
power. These places, sedate or mildly frolicky – the level of design is
pretty high – are now embassies, including the Russian. No flags fly,
and no notice boards announce the extra-territorial slice of stucco.[8]
There are just a few patrolling policemen giving you glances. It is
quite a relief to go downhill to Kensington Palace where ordinary
people like Princess Margaret live.

8. One or two exceedingly expensive modern buildings have found their way in, notably the appropriately grey and secretive-looking Czech embassy by the north gate.

The Hoop, Notting Hill Gate   75   1J
Interiors: Robert Radford, 1960

The best modern pub interior in London. Here for once the Victorian tradition is truly re-interpreted, not merely cribbed in a few coy details. This pub went behind the details to the creation of the right sort of drinking spaces, and everything followed on from this. The plan itself is classically simple – public on one side, saloon on the other, and a splendid back bar from which both estates are visible. The mystery follows naturally from the different layers of space and other people in other bars, and doesn't have to be tickled up. And the pub atmosphere doesn't need to be worked at but grows up from the basic architectural decisions.[9]

9. Renamed Finch's. It was redesigned in 1986, and the 1960s interior was stripped out. The new pub is studiedly, if rather pallidly, traditional, even to the extent of having fluted wooden columns on the street-front.

Holland Park Mews   75   1H

Most London mews are more fun to live in than look at. But this one is a cathedral among mewses. A steep drop to the entrance arch at the west end, and a steep climb out and a wristy flick at the east end give it an individual signature. In between, the strange blend of mews life rolls on for something like a quarter of a mile: chi-chi cottages above, and specialist car repairers below.[10] Zone that lot, ye makers of plans! The cottages themselves are complete and personable little buildings, rather like the single-storey terraces of Dublin, reached by an outside staircase. The stucco entrance arch must see every variety of human and automotive temperament in the course of a year.

10. Now nearly all private garages.

Melbury Road   75   3H
Farley Court, Julian Keable & Partners, 1961
Park Close, Colin Wilson & Arthur Baker, 1960
Fildes House, Norman Shaw, 1877

Famous as a street of Victorian houses for artists and aesthetes. Yet, ironically, what now makes it most worth a visit is two groups of modern flats: Park Close at the east end, next to Holland Park; Farley Court at the west end, at the junction with Addison Road. While the Victorians were tying themselves in all kinds of fancy knots, this pair does a straightforward job simply. They have moral fibre, where the last century was sunk in soggy eclectic indecision. (There is plenty of today's soggy indecision around here as well, both neo-modern and neo-Georgian.) Farley Court is six-storey, with a particularly effective

nd tough-minded relation between the units, with their staircase-
inks. Park Close is a set of separate nine-storey blocks with tall-
runked mature trees close up to the walls. A simple trick, but unfailing
in summer or winter to weld the units together.

The only nineteenth-century building to stand up to this is Norman
Shaw's Fildes House (opposite Park Close), which scorns surface
tricks, and lets the building's various purposes grow into an asymmetrical group rather like one of the original London Board Schools.
Yet that puzzling man also produced No. 8, just down the road, which
is full of surface tricks.) William Burges's own house, No. 9, next to
Fildes House, turns a bleak face to the outside world, though the inside
must be full of marvels. It is padlocked and seems empty, now; it must
be kept.[11]

1. The road has been partly renumbered. Fildes House is No. 31, Burges's
house has survived to become No. 29.

Leighton House
75 3H
Lord Leighton, nominally George Aitchison, 1865 onwards

This is not just one more museum. Lord Leighton's house has the
wholeness and excitement which is so conspicuously absent from his
paintings. He brought in a lot of genuine bits from the Middle East,
but the effect is purely Victorian. The old work acted as a springboard –
or more accurately a fuse – to send off designers like William de
Morgan and Leighton himself to the essence of nineteenth centuryness
the nominal architect Aitchison seems to have been brought in only
to ensure that the decoration didn't fall down). Here you can really see
what they were at, and like all true essence it seems quite natural.
Rich but not indigestible, rhetorical but not posturing. And above
everything else, harmonious, one world; nobody looking over their
shoulders like frightened mice. In a decade and a city controlled by
frightened mice, the point is worth making over and over again.

The Scarsdale
75 3J

Edwardes Square and Pembroke Square have been extruded into
notability because of the mediocrity of most things built since in this
part of the Royal Borough. This pub, midway between them, can stand
on its own feet. Nothing but one end of a terrace, three frilly iron
porches and a lucid arrangement of dark, comfortable bars behind – a
Victorian prototype of the Hoop, Notting Hill Gate.[12] So hard to do,
so simple once it has been done; the Scarsdale deserves particular
credit for staying intact in such a fashionable area. Perhaps it is so far
up in the world that its inhabitants no longer have to prove anything.
There is a genuine forecourt with open-air tables, and to sit out here
on a summer day with the foreground all green and airliners from
every country turning finals on London Airport is an exhilarating
cocktail of an experience: metropolitan, up-to-the-minute, relaxed,
and pure cockney, all at the same time.

12. Now only two porches, and the bars all combined into one space, though still pleasant and cosy.

CHELSEA AND WEST KENSINGTON

Chelsea 76

Chelsea is only relatively remarkable. Compared with the bow-fronted deserts of north Fulham, it is full of character; looked at coldly, it is made up of a few pretty bits set in an unlovely mixture of the utilitarian and the genteel. The trouble is that there are no eccentric buildings to match the eccentric people. King's Road sums up the social aorta of Chelsea perfectly: full of idiosyncratic life, yet without anything in the buildings to express it. The uneven shape is good, but the traffic boys would like to straighten that up, instead of diverting the through traffic, which makes any idea of a unified Chelsea impossible. What makes this all the more sad is that the Chelsea recipe is very exciting. It is still all mixed up, with rough and smooth side by side, and it seems incredible that such a natural centre and basically pleasant shape as World's End should have existed for a century without any recognition of its potential.[13] Only the pub has taken its chance, and that has been left out in the cold by a new dead straight streetline.

The late-nineteenth-century houses and studios are not much fun; the picturesqueness is applied, not instinct. Chelsea's high spots come from the unselfconscious Georgian cottages, now jerked violently up the social scale. They never make a connected system, and the Chelsea views which have edged into a hundred British films need to be carefully chosen. One is the L-shape of Lawrence Street, just at the back of the Albert Bridge, with Judge's Walk running off it. Another, unexpected and very much London, is a tiny enclave (Billing Road) crammed in between a railway, Brompton Cemetery and the Chelsea football ground.

13. With the exception of the pub, the old World's End was swept away in the building of the World's End housing estate. Today it is little more than the point of collision between the estate and the less fashionable end of the King's Road.

Sloane Square 76 4D–E

Apart from the traffic, Sloane is one of the most attractive squares in London. Many of them, and some of the venerated ones, are simply dreariness given another shape – the palm goes to Bonnington Square in Lambeth, which is quite an experience if you are expecting something mellow. But here, the space is right, the plane trees are right, the site is right, with London's most established *avant-garde* theatre, the Royal Court, facing Peter Jones, built as London's first modern glass wall in 1936 and still capable of giving a kick by the bulgy way it rounds the corner from King's Road. The square needs joining to both of them, instead of being misused as a traffic roundabout, and then filling with kiosks, a café, more seats. Here really is one of he few sites of London where that wistful dream, a 'Continental' tmosphere, would spring up naturally. Already, once you have dodged he No. 11 buses in their gloomy convoys, the central space is elegant nd welcoming just for its shape: a positive incitement to stop and talk.

o Bourne Street   76 4E

The kind of building whose personality outweighs its faults of detail, o that it sticks in the memory when bigger and better designs fade. 3ulky, and improbably slate-hung, in a nicely humble wedge between Chelsea and Pimlico which has not (as yet) been taken up too far. It nakes Voysey's point of forceful simplicity better than any of the Voysey houses in Central London.

Chelsea Barracks   76 5E
Tripe & Wakeham, 1962

This headquarters for the Coldstream and Grenadier Guards is content ust to be itself, and let quality come out of the barrackness. This was he recipe for Georgian military buildings, and it has worked again ere. One immensely long five-storey block facing the parade ground vith the scale that modern architecture in Britain has tried to get so ften and so unsuccessfully. Subsidiary blocks in approximate sym-netry in front, two towers of flats behind. Finesse or adroitness matters nuch less than this basic honesty. In a world of architectural charlatans his is an open-hearted handshake.

Chelsea Hospital Stables   76 5D
Sir John Soane, c. 1810

omething near a miracle, to be had any day for the asking by stopping ff a bus at Royal Hospital Road and walking down West Road. A lear, Euclidian proof of the argument of this book, that $2+2=5$. oane had absolutely nothing but the texture of yellow bricks to play vith, and created a power-house out of London stocks. An arch framed y arches for an entrance – no columns, no architrave, no cribbed letail. Instead of an archway through, there is just sky and then a urther arch, one brick thin [49]. It is all there: the rules of scale and roportion, plus the magic quality which converts a literary exercise nto a poem. You can analyse till the cows come home and you still von't arrive at the truth of this, mate. But someone on the wrong side f the G.C.E. might get there, just as T. Carlyle, Esq., did with the nain buildings ...

Chelsea Hospital   76 5D–E
Sir Christopher Wren, 1682–91

.. in one of the few architectural judgements that will stand endless epetition:

had passed it daily for many years without thinking much about it, and one day I began to reflect that it had always been a pleasure to me to see it, and I looked at it more attentively and saw that it was quiet and dignified and the work of a *gentleman*.

What else is there to say? Only an amplification, more necessary in 1960 than in 1840: that it is Nature's gentlemen that are meant, not Debrett's. So the Hospital's virtue is not excessive polish, but excessive politesse: the courteousness that can brush off loudmouths by the enormous stature of its own nature. Beneath this promise, and not explicitly expressed, is immense power: invulnerable because internal. Where Vanbrugh needed to emphasize his chimneys, Wren plants them down just as powerfully, yet unemphatic; this is probably the best place to feel his wisdom and calm authority. The street front depends on the understated rhythm of hall and chapel windows; on the garden side the wings take over, prodigious expositions of themselves and nothing more. End, side, roof, dormer, chimney: long-service medals all round.

Chelsea riverside   76 6c
Albert Bridge, 1873

This is Whistler's Thames, though Old Battersea Bridge, a wooden mirage, went in the 1890s. In a mist, the illusion is still there. But something harsher and deeper has come over the river since then. It is one of Whistler's symphonies, still, but the key signature is mud and dirty stock brick. The time to see it is in the afternoon with a warm front coming in, and the sun like a blob of melted butter shining down on the oily, sullen river. This is a working place, with flour mills for a frame.[14] Battersea Park and its funfair, an intellectual idea of enjoyment if ever there was one, looks ridiculously out of place. The whole thing hinges now on the Albert Bridge and the splendid rough shapes of Lots Road Power Station. Both are perfect examples of buildings full of character yet without any formal architectural merit – and so much the worse for formal architectural merit. Lots Road does without effort what a few modern designers just manage by using all their faculties: the Albert Bridge is a proper exchange for Old Battersea, absurdly over-spiky and over-strutted. Even then, troops must break step when marching over the bridge: a notice says so. It must be kept, as a recognition of frailty and absurdity, a manic shriek against the solid mill walls. No replacement will do; to see an ordinary suspension bridge, flick a glance downstream at the 1934 Chelsea Bridge, full of good taste. And then look back, into the sombre greatness of the curve round to the chimneys, filled with houseboats in the sort of organic pattern that the whole of Chelsea ought to have but doesn't.

14. i.e. the R.H.M. mill in Battersea, and the white building at Chelsea Wharf, formerly a Spillers French mill, now converted to other use. Lots Road Power Station is visible beyond Chelsea Wharf. Battersea Funfair closed in 1976.

[St Luke Chelsea, Sydney Street
James Savage, 1821
76 5C

Something to ponder. A famous church, the first in England to set about the Gothic Revival in earnest. Hence a place in the history books and some admiration. Yet the building itself is one of the most loveless in London, the details mechanical, the spaces expensive and empty. For a century and a half, St Luke's has been getting away with fraud on the strength of being the first to do something – a dubious distinction, here – and because a lot of money was spent on it.]

King's Arms (Finch's), 190 Fulham Road
76 6A

With all the charades that are put on London for people to posture in and think themselves odd, it is more and more difficult to provide for the real thing. This place is really odd – naturally odd and eccentric – and feels quite different from the pubs that are trying it on. For one thing, it is still rough; and for another, the local cockneys haven't been driven out. They coexist with the wildest *avant-garde*, and with yours truly, in season, scribbling these notes in an uneasy no-man's-land. (No. That's unfair. No-man's-land, certainly, but not really uneasy. This pub has got the secret of live-and-let-live.) Almost wrecked a year or two ago by a kill-with-kindness restoration which left all the old shapes and loaded bilious colours on to them – the blue-green tinge behind the bar is all too clear an example. But the people keep the spirit going.[15]

15. Thirty years ago it was one of the favourite and most fashionable pubs of artistic Chelsea. In more recent times it has dropped into relative obscurity, but it retains something of its old décor, with its bare wood floor, Victorian advertising mirrors, and general ruggedness.

24 Hereford Square
Colin Wilson & Arthur Baker, 1959
76 4A

If English architecture were in a healthier state there might be no need to include this building, because it would represent the average and one like it should turn up in every High Street. As things are, it is worth a special visit to see how a modern building can fit in to one corner of a stucco Kensington square without forced compromise or forced individuality either, just by being itself. All the architectural points are made too, such as indicating on the outside the size of the unit inside (flat or maisonette), but they are not laboured or shown off. Here modern architecture has at last arrived at maturity; most of all perhaps in not needing to insist on its modernity.

Bousfield Primary School, Old Brompton Road and The Boltons
Chamberlin, Powell & Bon, 1955
76 5H

Exhibitionism is masquerading as originality all the time in British architecture. God knows why, because here of all arts the shallow is shown up in ten years or so – who would look at most of the talking-points of the 1930s now?

By contrast this school is truly original, and although its paintwork may become dirty and its glass walling look splotched, the imagination behind it will never tarnish. Here, for once, a genuine joy in building, like one of those gurgles of uninhibited delight that come out of a full-bodied lady who doesn't give a damn. Nothing shows it better than what you can see as you walk up from The Boltons. First a view of the entrance achieved by replacing the wall with a water splash. You can trespass if you want, but you get your feet wet; the architects gleefully reported a few years ago that until then only school officials had managed to fall in. The wall begins again as you go towards the corner; but there is a slit at eye level, and you can peer in to see what the architects have made of what might have been just another bit of West Kensington. A passage burrows under the taut two-storey classroom; facing it, splayed all round the corner, are tiers of seats, making a Greek amphitheatre – and more to the point, a splendid playground, fount for a hundred new children's games: 'Who's higher than me', and so on. After all, what else is the House of Commons, except that the game is played in reverse, as is appropriate to humans of great sophistication. Everything feels as though it was done *with* the children instead of for them.

[Earls Court and Empress State Building   75 5J

Earls Court is a hippopotamus in the water hole, rearing up above West London, that ought to have grass all over it. The Empress State Building (!) is a Wimbledon housewife twenty-six storeys high, lifting her little finger as she drinks the tea (it ought to have a crop of trees on top like Vanbrugh's Eastbury). Between them they are certainly the longest joke in London, an ineffable and purely visual joke, two monsters desperately needing to grow more hair. London owes them more for being like this than it would if they were models of elegance.]

St Cuthbert, Philbeach Gardens   75 5J

H. R. Gough, 1884
Screens, pulpit, lectern, Bainbridge Reynolds, 1887 onwards

In a backwater, sandwiched between Earls Court and the Cromwell Road. The outside, bald and bricky, may not tempt. The inside will engross: a High Anglican temple, sombre and indrawn, the exact opposite of Comper's soaring lark-cry at St Cyprian, Marylebone, though both reflect the same leaf on the same branch of Christianity. A rood hangs in the air, a vast reredos looms in the background: English pomp and English melancholy. The architect, the son of that Gough whose partner was the wild Roumieu, provided a decent rich background. The woodwork added atmosphere but no more. What lifts the church into being something special is the glittering talent of

Bainbridge Reynolds. In items with antecedents, like the sedilia and the pulpit, it is no more than talent; but in the screens to the chancel aisles and the organ, and especially in the lectern, his genius could cut loose. Here, for once, is a genuine English Art Nouveau, and an inventiveness equal to that of Mackintosh. None of the obvious Art Nouveau signs appear; instead they are ploughed in, metamorphosed, become wiry and rope-like. The lectern, vibrating with energy, tingling to the tips of its wide candelabra branches, is the exact opposite of the milksop nonsense that the Arts and Crafts movement became. A communist might take off his hat in front of it; and the daintiest of country ladies might blush at the echo of remembered passion. Old Skelton would know, and old Pope and old Byron: stretch and barb, nothing soft.

Three Kings, West Cromwell Road and North End Road

Richardson & While, 1902

75 5H

A big surprise just round the corner from the cut and thrust of the Cromwell Road. It would need a firm resolution to resist the call of the entrance in North End Road which sucks rather than beckons. A splendid volute, all wood and glass, draws you into the recesses. The same old principle of the Baroque frontispiece: a door is not just a door, any more than a pint of bitter (which is very good here) is just alcohol.[16] The inside has been impaired by redecoration, but everything is still all there, including a labyrinth of bars each with a different clientele. It deserves to be restored to all its Victorian sparkle and would then be one of the best pubs in London.[17]

16. In 1967 Ian Nairn added: 'I am hoist by my own exuberance here; for I now learn that the door was not originally part of the pub at all. It was, of all things, a tea shop!'
17. It is now two rooms only, the larger of which recedes into remote candle-lit depths. The oval bar offers an enormous (perhaps over-ambitious) range of cask beers.

6 Thames-Side West: Putney to Staines

One loop north to Kew, one loop south to Kingston, then north again to Windsor. In spite of being submerged in London's growth, the riverside places have kept their own identity very well. Hardly any of them exploit the river, yet they are all affected by it, in completely different ways: Richmond, Petersham, Hampton Court, Chertsey and Chertsey Bridge, Windsor. It is a tip-and-run technique, very English, the opposite of the long *quais* along the Seine in the western suburbs of Paris: the best example is at Twickenham. Perhaps because it is never fully displayed, this comparatively puny river has an effect far beyond its size. Far more could be done to accentuate the differences, and multiply places as enchanting and absurd as Eel Pie Island.

SOUTH SIDE: PUTNEY TO KINGSTON

1a Fitzgerald Avenue, Mortlake   90 3A

A wonderful toy fort made up of genuine bits and genuine fantasy, in an uneasy bit of suburbia between Barnes and Richmond. The frontispiece is a huge Wren-style door dated 1696, but there are columns and battlements too. Nothing could better show the sparkling, original, Vanbrugh-Castle impulse to build your own separate fort – just as the surrounding houses show the terrible things that happened when this most individual of impulses was met by mass-production and the commercial instinct. 'Have your very own personalized dream-fort' as those lost fifty states across the water might put it.

Kew Gardens   72–73 7E–F
                                                                        88–89 1–2E–F

An astonishing three-penn'orth.[1] Apart from the plants, there is a chubby seventeenth-century merchant's house (Kew Palace), a set of Georgian temples, a remarkable nineteenth-century lodge and the Palm House. The gardens were originally a royal park, and the temples are left over from this, all done by Sir William Chambers. This kind of civilized small-talk was exactly his *métier*. Bellona Temple,[2] on its hill, is a perfect summary of these academic manners, but the effect is killed stone dead by the crass Victorian gables leering over the wall from Kew Road. The landscape part has been chopped up too much to read properly, also. But Chambers's titbits are good things to have around: and so is the Pagoda, gaunt as an ostrich, down at the south end of the gardens. There, the fancy is spread too thin, and what results is a water tower with sets of inexplicable eaves all the way up – and a colour scheme of dark blue and pillar-box red. There used to be eighty dragons on top, which would have helped.

The nineteenth-century lodge is next to the Marianne North gallery, and is also visible from Kew Road: an extraordinary Queen Anne building by Nesfield, Norman Shaw's early partner. The little building, with its great grave hat of roof and chimney, just like a solemn child, has all the presence and personality which Shaw angled for and often failed to achieve. The deadpan overstatement which must conceal a huge sense of humour is worthy of Vanbrugh at his best: the precision is Nesfield's own.

And finally there is the Palm House.[3] How on earth can I convey the utter originality and unselfconscious perfection of this building; nearer to a beautiful animal or to one of the plants it encloses than to the fumbling, guilt-laden compositions of architecture. The designer was an engineer (though Decimus Burton hogged the credit, to his shame): Richard Turner of Dublin.[4] He must have been a mad starstruck Irish poet as well, because he came up with one of the few completely original buildings in the whole of architecture. Compared with it, even the Crystal Palace seems like a classical reminiscence. The whole design is built up with curved sheets of glass: one big curve in the wings up to the clerestory, another from there to the central dome. It is right outside architecture, autonomous; and the feeling is overwhelming when one goes in, with foliage up to the roof and the gentle, fresh perfume of the leaves and bark. You can get up in a gallery under the dome; leaves below, glass all round, and an unearthly peace that is quite unexpected, even in these extraordinary circumstances. Go afterwards – a long time afterwards – into the Temperate House to see how a mediocre designer can demean even this recipe.

1. Now 50p; still pretty astonishing.
2. Near the Victoria Gate. The visitor needs a detailed map to get the best out of Kew: the Gardens sell one, beautifully done, for 40p.
3. Closed for restoration – stripped to the bones, a sad sight. It will reopen in 1988 or 1989. Interest for the moment has turned to the new Princess of Wales Conservatory: technologically advanced, architecturally deferential, as is only right.
4. This is still a contentious issue. The prevailing view is that Burton deserves credit for the curved design, Turner for the engineering which ensured that the design was both realizable and flawless.

Richmond   88 4–5D

Funny, louche, subtle. A bit of Wimbledon, a bit of Windsor and a disturbing whiff of Soho or Brighton. Where most towns around London are all too simple, this takes a lot of getting to know. And the farther you go, the odder it becomes: some of it is very odd indeed. The shape is all unexpected too. A narrow main street with the traffic tied in knots, then careful alleys off to the west which lead to an enormous square green which has everything: Maids of Honour Row, Victorian villas, a blowsy Edwardian theatre. If you like human crossword puzzles, then try solving this one.

Asgill House and Richmond Bridge
88 5C

Asgill House: Sir Robert Taylor, c. 1765
Richmond Bridge: Kenton Couse and James Paine, 1774

Off the north-west corner of Richmond Green, Old Palace Lane runs
down to the river, more cosy now than it needs to be. It leads past a
pub, which is handy, and comes to an abrupt end at the water. On the
left is Asgill House, a jewel of a riverside villa. Just like Ely House,
Dover Street, this is Sir Robert Taylor staying exactly within his *milieu*
and doing it superbly. Not a detail out of canon, not a detail out of
place either.

It looks out on a scene not mentioned in the elegant books of prints.
A railway bridge, a road bridge, a lot of ladies fishing, and an asphalt
footpath running up towards the only real bridge at Richmond, the
old one. In fact the only bridge between London and Marlow to take
account of the river as a personality, not an engineering problem. The
five graduated arches are partners with the glittering water, and lose
no excitement by the gesture, just as the minuet with its utterly formal
plan can act as container for the most exuberant high spirits. Between
them, Asgill House and Richmond Bridge spell out what we have lost
since the eighteenth century: not surface politeness, not a way of
designing, but wholeness of vision.

Richmond Hill
88 6E

The eighteenth century was enthusiastic, here, and it was usually right
about landscape. The astonishing thing is how green the view still is,
when several hundred thousand people must be living there. Nothing
can break the shape of the river and the trees around it, the centre of
the Improver's picture. The best view is by the direction indicator,[5]
and it has to be chosen pretty carefully to prevent one intrusion or
another nudging into the frame. If you walk downhill the view quickly
foreshortens into placidity; the excitement is then in the opposite
direction, where the Georgian and Victorian houses have their ground
floors completely obscured by low hedges on the edge of the road, an
effect which sounds banal in description but isn't. The continuous
parade of airliners on the way into London Airport helps by expressing
the Middlesex flatness, rolling away beyond the river.

5. Now marked by three pictorial panels.

Richmond Park
89, 105

This is far more than just another public open space. Like Windsor,
it is a Tudor chase, unimproved and unenclosed: big old trees on
brackeny hillsides. The irony is that it is now completely surrounded
with buildings: Richmond Park is antique but not artificial. It is the
deer and the few eighteenth-century villas which seem normal and
permanent, the airliners and the bizarre skyline of Roehampton which
seem ephemeral. The variation of landscape achieved with just a few

feet either way is remarkable, and so is the sense of isolation. Not illusion, an attempt to suggest that London is a hundred miles away, but the sense of an incredible survival, with London all-too-obviously on the horizon. Like the Saxon logs of Greensted nave, how on earth did it manage to stay untouched?

Petersham   104 1E

Greater London has some murderous slices of traffic, but this must be one of the most cruel. Petersham is the best place near London to feel the relaxed, sinuous sequence of big eighteenth-century houses behind walls and trim hedges. Or rather, it would be if there were not a continuous stream of lorries and buses (from Richmond to Kingston) with *homo sapiens* squashed on to a few inches of pavement. How the village has stayed intact is a miracle, and a by-pass is essential.[6] Dodging between the Fordsons and Leylands you might be able to get a glimpse of the handsome sobriety of Rutland Lodge, and the complementary curlicues of the iron gates to Montrose House, opposite. Away from the road there is a network of narrow lanes between high walls, the basis of an enchanting place. The river is a few yards to the west, Richmond Park a few yards to the east. Potentially, Petersham can't lose. It even has two weird churches. The old building on the west side of Pandemonium Alley[7] is one of those haphazard accretions that the Victorians occasionally overlooked. More odd than attractive, here; the designers seem to have been obsessed with rents and could only solve their difficulties by making the building much wider than it is long. The other church – All Saints – is in Bute Avenue, a cosy cul-de-sac east of the centre: tall and full of avid terracotta (by John Kelly, 1907), an astonishing thing to unload on to such a polite place. Quite a good joke, now, but once is enough.

6. There is still no by-pass, unless you count the M25.
7. Unmarked: it emerges by Petersham Nurseries on the main road.

Ham Common   104–105 3–4 D–F

Big and resilient, as indestructible as a rubber ball. Earlier days planted avenues across it, and the twentieth century has underlined one of them with a stream of traffic; but the place still lies determinedly east to west, athwart everything. Obstreperous, a big friendly dog that just won't go away. The west end is a film set of the home counties: comfortable houses behind fences and hedges, all in place and hence free to be any shape and style. The east end has strayed over from Richmond Park, thicket and bracken. Yet both are contained and controlled by the overall shape, where so many greens around London have given up the fight and surrendered to what is around the edges.

The edges here include one outstanding old building and one compelling new block of flats (and Parkleys (below) is just beyond the southern end). The new landmark is Langham House Close,* by

* South side of the smooth west end.

Stirling & Gowan, 1958: the first building in a new tough style which
was as much a reaction against well-meaning vacuity as the Angry
plays and novels. The fierce but not overbearing yellow brick and
exposed concrete still make their protest straight.

The old building is Ormeley Lodge,* early Georgian to its fingertips,
an epitome of all the Chesterfieldian virtues. Five bays of brickwork
between giant pilasters; but within this bald description there is complete freedom and subtlety. The bays are grouped 2:1:2, the windows
laced together with red brick against the brown-brick background.
The centre is a deliberate understatement, as English as could be,
which in its way becomes as effective as the most elaborate cartouche
of ornament. Not the stultifying stiff upper lip, but a natural restraint.
And all of this, to judge from its detail, was done by a mason-bricklayer,
paid by the square foot. One of Nature's gentlemen, in that case.

Parkleys, off Upper Ham Road, Ham Common   104 4D–E
Eric Lyons, 1954–6

The first of the Span estates, now ten years old and wearing well. All
of it is pretty, and the unforced decorativeness seems as fresh now as
when it was new. The tangle of interconnected courts in the centre
(their names, unfortunately, are Brooke, Marlowe and Spenser) is
something far more than pretty. Here is mid-twentieth-century space,
as distinct as Baroque space or Romanesque space. It is defined yet in
flux: each two-storey tile-hung court has its own shape, yet each has
views out to other courts and to the outside world. The outside world
is quite a surprise, here; the northern fag-end of Kingston is like the
jungle at the edge of a superficially European town in Central Africa.
You cannot fix any view or axis, it is all movement and changing
balance of buildings and decoration; yet the whole unit is piercingly
vivid.

Coombe (north-east of Kingston,
north of Coombe Lane)   106 7A, etc.

One of Surrey's lush, leafy and expensive suburbs; roads winding
amongst a jungle of rhododendrons, and houses of all shapes and styles
peering out. Now, at last, they include good modern houses, especially
along Coombe Hill Road.[8] But any style would fit into this dream-like
meander where bricks and leaves amalgamate. The casual visitor need
not feel uncomfortable, even though a new house here might cost
£16,000 or more.[9] Coombe, like St James's, is rich enough not to have
to put on airs.

8. Ian Nairn had particularly in mind a group of four houses (Fair Oaks etc.)
towards the eastern end of Coombe Hill Road.
9. The casual visitor is more likely to feel uncomfortable today, with every
road guarded by 'Residents Only' notices. And the cost of a house here is likely
to be £300,000 or more.

* North side of the rough east end.

Kingston upon Thames   118 2D

Without any doubt, the best town centre near London; in fact, one of
the best in the country. The first view of the triangular Market Place
seems too vivid to be true: the Market Hall, fussily Victorian, surrounded by stalls; the Church tower behind to the right, half screened
by trees, a wonderful half-timbered 1929 Boots[10] behind to the left.
Everything going on together, clanging like a peal of bells. And this is
only half. Another triangular market place, the Apple Market, dovetails
with the main space to make up a square. Buildings separate them
except for one narrow alley (Harrow Passage). Here and There, with
the There a reflection of the Here, like meeting the younger sister of
the woman you love. Another alley (King's Passage)[11] runs west from
the Market Place straight down to the Thames – no railings or notices,
just water at the end of stairs. And all this takes up approximately the
same area as one of the roundabouts on the Kingston By-pass.

10. Now Next.
11. Between Woolworth's and the Bradford and Bingley Building Society.

NORTH SIDE: FULHAM TO TWICKENHAM

Fulham and Putney   91 3G

Old church towers on either side of Putney Bridge are kept company
now by tall office blocks, part of the attempt to relieve the pressure in
Central London. One of those areas which could be marvellous but
isn't: as well as the contrasted buildings, the Putney side has a bustling
High Street and a medley of boat sheds, the Fulham side has a park
with splendid avenues of plane trees and the meek old buildings of
Fulham Palace, the home of the Bishop of London. Too many authorities involved and not enough imagination.

There are more specific reasons for going to Fulham. One you will
see as soon as you go in the north door of the church: the tablet to
Elizabeth Limpany (d. 1694). The stone cartouche is staid enough but
it has a huge carved wooden surround, the size of a reredos. This is a
sumptuous expression of the exact high point of English wood-carving.
Technically just as brilliant as Grinling Gibbons, but more flow in the
design and more personality in the lovely cherubs' heads.

After that great-hearted extroversion, there is something very
different under the tower. Viscount Mordaunt (d. 1675) postures on a
pedestal, the height of neurotic mannerism, brilliantly and wildly
carved by Bushnell, with a Van Gogh-like feeling of unbalance only
just restrained. This is good enough, but the real monument is the
bulgy main pedestal answered by obelisks on equally bulgy bases, set
diagonally. One has a pair of gloves thrown down on it, the other has
a crown. Everything gloomy and violent, and as direct as an explosion.

Hammersmith Flyover   74–75 5E–F
L.C.C., Architect's Department, Special Works Division, 1960–61

Exciting to drive over, if you can spare a glance, level with the affronted blank clerestory of the church. But the real excitement is underneath. The flyover is carried on segmental spans between a single line of columns. Horizon to horizon is circumscribed by this nervous structural under-belly, grooved and finny, never overbearing even though it is the biggest thing in the view. The concrete work has the same kind of humanity as Charles Holden's early Underground stations. The space underneath makes a shady car park, at the moment; but better things would be possible – an open-air market, for one.[12]

12. It is still a car park.

Hammersmith: King Street) and the Salutation   74 4D–E
Pub by A. P. Killik, 1910

King Street is like Rye Lane grown up. Just a busy, straight shopping street: but this is the one that is exactly right. The shape (height to width) is right, the rhythm of shops along the street is right, the shop decoration fits the place exactly; as at Peckham, the new styles of lettering on shopfronts are used with real gusto.[13] Best at the east end, near the Broadway, but it's worth carrying on west to the Salutation, opposite the stodgy pre-war town hall. The pub was built in 1910 by Fuller's of Chiswick, a colour scheme that you would not credit until you have seen it: a little mellow red brick and a lot of glazed tiles in a literally ravishing mixture of mauve and sky-blue. The effect is as delicate and penetrating as a Seurat, and quite an eye-stopper if you come on it casually when driving west out of London, as I first did.

13. Pretty well done for now, with elephantine new buildings, one-way traffic, and shopfronts like everywhere else. East of Studland Street there is just enough left to imagine what it must have been like; and the Salutation has survived.

Upper and Lower Mall, Hammersmith   74 5C–D

This is potentially the best of London's riverside. The river is immediately there, down steps, and you can walk along the foreshore at low tide – but be careful; one set of steps leads to a houseboat which declares that 'Trespassers will be drowned'.[14] There are riverside pubs, good old houses, and enough genuine people around to ensure that it will never go the way of Chelsea. The trouble is that Lower and Upper Mall are separated by a stretch of public garden. This is the site of the creek, filled in before the war and then made into an axis leading to the neo-Georgian town hall. But since the war the Cromwell Road extension has sliced across it, parallel to the river, restoring the old unity by accident. Riverside building linking the two walls would make the parts come together and still leave space for the gardens.

The walk can be carried on west, *diminuendo*, along Chiswick Mall, which for all its pretty Georgian houses is not much more than a nice suburban road which happens to have the river Thames on one side of it.

14. Gone. Perhaps the owner met his match, or was finally arrested.

Bedford Park   73 3–4K and 74 3–4A

The very first arty suburb, now only a leafy hiatus between Chiswick and Acton. It was laid out by Norman Shaw, and it shows his surface cleverness and inner emptiness very well. His group of church and Tabard pub – the name hits off the place a treat – looks as jaded as last year's fashions: there is not enough in it to stand up. But what does stand up is Voysey's wonderful house, No. 14 South Parade. Tall, narrow, uncompromisingly bare and a permanent reproach to the slack gables around. Built in 1889, it was his first building in a personal style and it has a punch and freshness which he lost in his later and bigger houses. This is Art Nouveau to its bones without using a single Art Nouveau mannerism, and its true children are on the Continent, at Brussels and Darmstadt.

Chiswick House   74 6A
Lord Burlington and William Kent, 1720–30

Lord Burlington may have been an aesthetic autocrat to his followers, but he was a personal and original designer himself. Chiswick [72 and 73] was his own house and he designed something far more than a copy of Palladio's Villa Rotonda. Palladio's harmony and sun-trickling mellowness have gone completely: instead there are staccato details and violent changes of scale. Mantuan violence, not Vicenzan harmony. The best place to feel this is the south front, towards the lake; a taut thin door under huge windows, smooth stucco capped by a crop of obelisks. This is in fact only ten years old: a really brilliant reconstruction done after the wings were demolished. Another building would be ruined by taking the additions away; at Chiswick the original design was so important that any amount of copy-work would have been justified.

Oddest of all is the main entrance under the portico: a dramatic, windowless cleft burrowing into the heart of the house. Mannerism could hardly go further than this secret, unostentatious penetration into the womb of the place. (The visitor today arrives by the plain ground-floor rooms and an equally unostentatious spiral stair.)

Once inside, by these sneaky portals, there is magnificence without limit. The first room is the central rotunda, and only here can any trace be found of the unemotional classicism which Burlington advocated and inflicted on England. The rest is barbarous grandeur, one of the triumphs of eighteenth-century decoration in Europe, never mind Britain. Beyond the rotunda is the three-part saloon. The central rectangle has apsed ends with openings through to an octagon and a circle. And as the rooms get smaller, the scale gets bigger – something which is caught exactly by Gordon Cullen's superb drawings in the official guide. Here, one and sixpence brings a set of graphic masterpieces as well as information.[15] Monstrous big doors on a curve, their open pediments leering at you. Cherubs and swags of incredible density, with all Inigo Jones's ability to suggest solid space. (In fact some of Jones's designs for ornamental details were re-used at Chiswick.) The rooms curl back left and right from the saloon, ending in two intense closets on either side of Lord Burlington's cleft into the building. Here, richness is achieved by the simplest means of all: wallpaper of such intensity that the whole room vibrates with colour: green and white in one sequence, red in the other.[16] Oh, those English, with their placid exteriors and all that passion underneath. The incredibly rich and complex ceiling of the Blue Room is English secret avowal at its most vivid, spoilt only by an awful painting by William Kent. Yet it must have been Kent's magniloquent decorative sense which created this room, and all the other rooms, in the first place. That's life.

The gardens are Kent's too, and historically important. But no fun, partly the result of trying to cram a quart into a pint pot, partly due to their dog-eared condition. Kent needed more space to do his best, whether it is seductively curvy like Rousham or stark and grand like Holkham.

15. Still available, price 85p.
16. The colours are becoming faded and shabby, but no doubt Chiswick's turn for redecoration will come.

M4 extension, Chiswick–Langley   73 5F, etc.
Sir Alexander Gibb & Partners, 1964

A leviathan rearing up out of the mediocrity of the Hounslow By-pass, dwarfing the road for more than a mile and then sheering away across country, near Osterley.[17] The blunt concrete T-pieces have brought back a scale without brutishness that has been missing since the Victorian viaducts. Threading your way underneath is an exciting business, especially around the interchange near Lionel Road. Ramps up, ramps down, and this superhuman march of concrete beams as far as the eye can see. Technology in the raw, where the Hammersmith Flyover is technology controlled and civilized: and each right for the site.[18]

17. It sheers away across a girder bridge which strides just over the roof of a small factory in Boston Manor Road – a particularly audacious gesture.
18. Perhaps appropriately, the concrete has stained more here than on the Hammersmith Flyover, and graffiti artists and bill-posters are more active.

Brentford   72 6–7D–E

A tragic traffic-laden place, as you go through it on the main road. Battered and doomed stock-brick houses yield to shoddy modern improvements, with nothing to show that this was the capital of Middlesex. Yet, potentially, one of the most exciting towns near London. The main-road traveller can get some idea on the eastern approach (the traffic will give him ample time for study) in St George-by-the-Gasworks, A. W. Blomfield's fiddly Victorian church, now a piano museum, thrown against the majestic sixteen-sided gasholder that compromises the view from Kew Gardens. Both are likely to come down – a pity, because the contrast is really moving.[19]

For the rest, you need to be out of the car. North to The Butts, a secluded leafy square criminally treated by the local authority, with a sea of asphalt in lieu of the delicate floor-surface that it needs, and some of its buildings in a bad way.[20] Then south to the really spectacular bit, down Dock Road or Catherine Wheel Road. This is where the Grand Union Canal meets the Thames, hence one of the busiest canal wharves in Britain. Art has never touched it – a good job, until art learns its proper position; this is a marvellous place in the raw. Water bubbles down spillways, sheds hold all manner of materials, wide boats bob up and down, a railway shed the size of a terminus rears up on the other side of the canal. It is as diverse yet as harmonious as the dawn chorus of birds in a London square.[21]

19. They are still up.
20. The buildings appear to be in reasonable condition now, but the asphalt floor persists.
21. Worth seeing now only for its air of melancholy decay. The water still pours through weir and lock-gates, but there is no bustle, no trade, and no railway shed. Aquatic life of a different sort goes on nearby, in the marina at the end of Augustus Close, which replaced the railway; but it is not worth a special visit.

The Beehive, Brentford High Street (corner of Half Acre)
Nowell Parr and A. E. Kates, 1907   72 7D

An elaborate in-and-out kind of building, which includes a stone beehive high up. The ground floor is a song: Fuller Smith and Turner's designer was ringing the changes infallibly on coloured tiles – green and mottled blue – on Art Nouveau lamps, on two or three very personal styles of lettering. Here is a complete person producing a complete personality. There just don't seem to be the same number of real people around any more, especially amongst the designers of pubs.

Syon   88 1C
Decoration, Robert Adam, 1761 onwards
Greenhouse, Charles Fowler, c. 1830

A secluded park in the heart of Middlesex, with strange animals such as the Gillette tower peering over the boundary wall. From outside, there is nothing to attract in the house: blank and quadrangular, with gruff battlements, the result of a making-over of a Tudor house in the 1820s. But before that, in 1761, Adam had been called in to design a suite of rooms – he wanted to cover over the whole centre with a rotunda – and this is his best sequence near London. It is emphatically a sequence; the rooms are related to each other, each space is meant to be experienced with the memory of the last and in the expectation of the next. The total effect is far more than individual excellence: but even as isolated units, the Ante-room and Dining-room are two of the best things that Adam ever did.

The sequence begins with the entrance hall; big, white and rebuffing. Here is the theme but not the orchestration; and without colour the deeply cut plasterwork looks unpleasantly sharp and slick. Perhaps this is deliberately done to clear the palate, because the Ante-room, next door, is glorious. It could have been done only by Adam: a rich, feminine colour scheme of gold and blue-green, with his favourite trick of a double wall, achieved here by a complete set of gilded columns standing forward: quite a place for a sherry. And next door, quite a place for dinner. Bigger, more regal, allowing the fittings to tell more, because the room is experienced for a longer time. White and gold, relieved by niches painted with a glorious blood-red marbling. Either end is apsed with a screen of columns in front, so that you can be inside and outside the room at the same time. Beyond that, the Withdrawing-room. Here, after dinner, the focus has shifted to humans – Adam was never just a decorator of space – and the room is quiet and rich, with deep red silk wall hangings – and, alas, a depressingly vapid Etruscan ceiling by Angelica Kauffmann.

Beyond this, the last of the public rooms, is the Library. This was the Tudor Long Gallery, and Adam wished to reverse its role completely, from continual motion into an aggregate of leisurely bays. So he snipped and embroidered from end to end with incredibly pretty small-scale plasterwork and a colour scheme that is almost a signature: white, gold, pink and pastel green – though, oddly enough, no screens of columns, which could have tamed the space even more. As a room it is not a complete success; but again, Adam was aiming at a mood as well as a space.

The other thing to see at Syon is the greenhouse [71], as memorable as the house. How it has remained out of the limelight, when every construction of Paxton's is rigidly documented, is a mystery. It was designed by Charles Fowler of Covent Garden and Exeter Market and he brought off a tremendous *coup* by treating it as a complete neo-classical house – centre, quadrant wings, end pavilions.

Nothing is forced, though; the glass and ironwork is so elegant that the greenhouse floats and what might have been an unhappy compromise becomes a Regency *soufflé*, as light as the Brighton Pavilion. The strength behind Fowler's sensitivity is amazing: the central rotunda is a vegetable dance, far removed from Paxton's seriousness. The huge iron columns seem to have been intended from the first to be covered with foliage, so this wonderful Schubertian frolic looks back to the eighteenth-century follies and forward to the Crystal Palace all at once. A golden moment, combining the taste of one century and the enterprise of the next.

Crowther's Yard, London Road, Isleworth
88 1B

It advertises 'ten acres of antiques', and this is no boast. Crowther's Yard is a crazy garden cram-full of architectural fragments – everything from cherubs to garden temples and Georgian shopfronts. It is a continuous set of flash-backs to every bit of old London you have ever seen, packed in surrealist relationship to fragments from India, garden statues, slices of manor-house. Some of the stuff is very beautiful, some of it is a joke, all of it is for sale, though I suspect Messrs Crowther must be very attached to some of their more artful arrangements. It is difficult to believe that a main road is just over the wall. (The yard is attached to Syon Lodge and the entrance is a fairly inconspicuous hole in the wall fronting London Road. You are free to walk around.)[22]

22. The business – now known as Crowther of Syon Lodge – has been rationalized, and reduced to about two acres, and in the process may have become more serious-minded: just the place if you want to buy a period garden ornament; less so if you are only out for a child-like wander.

Osterley
71 5–6H
Redecoration, Robert Adam, 1763–77

Like Syon, a quadrangular Tudor house. Like Syon, drastically remodelled by Adam in the 1760s and 70s. Yet at Osterley everything has gone wrong, where Syon is one of Adam's triumphs. The worst side of his nature comes out, all fribble and fuss. The idea of inserting a full-scale portico into the entrance side to let air into the sullen brick keep was superbly imaginative; yet the effect is relentlessly eroded by the niggling small-scale detail, always using several short words where a long one would have done better. And the rooms inside are isolated cells, rather than the powerful sequence of Syon. The Etruscan Room is an interesting idea spread far too thin, and one has to go to James Wyatt to see how it should have been done. Even the park is gaunt and at odds, with semis peering in all around the southern boundary.

There are always compensations, with Adam. Here, there is the State bed, designed in 1776; a majestic domed four-poster, with his sensibility this time acting in the right way by preventing any heaviness, exactly balanced between a sense of occasion and a sense of humour. The tapestry room, next to it, is a superb invention, the whole space vibrating like a single chord. Adam's greens and pinks on the ceiling are a treble to the deeper reds and greens of the Gobelin tapestries which fill the walls. These were designed by Boucher, and his overblown style has been fined down into balance by the astringent tapestry technique. *Galanterie* could hardly be better expressed.

Twickenham river front
104 1A, etc.

Twickenham's riverside is a continuous experience, and as such worth ten of the isolated pretty bits that survive in the home counties surrounded by traffic, car parks and pointers to photogenic views.

It begins only a few yards from the clogged shopping centre, down

Water Lane or Bell Lane. There was some bombing here, and the area has been left to decay instead of being put on its feet again. The borough council now have comprehensive proposals for comprehensive beastliness: long may they be postponed.[23] Straight away, there is the footbridge to Eel Pie Island, quite an elegant concrete design (1957) which is not wearing too well. Eel Pie Island is one of the private worlds that London excels in and that modern planning abhors. No cars, but boatyards, shacks, every man his own eccentric.[24] One of them, Hurley Cottage [55], is so pretty and so beautifully painted in blue and white that it would be worth a special visit to Twickenham on its own account.[25] Places like this produced the kind of person that sailed the little boats across to Dunkirk and we'd better not forget it.

Back on the shore, the river walk proper starts at the church: exactly the right beginning, one of the best examples near London of crude architecture making good townscape. A simple, fifteenth-century ragstone tower, a standard type along the Thames valley, was delivered into the hands of John James in 1714. Sublimely self-confident, he rammed a plain brick box on to it; the sides pedimented, the rubbed brickwork beautifully done. The combination is marvellous: two ordinary people coming together to make an out-of-the-ordinary marriage.

Beyond that, all walls. This is very English, the opposite of the esplanade technique. The river, sometimes out of sight, is never out of mind, and meanwhile the foreground is continually changing. Walls and trees, as leafy and apart as anywhere near London, then suddenly Sion Row on the left-hand side, a brick terrace of 1721 straight out of Westminster. The river comes back immediately afterwards, with a ferry to Ham and a good riverside pub, the White Swan, where the bar is just the right height to look across the water, and the beer (Mann's) is good too.

After that, walls and trees again, closing in even closer than before. Round a bend, and under a footbridge, and there is a view over the left-hand wall of the octagon of Orleans House, a grand solid piece by Gibbs, 1730, designing with Baroque swagger instead of being confined to the Palladian rules.

Now, at last, the river appears in public. The transition even now is delicate, not crude – a lawn with a double avenue of trees along the riverside. It is ten times more effective through being reached after this thrilling strip-tease.

Here, the road turns left and can be followed right and then left to Montpelier Row, another of these elegant terraces bedded out from London in the early eighteenth century. The urban scale can never have been disturbing because the thing is done with so much intention; not a careless speculation, as the Victorian terraces were. The builders cared, however inarticulately, about the life that was going to be lived in their buildings. The present-day equivalent is Eric Lyons and his Span estates.

Straight ahead, and a worthwhile climax, is Marble Hill [75]. This was designed by Roger Morris in 1728 and makes an odd contrast with the Orleans House octagon. For here is a third-hand design (Palladio via Lord Burlington) carried out by a natural copyist. Originality doesn't matter. What does is the exquisite realization of the original compactness and squareness, set in a free English park instead of beside the Brenta. There's room in the Pantheon for both this and Hawksmoor's giant flights of fancy. What there is no room for is slavish copying just to be in the swim, or slavish originality just to be different. The river front at Marble Hill has a little too much window space, but the pilastered entrance side is perfect, one of those rare buildings in which you could not wish to alter anything. Painted grey and white, the model of dignified graciousness, the final effect is neither English nor Italian but Dutch; the wavelength of the Dutch national anthem, or one of those villas lining the Vecht between Amsterdam and Utrecht.

23. They did not come to anything.
24. Nevertheless they have picked up the affluent middle-class habit of fending off outsiders with 'Residents Only' notices.
25. Now brown and yellow; less pretty.

[Strawberry Hill, Waldegrave Road, Twickenham 103 3K
Various architects, 1747–76
Horace Walpole's stucco fancy is now part of a R.C. Training College, perfectly kept up. Though it is not open to the public, I think that the owners would look kindly on serious requests to see it.[26] Well worth a visit, for it is far prettier and less finicking than you would expect from reading Horace Walpole's journal or biography.]

26. It may be visited on Wednesday and Saturday afternoons, by appointment only: contact the Principal's secretary, St Mary's Training College, Twickenham (01-892 0051).

Hampton Court[27] O.S. 176 15:68
Henry Redman, 1520s; John Molton 1530s;
Sir Christopher Wren, 1689–1700
The English Versailles. But whereas at Versailles the palace is the culmination of the aristocratic town, here it is an unexpected interruption of outer Middlesex. First of all avenues of trees, too straight and too near London to be in the Green Belt, and then the long, comfortable brick sprawl of the palace itself. Temperamentally, we are not up to the Sun King just as the French could never match Bath or Regent's Park. Hampton Court could be lived in today without too much alteration; Versailles would be inconceivable even for de Gaulle.

It consists very roughly of three courtyards. The first two are Tudor, the third is Wren's. But the Tudor parts are of two dates too – Wolsey in the 1520s and Henry VIII ten years later. And in a way the difference between these is more radical than the difference between Henry VIII's work and that of Wren. Wolsey's palace was – and is – a remarkable thing; astonishingly mature and relaxed, the exact opposite of the rigidities and displays which newcomers usually prefer. From the second man in the land – 'Why come ye not to court?' 'To the Kynges Courte? Or to Hampton Court?' as Skelton maliciously wrote – who started life as a butcher's son, it is at least very unexpected. Wolsey's mason was probably Henry Redman, who designed the original parts of Christ Church at Oxford; and he quite happily set the gatehouse of the inner court asymmetrically, and let the windows work themselves out how they would. The palace was for living in, and feels more like the quads of a university or the spaces of a country town than a focus of ceremony. It is in fact almost too relaxed, for all tension has drained out of the design as well.

Henry VIII's approach was very different. He obviously felt the need to prove something, and thumped down a Great Hall in Wolsey's comfortable second court,* breaking into the skyline as gracelessly as the Shell Building does into London's shape today. Inside, the contrast is even more telling. Wolsey's decorators were content to slip gently into Renaissance detail as the rest of Europe did, and the ceiling to the Chapel Royal has a wonderful golden flicker to it, the hammer-beam roof accepting easily such classical features as cherubs and egg-and-dart mouldings. Henry, on the other hand, had by 1535 turned his back on the Renaissance. Everything had to be demonstratively English, and so his Great Hall has a strict Gothic hammer-beam, showy and cold-hearted. No Popery.

After this authoritarianism, Wren is a relief, even though his designs are more obviously formal. A humble man building for a humble king; both would probably have been happier with something like Chelsea Hospital, and the swags and garlands have an uneasy look to them. The four-storey ordonnance looks even odder, far from the polish of Perrault's Louvre – though not so far from the lumpishness of the Versailles elevations. Cibber's wonderfully live carving on the east front pulls it through, plus an engaging unpretentiousness – Wren saying in a polite, deprecating voice 'This is only a matter of funny hats, really!' The formal avenues radiating out from it have the same almost amateur air of playing at soldiers. Wren's natural mark would have been nearer the regulated but not regimented growth of the famous vine, planted in 1768, and now not so much a plant as a good-sized room roofed with grapes.

Next to the vine, the Orangery: a long austere room full of Mantegna, a sequence of nine paintings of the triumph of Caesar. Or rather, Mantegna repainted by Laguerre, and a great disappointment after the National Gallery.[28] Plump pudding faces peer out where you expect

---

* The gatehouse here has fancy Gothic detail put there in 1732 by the genial William Kent: the exact beginning of Gothic Revival as a giggle.

real people. Only one painting (*Corselet Bearers*) gives a proper idea of his genius: every figure and object thrillingly separate, individual, yet subordinate as well.

Nothing as good as this turns up in the State Apartments. Wren's rooms are desperately dutiful. Verrio's paintings in the staircases are barely that, Lely's *Beauties* show a collection of podgy and interchangeable bitchiness which it would be hard to improve on at a West End party. Only bits need to be picked out – the inside of the Great Hall and Chapel Royal, mentioned earlier; a sweet octagonal room, probably done by William Kent, which was the Queen's chapel, and an even sweeter sixteenth-century one called Wolsey's Closet, opening off a gallery and easy to miss. It is as though you were inside a jewel-box: linenfold and paintings covering the walls, and an incredibly pretty Renaissance ceiling. It is hard to reconcile with an arrogant go-getter.

Two other things must be seen. Both of them can be looked at from outside the grounds, which are open free until dusk – a marvellous thing if you have no money and an urge to see buildings. Tijou's iron screens have been collected at the riverside end of the Privy Garden and can be seen from the towpath. They are probably the most spectacular thing at Hampton Court; extreme virtuosity always harnessed to a purpose beyond itself. Tijou managed to create in two dimensions the heavy luxuriance which Grinling Gibbons mastered so well in three. At the same time, it completely stops being iron and never stops being iron: virtuosity burrowed right down to the common ground where all art meets.

The other thing does for the vegetable world what Tijou did for the mineral. Bushey Park, north of the lion gate and the A308 to Kingston, was laid out as the most ample of all English avenues* – five rows of trees on each side, deer nibbling in and out, and a big *rond-point* part of the way along with a pool in the middle. Man proposes, and a noble enough proposal. Nature takes over, but heeds man's direction. All you see now are the glorious trees: but they would not have been so glorious without the initial design. As a symbol of Hampton Court, and of the whole of England, you could do worse: the tree allowed to grow freely, but to man's pattern. Every hedgerow oak does the same.

27. The fire of Easter Monday 1986 damaged the Cartoon Gallery and three other rooms in Wren's part of the Palace, but the specific items mentioned in this entry were not damaged, and are still accessible.

28. No longer a disappointment; they have been restored, and Laguerre's overpainting has been removed, so skilfully that a distinguished American art historian, on seeing one of the paintings after restoration, is said to have staggered and turned pale, as though he had seen a ghost. One unrestored painting, too far gone to be rescued, is displayed to show how they all used to look.

* Wren intended this to be the grand approach, but things turned out differently. Bushey Park leads nowhere much, now, and this is very English too.

Hucks' Chalet, Hampton   O.S. 176 14:69

A jolly good absurdity on the traffic-ridden road between Hampton
Court and Hampton village. Messrs Hucks are boatbuilders, and in
about 1900 they decided to house themselves in a Swiss chalet. Scorn-
ing pastiche, they brought one over from Switzerland, and here it is:
three frilly well-oiled wooden storeys that can give you quite a turn if
you aren't expecting it. In the end it looks more like the superstructure
of a paddle-steamer than something on the outskirts of Interlaken; not
so absurd after all.

Garrick's Villa, Hampton   O.S. 176 14:69

The actual objects are still all just as they were in the eighteenth
century. River, lawn, Capability Brown's grave octagonal temple, the
best kind of dumpling, and the villa itself in the background, with
Robert Adam's very earliest attempt at decoration stretched across it.
But between villa and lawn is an endless cavalcade of cars. Between
Thames and lawn is an ugly concrete-and-wire fence. The lawn itself
is cluttered with fussy seats.[29] There could be no clearer exposition of
the way that apparent trivialities can diminish the personality of a
memorable place. The best view of it is from the Surrey bank where
Hurst Park racecourse used to be.

   The traffic at Hampton is truly unbearable, some of the worst near
London, and makes it impossible for the village to develop as it ought:
as a pleasant riverside place built up consistently back from the river-
banks. The traffic must go before Hampton does.

29. There is now a decent white-painted metal fence by the river's edge, and
the seats are discreetly sited. But the cavalcade of cars persists.

Esher Old Church   O.S. 176 14:64

An astonishing, genuine touch at the very centre of Esher's raddled
gentility. Just when the mixture of traffic, neo-Georgian stodge, and
recherché fragments becomes unbearable, this lovable old building
turns up – at the back of the main crossroads behind the Bear car park.
It looks like a jobbing builder's sample card of materials – church,
flint, tiles, stone slabs, weatherboarded belfry, all set off by the chop-
pish brick transept built in 1725 to house the Newcastle Pew. Inside,
this announces itself with pediment and columns so chaste it seems
impossible that Vanbrugh could have designed it, so fierce that perhaps
he might after all. By the time you reach Esher driving out on the A3
from London you are really in need of this.

St George's Hill, Weybridge   O.S. 176 07:62

Superb in any weather, the kind of suburb that Surrey was made for.
Steep hills, big pine trees, curving views along the golf-course greens,
expensive houses tucked up in the bracken and rhododendrons. Yet

not a hint of ostentation, or its genteel inversions. This is fresh and sparkling, and it has the kind of wealth that makes the onlooker feel included in the party instead of generating envy.[30] The easiest way in is from B374, the Weybridge–Byfleet road. The signpost is to St George's Golf Course and the Hill waves its enchanted wand straight away, with a cosy cottage and Tudor brick arch at the entrance.

30. Not for the likes of you and me any more. Fierce notices at the entrances threaten prosecution and security patrols to any outsider venturing a toe over the threshold.

Shepperton village square   O.S. 176 07:67

In the north of England this might be passed over: in Middlesex it has got to be noticed. But only in one direction: the view in to the square, with the old church at the end, cottages along the sides, and a road beyond which meets the river head-on because it takes a sudden bend here. Look back, and the whole thing disintegrates, dominated by an ugly, fragmented splay corner which carries a continuous stream of traffic.

Chertsey   O.S. 176 04:66

An extraordinary place to find mid way between Weybridge and Staines. It feels delicate, long-established, the opposite of the shopping-arcade town.[31] Victorian Surrey must have been like this, revolving equally around sleepy local industries and the trains to London (and here, bless us, *both* platforms take you to Waterloo).[32] The plan is simple but rich, just the thing for a small town. The three streets meet in a T-junction by the church and the Victorian town hall, a jolly Italian design which sits in the street as easily as it would in Lombardy. The fourth arm is a long straight footpath beside the churchyard. It leads to the quiet sector of Chertsey: cottages, the pathetic remnants of the enormous abbey, then flat Thames water-meadows.[33] In reverse, the transition back to bustle is just as exciting. Many places which boast of picturesqueness or antiquity are far less satisfying than this.

31. Its delicacy has been marred by a relief road with new car parks and supermarkets.
32. And still do, but now only indirectly.
33. Some of the cottages are boarded up, and the water-meadows now have the M3 running slap across them.

Thames-side,
Laleham to Chertsey Bridge   O.S. 176 05:69, etc.

This is the only place near London where a country lane runs beside the river. Placidly memorable, with only a strip of green between road and water: houseboats, fishermen, the flat Surrey shore opposite, a good place for half-sensations: nostalgia, or faint regret or *accidie*. And the effect is just about obliterated by a waist-high fence between road and lawn, and a ferocious crop of *No Waiting* signs on poles.[34] This is just by-law stupidity: a low fence stops cars just as well as a tall one, a ditch as well as either. And as the essence of the place is somewhere for recreation, better to make the whole road one-way and allow parking on it.

At the south end Chertsey Bridge is another of those places with a lot of local character that nobody has bothered to translate into shape. If they ever do, the Bridge Hotel is a wonderful basis to start from: a Regency house with an enormous verandah that could have come straight from the West Indies.

34. There are fewer poles, but the fence is still there. The effect is complicated today by a camp-site just off the road, and by the M3 leaping across road and river.

Littleton Church   O.S. 176 07:68

Very much Middlesex, jammed between the Shepperton film studios and the grassy wall of a reservoir. It would take more than that to spoil the outside. Four different kinds of stone, vermilion Tudor brick in the tower and clerestory, and vermilion tiles all over; the Middlesex trade-mark. A chord from Mozart's Wind Serenade might describe it; it wouldn't harm a fly. The altar rails are the best thing inside: Flemish Baroque, utterly un-English in the florid carving, and utterly un-English too in the lack of expression in the cherub faces. The nasty taint of the Counter-Reformation and mass-produced images breathes even through carving as technically brilliant as this.

B379, Staines to Stanwell   O.S. 176 04:72, etc.

Monkeys-on-typewriters, the many and varied needs of outer London throwing up a man-made combination which is already intriguing and could be superb. The road runs in a narrow cutting between steep grass banks which have sheep grazing on them to complete the surreal feeling that this ought to be in the West Riding. A 132-kV electricity grid line marches down the middle, and the result is a memorable discordance – so far, without a contemporary Repton to orchestrate it. The valley is formed by the retaining walls of two reservoirs. They are mostly inaccessible, but a footpath runs up on the eastern side to a landscape which is magnificently absurd. The foreground is all water, twenty feet above the surrounding Middlesex plain, so that only the roofs of houses appear above it; a very unsettling effect. The footpath sets off undeterred across the middle, heading for Stanwell, full of birdwatchers – this is London's backhanded way of making a nature reserve. And over to the north, between the houses and trees, the giant tails of the airliners glint as they move around the London Airport perimeter track. The Middlesex landscape has been shaken up and re-made by the Mad Hatter: and the result is some compensation for the twenty miles of building, most of it dreary, between here and Piccadilly Circus.

St Mary Woolnoth

2 and 3. Wren, City and West End: St Mary Abchurch and St James Piccadilly

4. Queenhythe [cf. 90]

Skinners' Hall

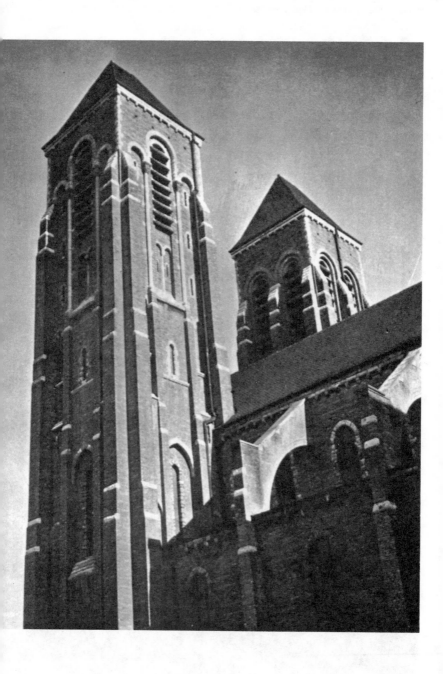

17. Towers: Westminster [cf. 91] and South Tottenham (St Ignatius)

8 and 9. Death masks of Henry VII and Elizabeth of York, Westminster Abbey

12 and 13. The Houses of Parliament, upstream and downstream

14. St John, Smith Square, and Lord North Street

15. Portland House from Victoria Station

16. Carlton House Terrace

17. Pall Mall: the backside of the clubs: Reform – Travellers' – Athenaeum

18. St James's

nd 20. Contrasts: New Zealand House (*left, at back*)
33–5 Eastcheap (*above, right*)

21. Trafalgar Square from the roof of New Zealand House

22 and 23. Pubs: The Salisbury, St Martin's Lane (*top*),
and The Victoria, Bayswater

24. Regent Street from Piccadilly

25. Somerset House

26. The Temple

27 and 28. Victorian passion: All Saints, Margaret Street, and St James the Less, Moreton Street

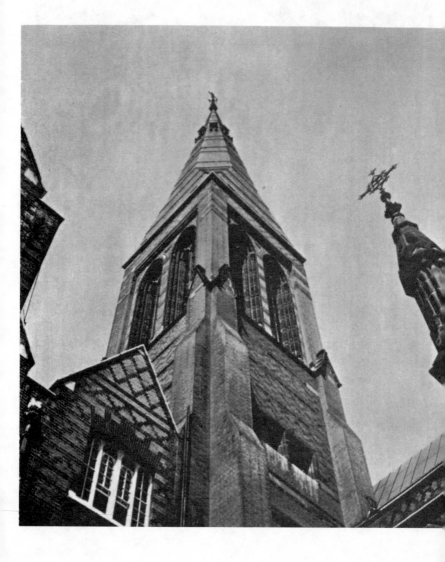

Regent's Park Lake and The Holme

St Mary-le-Strand (*top*)

Nos. 46 and 48 Portland Place

32 and 33. Four hundred yards apart: Chester Terrace and Park Village

Penguin Pool, the Zoo

37 and 38. London parks: Primrose Hill (*top*) [cf. 92] and Greenwich

39. Hanover Lodge, Regent's Park

40 and 41. Georgian Holborn – and its inhabitants [cf. 93]

42. Courtenay Square, Courtenay Street, Kennington [cf. 94]

44. Lodge Road Power Station,
St John's Wood

45 and 46. St Paul's from Bankside: display and vignette [cf. 95 and 96]

47 and 48. Upstairs and downstairs: Pelham Crescent, Kensington, and Whittlesey Street, Waterloo

49. Chelsea Hospital Stables

50 and 51. St Katharine Docks (*top*) [cf. 98] and Bow Creek off East India Dock Road

52 and 53. Hawksmoor in the East End: St George-in-the-East [cf. 99] and Christ Church, Spitalfields

Romford market place [cf. 100]

57 and 58. Thames: Battersea and Blackwall [cf. 102]

59 to 62. Four views of a cockney street: Rye Lane, Peckham [cf. 103 and 106]

5. Wandsworth Common

and 64. Asylum (Old Kent Road, *top*) and academy (Woolwich)

66 and 67. Modern humanity: Mayfield School, Wandsworth,
and Boundary Road flats, St John's Wood

68. South Croydon Power Station from Beddington Lane [cf. 104]

70 and 71. Nature in command and under starter's orders:
Stanmore Old Church and the greenhouse at Syon

72 and 73. Chiswick House, vista and detail

74 and 75. Georgian London: Islington (*top*) and Marble Hill, Twickenham

78 and 79. Barges for all: Greenwich Museum (King's barge) and Tottenham Wharf [cf. 107]

80 and 81. Blackheath Park and Blackheath

82. Charlton House

85 and 86. Essex churches: Leyton and Dagenham

87. Greenwich, midsummer evening

88. Dulwich College, midwinter

89. Royal Albert Dock, North Woolwich [cf. 105]

90. Queenhythe

91. Towers: Westminster [cf. 6]

Primrose Hill

93. 'Georgian' Holborn [cf. 41]

Courtenay Square,
Courtenay Street, Kennington

95-7. St Paul's from Bankside:
display and vignette
(1980s version) (*left*),
and original vignette (*right*)

98. St Katharine Docks [cf. 50]

99. Hawksmoor in the East End:
St George-in-the-East [cf. 52]

100. Romford market place [cf. 56]

101. Danger, cockneys at w●
Spiegelhalters', Mile End Road [cf.

102. Thames: Blackwall

103. A cockney street:
Rye Lane, Peckham [cf. 59]

104 and 105. Site of South Croydon Power Station [cf. 68]
and Royal Albert Dock, North Woolwich [cf. 89]

Rye Lane, Peckham [cf. 60 and 61]

107. Tottenham Wharf [cf. 79]

7 East End and East London: Whitechapel to Romford

EAST END

Of all things done to London in this century, the soft-spoken this-is-good-for-you castration of the East End is the saddest. All the raucous, homely places go and are replaced by well-designed estates which would fit a New Town but are hopelessly out of place here. This is a hive of individualists, and the last place to be subjected to this kind of large-scale planning. Fragments survive, and the East Enders are irrepressible – and no doubt satisfied by the undoubted increase in material amenities: but they could have had so much more, so easily.

North of the East End is an uneasy, mingled area. Political and racial feelings ran high before the war and still do in Dalston, Hoxton, Hackney and Stoke Newington. To look at, the area is an intriguing mixture of large- and small-scale, but the edginess discourages exploration, where even the roughest bits of Stepney have a kind of welcome.[1]

1. POSTSCRIPT 1987. Twenty years later the fragmentation of the East End continues, and much of the area to the north is in decline. The main exceptions are those select corners – large parts of Islington, parts of Limehouse and the old docklands, increasingly numerous enclaves elsewhere – which have been 'gentrified', i.e. colonized by enterprising members of the professional middle classes. The ethnic mix over the whole area is complicated and diverse, and is marked by the appearance of mosques, Greek and Turkish restaurants, Asian businesses and the occasional Sikh temple.

St Katharine Docks   148–149 1–2F–G
Thomas Telford, 1825–8

Austere yellow-brick warehouses rammed in tight next to the Tower. St Katharine's Way plunges down on the east side of Tower Bridge and provides one of the biggest contrasts in London. It takes a running jump into dockland from the politeness of the City: the road winds round a stupendous retaining wall to a swing-bridge over the dock entrance which is the only place where the basin can be seen properly. If these gaunt masterpieces lose their usefulness as working docks they should become London's marina [50].[2]

2. The dock has indeed become a marina. The only survivor of the old warehouses is the Victorian Ivory House (1850s, by George Aitchison Senior). It used to store ivory (hence its name); now it contains luxury flats, shops, and a yacht club. So it has been preserved, at the cost of being prettified. The surrounding buildings are an uneasy mixture. The World Trade Centre's Europe House, by Andrew Renton, is a good, strong, 1960s building faced in brown pebble aggregate. The Centre's International House is an attempt to

recreate the demolished Warehouse B (originally by Philip Hardwick), but in the wrong colour brick, and with a modern roof. The London Commodity Exchange, north-east of the dock, is in a vaguely sympathetic style, but in yet another colour brick. The Dickens Inn is a conversion from a timber-framed brewery building.

The character is, of course, no longer dockland: St Katharine's now belongs firmly with the Tower as a place for swarms of tourists. It is hard to argue with financial success and lots of people enjoying themselves, but one feels that something fundamental has been lost.

St George-in-the-East   143 9J
Nicholas Hawksmoor, 1715–23

A ruin among ruins, in the lost part of Stepney, south of Commercial Road.[3] The old life has gone or been deliberately killed, the new has not yet come up with any pattern or buildings worth twopence. It makes no difference to Hawksmoor's bizarre poetry. This is probably the hardest building to describe in London; it is an entity like a hand or a foot, total shape and total atmosphere [52]. It just doesn't have separate parts. The difference between the tower here and that of Limehouse Church is extraordinary. With the same basic plan, that remains a collection of parts, this has all the details ingested, fused together; impossible to consider the astonishing coronet of columns at the top – a steeple *flambé*, as it were – without being struck by the tense grooving in the pilasters lower down which slew a square tower into looking rectangular. Impossible really to look at the tower in isolation at all, apart from the four sinister pepperpots above the nave. This is a stage somewhere beyond fantasy, which is always comfortably related to common sense: it is the more-than-real world of the drug-addict's dream. Hawksmoor might possibly have referred to it as a little fancy.

3. Despite the reference to restoration on a notice-board outside, it is still a ruin, or at least a shell. A small, plain modern church has been concealed inside, using only the apse of Hawksmoor's building. It is practical for a small congregation, but not worth tracking down the key in order to see it.

Cable Street   143 9H–J

'Cable Street, the whore's retreat': a shameful blot on the moral landscape of London: an outworn slum area. Make your games. A small stretch of a long street (between Leman Street and Cannon Street Road) is all that is left of lurid dockland. Its crime is not that it contains vice but that it is unashamed and exuberant about it. Dickens could put it straight into *Oliver Twist*. Embedded in it are the hopeless fragments of two once splendid squares, Wellclose and Swedenborg, built for the shipmasters of Wapping when London began to move east. Those who could care about the buildings don't care about the people, those who care about the people regard the decrepit buildings rather as John Knox regarded women: unforgiveable blindness.

Nobody cares enough, and the whole place will soon be a memory.[4] As for viciousness, you can find as much at a council meeting or social evening. But there, of course, it is polite. I doubt if the efficient concealment of evil will be quite enough, in the next world.

4. Wellclose and Swedenborg Squares have been demolished, along with most of Cable Street. The area is predominantly council flats, but one terrace of Georgian houses survives in Cable Street, just east of Cannon Street Road.

Limehouse   64 6–7A–B

Limehouse was done for even before the war, by the wrong kind of rebuilding. Now there are gloomy hulks in last generation's fashion, ably followed into lifelessness by our present efforts. Fragments hang on: a glittering undertaker's shopfront (Francis and Chris Walters) in the very centre, the genteelly beat-up but still evocative back bar at the Grapes in Narrow Street, and always the muddy grandeur of the river which it overlooks. At least they can't zone away the water.[5]

5. The area is still largely poor and working-class, but parts have been gentrified, by the former leader of the Social Democratic Party among others. Hence the Grapes has gone up-market, with Rolls-Royces parked outside, and prints of characters from Dickens in the back bar. By contrast, Walters' unaltered shopfront has lost some of its old glitter.

St Anne, Limehouse[6]   64 6B
Nicholas Hawksmoor, 1712–30

Hawksmoor, limbering up for his great London churches; feeling his way, maybe startled by the implications of his own leap into space. St Anne's is a collection of disparate parts: near to Wren in the shoulders supporting the steeple, completely original in the turrets at the east end, feeling a twinge of gout in the dour windows along the sides. The inside was burnt in 1850 and rebuilt, so that the fittings are gone: but the plan is a similar half-way stage, with huge columns marching in from the corners but afraid of the consequences, drawing back from the logical conclusion of a Greek cross inside a rectangle. The steeple probably came later, and is pure Hawksmoorean invention, but still disparate. The bottom is one of those mysterious theorems by which Hawksmoor managed to prove that a square tower could look rectangular – the idea which he transfigured in Christ Church, Spitalfields [53]. The octagonal top is a staccato crop of columns and obelisks, with everything set diagonal and at twenty degrees to everything else – a near relative of St George-in-the-East. Both stages are marvellous by themselves; but they belong to different buildings – except at a distance from the river, when all this detailed carping is resolved and it becomes simply Limehouse steeple: Portland stone gleaming in the sun or glistening in the rain.

6. Recently restored by the London Docklands Development Corporation.

St Paul's Presbyterian Church, West Ferry Road, Millwall
T. E. Knightley, 1859   80 4C

I always expect this astonishing little building to have gone by my
next visit: it seems such an improbably fierce survival.[7] The chapel
committee chose the young Mr Knightley, who afterwards went on to
do many other things, including the old Queen's Hall and the late wild
Westminster Bank in Holborn (p. 91). Mr Knightley in turn chose to
recreate Pisa on the Isle of Dogs: a fussy piece of Romanesque, fighting
mad, polychrome from end to end. The front diminishes in arcaded
tiers, the four bays are given a circumstantial arcaded clerestory, slate-
hung for good measure. It is a very lovable firework, and needs to be
much better known.

7. It survives still, as an outbuilding for a crane and lifting service company
(opposite Claude Street).

The Gun, Coldharbour   80 2E

You will know a bit about East End topography by the time you find
this one. Coldharbour is a tiny loop road off Preston's Road, which is
the eastern entry to the Isle of Dogs, and the Gun is at the southern
end of it. Good hunting. It is a good friendly dockland pub that has
neither been irreparably spoilt by the brewers nor irreparably taken
up. The special thing, unsuspected from inside, is at the back – through
the Saloon in summer, down the passage past the Ladies and Gents
in winter. For the Gun is a riverside pub, and the particular bit of the
riverside is the sharpest part of the curve around Blackwall Point.
Nowhere is the muddy horizontal excitement of the Thames more
urgent than here, framed in a tiny terrace, the curvature making sure
that the maximum amount of swift-running water stays in the view.

Bow Creek   65 6–7G

This one is down Leamouth Road, a right turn off the main Tilbury
road between Poplar and East Ham. A long straight street at first, with
the wall of the East India Dock for company [51], then a bend, an
opening out, and on the left a sudden smudge of green. It is the loop
of Bow Creek, a fag-end of railway sidings, with muddy water seeping
up each side. More than sudden: an apparition, miles from greenery
in any direction; and not any old apparition, but a directed, offered-
up bit of grass, forced into prominence by the shape of the river, and
the fiercely industrial surroundings.

Mallinsons' Timber Yard,[7a] Parnell Road   64 1B

Fancy roofs are a fad these days, sucked out from reluctant engineers
by designers who think that they make 'pretty shapes'. This one, for
a change, is used unselfconsciously and naturally, as Telford might
have used it, to cover space cheaply and lightly in a set of hyperbolic

paraboloids whose up-tilted ends give the height needed for roof-lights. The walls are slatted timber, the article stored is timber too. The result is a timbery essence, an animal which has grown a covering shell to stop itself getting wet. A whole city can be built up in the same way. In a quiet bit of the East End, south of Victoria Park; best seen in the week, when the yard doors are open, otherwise the structure may be hard to follow.

7a. Closed in 1986; to be demolished for housing development.

Tower Hamlets Cemetery   64 4B–C
Begun 1841

If Highgate is an anthology of horror, this teeters between still melancholy and a grisly cheerfulness. A few areas are kept up, and used for new burials; the rest is an astonishing wilderness. Row after row of East Enders, jammed together. Around them, trees and scrub as thick as the undergrowth in Epping Forest. Man and nature have combined to produce a macabre case of statutory overcrowding, and the result has the same absurdity as a Resurrection by Stanley Spencer. The skulls obstinately refuse to show beneath the skin. But then again the path widens, the trees part a little, and you are in a soft Corot glade stuffed to the gills with the remains of cockney mums and dads. Far over in one corner there is an abandoned octagonal chapel: the whole place could be in Cambodia or Yucatan. In fact it is at Bromley-by-Bow. (Entrance from Southern Grove at the north-west corner.)[8]

8. The chapel has gone, and there are no more new burials. The cemetery has acquired a slightly sinister reputation as a haunt of muggers and glue-sniffers.

St Paul, Bow Common   64 5B
Robert Maguire and Keith Murray, 1958–60

One worth-while new church in a city-region of ten millions, at a time when France and Germany have dozens. Make what you like of the implications. Anyway, here it is, burningly honest but not aggressive, on a run-down street corner (Burdett Road and St Paul's Way) in Stepney. It is completely fresh, the perennial force seen again for the first time. Purple brick, a top-lit cube on a long podium, with a porch almost detached with quivering letters on it: *This is the Gate of Heaven.* And it is. Not one thing has come out of slickness or reaction or a wish to be original. Hence it is truly original, like All Saints, Margaret Street, a century before. Often locked, but it is worth digging out the keys, for it was built from the inside out, around a central altar. This is under the cube. Around it lights dance on a square iron frame, better than all the copies of parclose screens. Demure yet full of fun, reverent yet completely light-hearted: the place seems to heal you.

North Thames Gas Board,   64 5A
Ben Jonson Road and Hartford Road

A splay corner in a part of Stepney that is now changing from old slum
into new desert. A hundred years ago the gas people put up very decent
classical buildings, with a dressy Italianate block on the splay, like a
superior early railway station. Immediately behind, naturally enough,
they put up gas-holders, three times as high as the neat box in front,
like keeping a hippo in a patio garden. They are thrown together so
disarmingly that the eye accepts both; one of the best and most surprising cases of the architectural foil in a city which is full of them.[9]

9. The gas-holders are still there, but the buildings are gone except for some
fragments of wall.

Spiegelhalters', 81 Mile End Road   143 4M

Messrs Wickham, *circa* 1910, wanted an emporium. Messrs Spiegelhalter, one infers, wouldn't sell out. Messrs Wickham, one infers
further, pressed on regardless, thereby putting their Baroque tower
badly out of centre. Messrs Spiegelhalter ('The East End Jewellers')
remain; two stuccoed storeys, surrounded on both sides by giant
columns *à la* Selfridges. The result is one of the best visual jokes in
London [54], a perennial triumph for the little man, the bloke who
won't conform.[10] May he stay there till the Bomb falls. (A bleak thought
is that, if Messrs Wickham's problem had arisen today, smooth lawyers
and architects could probably have presented a case for comprehensive
redevelopment, and persuaded the council to use their powers of
compulsory purchase. Big deal; fine democracy.)

10. The joke loses a little of its force now that Wickham's no longer operate
the shop premises either side, but it is still obvious to anybody who looks
above the level of the fascia-boards.

Bethnal Green Church (St John, Cambridge Heath Road)
Sir John Soane, 1825–8   143 1L

Two of Soane's three churches in London suffer from incurably low
blood pressure (Holy Trinity, Marylebone, and St Peter, Walworth).
They have survived fairly well, and it is a minor tragedy that Bethnal
Green Church fell into the hands of S. S. Teulon, who had his own
fish to fry. For here, Soane really came to grips with church design: a
rough, tough little building using a post-and-lintel language outside
with complete logic yet complete originality. The tower is just the
opposite: illogic used to further one more of his journeys into space.
It is basically an outer square of attached corner columns, and an inner
solid square doing the work. But Soane created an artificial inequality
by doubling the columns along the sides, so that a whole set of tensions
is set up between the two squares. And after that he signs off with a

grumpy circular turret – 'if you want any more you can sing it yourself'. Inside, the vestibule is a marvellous room done entirely with plain arches in the same way as the Chelsea Hospital Stables. But beyond, there is only Mr Teulon, and the tragic swallowing up of one talent by another.

[Cluster blocks, Claredale Street and Usk Street   63 2H, 3K
Denys Lasdun, 1956–60

A lot of talk about the vertical re-creation of the old East End street, but not much performance in fact. Lasdun's talents seem to need expensive finishes – not necessarily a fault, just a difference. Meanwhile the old streets go down without a thought. If you want to like modern architecture, don't come to the East End.]

St Peter, St Peter's Avenue, Bethnal Green   63 2G
Lewis Vulliamy, 1840

As cheerfully incorrect as a building in the newly settled plains of Kansas. Usually, the style-revivers were haunted too closely by the books of architectural engravings. Here, the style revived is neo-Norman, and although Vulliamy had a big and serious practice, this building hasn't a care in the world. Flint, stock-brick, and stone to start with, the west front filled with narrow arcading. In front, a lean square tower turns octagonal without batting an eyelid: underneath the squinches a refined angel blandly displays St Peter's keys. Indeed, who would not open the doors to this feckless charmer? The Church of England, perhaps, for it is locked and empty. It ought to be preserved.[11]

11. It has been, and is in use again.

Balls Bros., Bethnal Green Road   143 2J

This is a real bit of Old England: honest, cantankerous and value for money: the opposite of the gimmick. It was built up by William Austin Balls, and his precepts and advertisements* hang all round the dark walls and above the bars, still subdivided, as they should be, to give a choice of temperament between Public, Saloon and Private. So they maintain what is primarily a wine-selling business in the middle of the beer-drinking East End with complete amity, because it operates on more levels than a company accountant would think of – the Balls family is very much in charge. The place is full of self-respect and the right sort of pride, so naturally it looks right. Obviously a good place to buy wine: but good beer and a good pub lunch as well.[12]

*For example: 'I take great care in the selection of my stocks to continuously maintain uniformity of style and quality. Wm. A. Balls.'

12. It is now the Old George, an ordinary undivided East End pub. Balls Bros. still run the wine shop next door. They also run wine bars all over the City, but these are not places to breeze in and ask for a pint of mild and a corned-beef sandwich.

32–4 Whitechapel Road   143 6G

I have been down the Whitechapel Road a hundred times, and still never noticed this until I went through Sir John Summerson's *Georgian London* with a toothcomb. What he says there is quite true: 'the most remarkable group of its kind in London'. It belongs to Messrs Mears & Stainbank, bellfounders, with a Georgian house to the street and a Georgian factory behind, facing Fieldgate Street. All the parts are admirably proportioned in space, of an order which would excite admiration if an eminent name were attached to the drawings. More important, they are proportioned in life. This rhythm of living-place and work-place is fundamental. It is the way every family business keeps up and the way most big business starts. If today's designers ignore it to follow a set of zoning rules as arid as the multiplication table, then it is the rules which are wrong, not life.

Christ Church, Commercial Street, Spitalfields   142 5E–F
Nicholas Hawksmoor, 1723–9

Mighty; Hawksmoor's biggest and grandest church, all built up on the scheme of the Venetian arch – three-part, with the centre higher than the wings [53]. But not 'composed'; transmuted somewhere right down in the blood so that the whole building becomes a living idea (just as St Mary Woolnoth is a living demonstration of cube inside cube: just as St Stephen Walbrook, however brilliant, is a composition). Centre and wings in the huge porch, in the relation of belfry to steeple; and, overwhelmingly, inside: aisles to central space, division of the chancel screen, divisions of the huge flat ceiling, the actual Venetian window at the east end: everything offered up: to God be the praise. Locked up whilst money is being collected for a restoration; if the Church lets it fall down it might as well present a banker's order for thirty pieces of silver.[13] For here *is* the faith, manifest.

13. The Church hasn't let it fall down yet, but restoration is proceeding very slowly. Meanwhile the interior has bare masonry and makeshift furniture, but is so magnificent, even in this condition, that it is worth going to some trouble to see it.

Spitalfields   142 4–5E–F

Doomed and grimly magnificent in its last tottering years, Spitalfields was an early-eighteenth-century New Town, just beyond the city. It went down as the East End grew up, and the big taciturn brick houses are now on their last legs: ironically it is the biggest area of its date left in London. Elder Street and Wilkes Street have hardly altered since 1750; unexpected treasure turns up, like the Great Synagogue in

Fournier Street and the Georgian shopfront at 56 Artillery Lane –
easily the best in London, with gusto as well as polish, now used as a
storeroom. The whole area seems bound to go, not only because
rehabilitation would be difficult, but quite simply because nobody
loves it.[14] Christ Church looms over the whole area, the meths drinkers
lie around near by: charity is far enough away and compassion even
farther. For tourists who visit the cheerful market at Petticoat Lane
(Middlesex Street) on Sunday mornings, this sombre ghost is just
beyond. It could even now be one of those living areas in the heart of
cities over which so many pious words are spilt at conferences.

14. A good half of Wilkes Street, together with Georgian houses in Hanbury
Street, disappeared to make room for Truman's brewery. The remainder of
Wilkes Street is half ruinous, half down. Elder Street has survived, with some
restoration and some repro infilling. The Great Synagogue is now a smallish
mosque.

Geffrye Museum, Kingsland Road   63 2F
1715

The museum is a placid set of period rooms, really intended to be a
history lesson for schools. It is the building which is worth a visit, in
an unloved bit of Shoreditch. Originally the Geffrye almshouses, built
in 1715, and then just in the country, a mile north of the City of
London. Only England could have produced such plainness combined
with such domesticity: there were fourteen houses originally, each with
its own front door. No ornament except for the most reticent of
pediments in the middle and the curly patterns of the plane trees in
the courtyard, which are now bigger than anything else. Everything is
tranquil and easy.

St Columba, Kingsland Road[15]   62 2E
James Brooks, 1867–71

A dusky, grubby working church that could as well be in the Ruhr or
an industrial suburb of Paris. Bulky and thick from the street: entrance
through a courtyard to one of Brooks's severe big interiors, all whitewashed now and used as an austere backcloth to a rag-bag of fittings,
as High as they can be without going Roman. But *used* is the word:
everything is here because it needs to be, and there is none of the
genteel swoonishness of High Anglican churches in the politer parts
of London. It is the medieval abbey filled up with eighteenth-century
fittings all over again, with the same lived-in atmosphere and the same
basic rightness of man furnishing God's house.

15. Now the Christ Apostolic Church Mount Bethel. It looks disused, but is
apparently run by African Pentecostalists.

St Barnabas, Shacklewell Lane, Hackney   47 4F
Sir Charles Reilly, 1910

It takes some finding, but is worth it.[16] In Shacklewell Row, off
Shacklewell Lane, and hidden behind the church hall. Even then the
outside is just a big plain stock-brick building, like a warehouse. The
inside is the best church of its date in London, sure in its domed
and barrel-vaulted spaces, incredibly fresh in its detail, concrete and
exposed yellow brick. England could so easily have stepped across to
modern architecture from here, instead of relapsing into an eclectic
fog. This is the kind of quintessential classical composition that
Lutyens tried for and never had the integrity to achieve. Only the big,
gaudy Adamesque screen jars: everything else is pure space; or rather,
something better – pure space charged with feeling.

16. The Rectory is in Stoke Newington, over half a mile away, so the only
certain means of seeing the church is to attend it.

Agapemonite Church, Rookwood Road, Clapton   31 7G
Frank Morris of Reading, 1895

Surrealism at the north end of Clapton Common. At first it looks like
an ordinary suburban church, middle-pointed and medium-spired.
Closer to, it has got colossal stone symbols of the evangelists low down,
and another bronze or copper set at the corners of the parapet. All the
other details are off-centre, too. And it turns out to be the Cathedral
Church of the Good Shepherd, the Primatial See of the Ancient
Catholic Church: a faint, low echo of Druids. I have never been able
to get inside.

St Ignatius (Roman Catholic),   31 6F
South Tottenham (High Road and St Ann's Road)
Benedict Williamson, 1894

Grandeur in mean surroundings: twin towers cleverly varied, rearing
up above the street [7], with far more meaning than the usual careful
English copy. This building means business; and the extra force hits
you straight away. The inside goes soft like a French or Belgian
nineteenth-century church, but the outside is worth a special visit.
Those forceful stone voussoirs will stay in the memory when Bodley's
cool calculations have all faded away.

Sheds at Ferry Lane Wharf, Tottenham   31 4H
Anonymous pre-war

If modern architecture is ever going to be more than an elegant cutlet
frill to chaos, architects had better start building like this, even if it
means forgetting all the aesthetic fads that they have ever acquired.
Hump-backed corrugated iron sheds, storing timber and paper alongside the Lea Navigation. Projecting hoists set up a slow, sure rhythm
[79] in which aesthetic decisions are made deep down in the bones,

not thought of afterwards. It is a grim irony that nobody seems to know who designed them. With all the pretentious nonsense of name-dropping, this is something really great whose authorship is already lost.

Pumping station, Green Lanes   46 2C
W. C. Mylne, 1854

No one like the Victorians for pumping stations. When they come plain, as they do around Staines, they are good straightforward industrial buildings. What happens when they come fancy can be seen by stupefied travellers on the way up from Stoke Newington to Manor House. Turrets of every shape and size, with a chimney in the tallest, attached to a big bare box with which the architect has had a little Tudor fun. The effect is very different from a straightforward folly. Like Vanbrugh Castle, the plainness and solidity argue a serious intention, and it leaves you with the disturbing feeling that if you saw it once too often it would seem completely natural.

Highbury Quadrant   46 3C
L.C.C. Architect's Department, Housing Division, 1955–7

An estate from the vintage years of the L.C.C. before it traded humanity for a change in architectural fashion and some tall slabs. Blocks of yellow-brick five-storey flats close up to old trees, interspersed with two- and three-storey red-brick terraces. Delightful to walk through, a real melting together of buildings and landscape, and a personal touch which runs through to the railings and paving.

Islington   46 7A–B, etc.

Georgian Islington, like Georgian Chelsea, is an overrated place, pleasant enough to live in but hardly worth a special visit. The houses were a neat and decent speculation, but the modest effect is eroded by heavy through traffic (Canonbury Square has streams in both directions and traffic lights in the middle) and also by the extraordinary Cotswold landscaping indulged in by the Borough Council. Along the banks of the New River the boulders and rockeries are odd enough to make a folly landscape in their own right, but in the plain Georgian squares they are hopeless. The best of the old part [74] is around the pedimented house in Alwyne Villas which is Sir Basil Spence's house and office,[17] but even here the genuinely Elizabethan Canonbury Tower manages to look like an advanced L.C.C. fire station of about 1900. The best effect altogether is not Georgian at all: the mid-nineteenth-century opulence of Thornhill Square, which with its rounded ends comes somewhere near the dignity of the west end of Glasgow. It also has a very skittish public library by Beresford Pite, 1906. Milner Square (below) is in a class of its own altogether.

Islington is the ancestor of the monotony of Victorian North

London. The Georgian parts are monolithic and humourless, quite different from the East End. The deserts around the Seven Sisters Road simply took the recipe and debased the architecture. This is the least friendly segment of London; go into some of the bigger pubs and you will soon find out.

17. The Sir Basil Spence Partnership still occupies the house at No. 1 Canonbury Place.

[Milner Square, Islington   46 7A–B
Roumieu & Gough, 1841

Not to be missed, in the sense that you ought to try Fernet-Branca at least once. A violent, deliberate reaction to the placid Georgian squares around, with the windows laced together in vertical bands. What plain brickwork is left is then carved up by sinister thin pilasters. It is as near to expressing evil as a design can be.]

Islington Church steeple   62 1B
Launcelot Dowbiggin, 1751–4

Only the steeple is old; the rest was blitzed and is now an unlovely hybrid. But Mr Dowbiggin's spire is a perfect example of Baroque blood flowing through Palladian veins. On top of a sturdy stock-brick tower he constructed his square-rigged fantasy, using no elements that Lord Burlington would not have sanctioned. But what he then did is another matter. This is exactly the same temper as Gibbs at St Martin-in-the-Fields; innocent, where Gibbs was cannily playing the market.

St James, Pentonville Road[18]   61 2K
A. H. Hurst, 1787

Shabby and dilapidated now, yet with proper restoration this could be one of the prettiest church façades in London. The central window framed by pilasters has a splendid racy rhythm to it, the yellow bricks are among the mellowest and duskiest in London, and the church is beautifully placed between big trees. The odd thing is that this unforcedly decorative result is actually a hybrid. The front was originally square and was only cut down between the wars, to provide the present elegant shoulders.

18. Demolished 1985.

Myddelton Square   141 1G–H
and Lloyd Square, Finsbury
W. C. Mylne, 1827 onwards and 1819 onwards

These are the only Georgian squares in Finsbury to have survived the war and local government. They need to be seen as part of an unselfconscious chain, not as isolated architectural specimens. In fact, their merit as places to live in is the lack of architecture. Myddelton Square is the plainest kind of four-storey brick Georgian with a joke

Gothic church in the middle. The size, the trees and the cheerful stumble uphill do the rest. Lloyd Square has the tightness of the terraces loosened by being made up of linked pairs, each with a pediment. The sight of them dutifully climbing Lloyd Baker Street, two by two, is like a parody of the Greek Revival. But what you remember is half a doorway, someone's curtains, the flicker of leaves in sunlight or wet bare branches. The underlying pattern is there all right, but it is never obtrusive. Finsbury's post-war housing, by Tecton (the best known is opposite Sadlers Wells), is just the opposite.

Finsbury Savings Bank, Sekforde Street   141 3J
Alfred Bartholomew, 1840

An extraordinary overwrought building produced by a thoughtful man (an early editor of the *Builder*) trying to will his way out of the nineteenth-century confusion of styles and finding that his brain became overheated in the process. The style is more or less Barry's, but with every detail screwed into place compulsively. Yet it is not hysterical, and each of its parts separately seems quite natural, such as the glass wall to the banking hall on the ground floor. What holds the design together is the splendid embossed lettering. After a century of sobriety we have seen fit to repaint it in lime green. This is a disaster which almost obliterates the building; it should revert to cream stucco forthwith.[19]

19. Not quite back to cream stucco: pale grey and white, with details picked out in black.

STRATFORD TO UPMINSTER

The bleak winds of East Anglia are blowing here, all right. One look at the 1-inch map will show what to expect: long straight terraces close in, interminable curvy estates farther out. The ground is flat and unresisting and sometimes produces effects of stricken beauty where the urbanization has been particularly harsh. Somehow, this unpromising formula has nurtured a vivid life, unblurred by thoughts of the Joneses, status and suchlike crap. There is Woodford, to be sure, but that is only an incident. Undifferentiated, borough succeeds borough, a dead level of environment. Luckily, human beings are resilient enough to take it.

Three Mills, Stratford   64 2–3E

Reached by road from Poplar, down Three Mill Lane; but the best way is to turn south off the main A11 near the Yardley factory, down Bisson Road. Half way down, right, a footpath runs along the Lea. Across the river is a wonderful factory that just growed, a building to confound the idea that corrugated iron is always horrible. It is all corrugated, with a kind of poetry for which nothing else will do, a

perpetual lean-to.[20] At the end are the Three Mills, or rather two of
them, dated 1776 and 1817, one with a sweet cupola attached. They
form a focus in the otherwise too-spread valley, a place like a village
green. They need attention, far more than some fussed-over piece of
half-timbering in the Home Counties; they tie a knot in the Lea valley
that potters through a dozen miles of outer London – a formidable
spinster, as it were, who needed a cuddle by gentle buildings to make
her complete.

20. Gone. The replacement is also corrugated, but unpoetically neat and
regular.

Abbey Mills Pumping Station   65 2▶
Bazalgette & Cooper, 1868

Abbey Lane is a short cut from West Ham to Bow that lets you in for
more than you expected. Specifically, what seems to be part of the
Kremlin, surrounded by trees. It pumps sewage and it was built in
1868 by Bazalgette of the Embankment. It pumps vitality too, and the
conviction you look for in Victorian churches and rarely find. If the
Russian shape of the main dome and the vaguely Moorish corner
towers had not existed, the nineteenth-century engineers would have
invented something like them. They were pumping sewage from a
great city – not an occupation to be disguised with terms such as
'rodent operative', but a noble function. The fifteenth century might
have called it God's bowels. The nineteenth kept enough sense of
occasion to make the inside, cross-shaped, into a kind of cathedral
scrolly ironwork, walkways, and a great dome. Outside, the chimney
has gone: the base remains like a kind of mausoleum.[21]

21. There is another chimney base beyond the central building. The Station
is not open to the general public, although specialist groups are occasionally
able to arrange visits.

Black Lion, High Street, Plaistow   65 2▶

This is the East End equivalent of the Crown and Greyhound at
Dulwich. Think of everything un-pub-like, put it together with flair
and there you are: one of the true modern equivalents of the gin palace.
Tiles and barge-boarding over the bar, glasses stuck on the ceiling,
coloured lights and wrot-work everywhere. Mirrors with leaded lights
and a pelmet on top, a bar front of exotic coloured photographs behind
a wrought-iron framework ... you name it, they've got it. And it's
marvellous, because it has gone back to the fountain-head of human
pubbiness, instead of sticking at some formula of details. (And also, to
be fair, because the landlord must be a remarkable person. There are
plenty of places in London where the same impulse has gone horribly
wrong.)[22]

22. The décor has changed beyond recognition. The pub still enjoys a good
reputation for food.

Stratford Broadway 49 7F–G

This is the real centre of the East End, now that Stepney has been broken on the planner's wheel. And a lovely shape it is too, when you can see it for the traffic: a long funnel widening and curling around one of the hungriest-looking churches in London (by Blore, 1834. It is usually open and the inside looks pretty ravenous too). In front of this is a colossal terracotta column to local Protestant martyrs, put up in 1878. Everything around is fussy, florid or full of goods, and only the new Co-op attempts a monolithic arrogance, jutting up into the eloquent envelope which is as vivacious as a Belgian *grand' place*. It needs caring for far more than most of the shattered towns of metroland: at the moment it serves as a one-way circus for the main roads to Cambridge and Norwich. With the through traffic out, and some care over new buildings, the people who use it would keep it swinging.[23]

23. Through traffic has been banned from one side, only to pour down the other in a torrent. The church (now usually closed), the column, and the buildings on the east side, including the florid town hall, are holding their own, but the Co-op started a trend towards large overweening buildings on the west. To the north and south the townscape falls apart completely, not helped by insensitive commercial development. In general, the Broadway has not been cared for properly, and no longer looks like the real centre of anywhere.

Leyton Church 48 2D

A huge surprise in the endless late-Victorian bow fronts of London-across-the-Lea. A village church [85] that gradually got bigger, and one that has never been rectified. A pre-war west porch adds itself unselfconsciously to the bits of 1830 and 1750, all shapes and sizes, as diverse as the characters in a saloon bar. This is something far more important than architectural style, and the kind of thing that was swept away in ninety-nine cases out of a hundred for the sake of 'correctness' or 'tidyness' – like cutting inches off people's heads to make things consistent.

Wanstead Church[24] 33 7K
Thomas Hardwick, 1790

The church is an anomaly, now, with the big house long gone, and leafy, spiritless terraces of the 1920s crept up across the road. It was built by Thomas Hardwick and, like all his other churches (St John's Wood or Marylebone), it has a lot of surface charm which evaporates when you realize the thin-lipped sod that lived underneath. Tidy and decent, and a nice, academic way with detail, but no more. Worth a visit, and worth hunting up the key (the nearest clergyman is at 114 Overton Drive)[25] to see the gorgeous pulpit. An octagonal bowl on a single stem, the joinery in perfect taste, is capped by a wonderful kind of Chinese hat, supported on palm leaves. It must be a job to deliver a humourless sermon from underneath this winking, twinkling top.

But the huge tomb to Sir Josiah Child, who died in 1699, looks exactly as if a self-made man had paid the top price per yard for servile adulation.

24. i.e. St Mary, Overton Drive.
25. The clergy are now half a mile away in Wanstead Place, near Christ Church.

Romford   O.S. 177 51:89

On four days a week this is an old market town caught up in London – a shapely market place [56] slowly disintegrating under traffic and shoddy redevelopment. On the other three – Wednesday, Friday and Saturday – the market has its own back. The whole town centre becomes a cornucopia: cabbages, remnants and transistors everywhere, the traffic fighting its way through but beaten easily by the relentless pressure of goods and shoppers. This is the immense potential implicit in the dreary pre-war terraces and semis of London's forgotten segment; and in fact land in the main street is as dear as anywhere in Britain. Petticoat Lane was never like this – or rather, it is, but without the little felicities of shape which grow on acquaintance – the long wedge-shaped street, the church set back, the old town hall at one end and the Golden Lion, still amazingly countrified (for how long?), at the other.[26] The town, as big as Norwich, is still only one building thick; if arcades could be driven into the back-land and stalls allowed to seep into them Romford could become an exciting place on every day of the week.

26. A hint of its countrified character still clings to the Golden Lion, but beaten about the head by loud music and games machines. The old Laurie town hall has been demolished, some clumsy new buildings have arrived, and the eastern end of the market place is abruptly closed by an ugly blue hoarding. But as compensation the through traffic is out of the market place, and there is a pleasant, if anonymous, maze of shopping walkways to the south.

Upminster Mill   O.S. 177 55:86
1799

A great surprise amongst all the pre-war villas: big, stark and well kept up. Octagonal weatherboarded body, complicated curved weatherboard cap, everything as trim and crisp as the hull of a ship – a good reminder that windmills were vital factories, not picturesque accents in the landscape. (Just north of the main Hornchurch road, about 500 yards west of Upminster's central cross-roads.)

Cranham   O.S. 177 57:86

Of all the ways in which London meets its countryside, this is the least credible. When the Green Belt came into force in 1938, the outward swell of building stopped dead, two fields away. So you can look back to the serried roofs from what is still an unspoilt Essex hamlet – farm, house, rectory and church (unhappily Victorian) in a big leafy churchyard. Essex doesn't go in for cosification, so this is still rough and honest. There is a terrifying forty miles of solid brickwork behind those demure-looking semis half a mile away. You feel as Canute might have on the beach, but unexpectedly successful. (Turn south off B187 just before the railway bridge.)

8 Thames-Side East: Deptford to Dagenham

The working river, sinuous loops of greasy water thick with boats. As one of London's basic units it is magnetic and almost inaccessible. The final thrill of getting to the waterside, without signposts and after many false starts, never palls. Most places along the route are utterly obscure; but sandwiched between power stations there is the astonishing cartouche of Greenwich, easily the best thing of its kind in London. Down-river there is a provincial city of great character, mysteriously transplanted from the Midlands and named Woolwich.[1]

1. POSTSCRIPT 1987. No great changes to the more notable buildings. But a profound change in their midst, as they stand either side of empty docks, and of an idle river disturbed by little more than the occasional pleasure-boat. It amounts to the end of a history going back at least 400, and arguably 1900, years.

SOUTH SIDE

Deptford Town Hall   96 1A
C. E. Rickards, 1905

The jolliest public building in London, dashed off by an Edwardian genius, Charles Rickards, who could overturn classical rules and – like Wilde – make a masterpiece out of the paradoxes. Something for everyone here, with abundant maritime illustrations and naval dates (1537, 1652, 1805) sprayed all over the façade. Odd enough they look, in the landlocked traffic-block that is today's New Cross. But the gusto will never look odd, nor will the infectious topsy-turvy composition that starts with vigorous horizontals and a bow window, and ends up with a great lid of a pitched roof sheltering (what else?) a relief of men-of-war – well carved, like everything else on this expert confection. Edwardian England meant many things to many people. One of them, undoubtedly, was gaiety; and here it is.

[St Paul, Deptford Church Street   80 7C
Thomas Archer, 1712

A fascinating comparison with Hawksmoor's great churches, built in the same style and for the same clients (Queen Anne's Commissioners). The trouble here is the same as at Smith Square; Archer's detail is forceful enough and original enough but has nothing behind it, where in the maddest of Hawksmoor's designs there is always architectural and religious logic. This is rhetoric where there should be poetry, one of Guido Reni's towering but empty compositions. Notices inside say brusquely 'Silence': and this is exactly the building's effect, slapping into submission with giant columns and a thick, richly carved ceiling. And again – and again unlike Hawksmoor – the submission brings no reward, only bleak acceptance. The church is sombre, the churchyard is sombre even in sunlight, the people in the churchyard are sombre. The whole thing is one of London's least accommodating places.][2]

2. The notices have gone and, architecture apart, the church is friendly and apparently flourishing, while the churchyard is softened by a border of municipal flower-beds.

St Nicholas, Deptford Green   80 6c

A chubby brick church of 1697, blitzed in the war, now repaired and hard to get into – usually the churchyard is locked, but never mind the church. Immediately behind it is a whopping power station, and the foreground is a pair of stone skulls on the churchyard gates, so weathered that they seem disturbingly animal, the sharpest *memento mori* in London [76]. Caught as the filling in this surrealist sandwich, St Nicholas has an effect which it would never have managed by itself.

Greenwich Market   80 6e
Joseph Kay, 1831

A wonderful Improvement, now insulted by a repainting in colours as phoney as a hair-rinse, when all it needed was solid cream stucco. Just a simple block, of the kind which today would be developed with off-hand slabs and cack-handed corners. Around it, smooth frontages, as good as Nash and better built. Inside, a market, reached by three alleys and an archway, all leading as well to a good pub, the Coach and Horses. Not colours on a map, not interesting items in the townscape, but a living unit, the heart of Greenwich. The inscription on the back of the archway says: 'A false balance is abomination to the Lord But a just weight is His delight'. Remember that, fashion-mongers, when the time comes to repaint this real place, and choose something less false and more just than the present slick and sickly lime green.[3]

3. They chose yellow ochre: still a bit strong.

Cutty Sark   80 6e

Cutty Sark has leapt like a dolphin into a concrete dry-dock next to Greenwich Hospital. The superstructure is impressive enough, but the really marvellous thing is the view from the bottom of the dock, reached by steps from either end. The part of the boat that nobody ever saw billows out in a proud copper sheath, as necessary as the shape of an aerofoil. The thing that Victorian architecture missed, and modern architecture has missed also (though modern aeroplane design has reached it because it had to): sheer need, pared of anything inessential. But sheer need on all levels – as much a spiritual need for the figurehead [77] as a functional need for the precise shape of hull.

Everything has got to be just where it is, and the rightness is worth more than any artificial tension. Inevitability; and you can try for it all your life and miss, like George Bernard Shaw.

Queen's House and Maritime Museum   81 6F

Inigo Jones, 1619–37

The Queen's House is the building with which Inigo Jones burst into the astonished seventeenth century. After three hundred years of imitation it is still astonishing, for a purity and strictness which never for a moment becomes impersonal or academic. The inside space of the Great Hall is a simple cube, with a gallery high up: yet it is incredibly urgent and forceful. Every doorcase has meaning, just as every capital of the Banqueting House has meaning. The cantilevered Tulip Staircase is not only an engineering feat but a lyrical quintessence, uncluttered by any backward glances. This is exactly the feeling of the best Renaissance designers in Italy, and Inigo's achievement is as good as that.

The Queen's House is now part of the National Maritime Museum, linked by colonnades to a pair of exhibition halls. These colonnades focus on the centres of the sides and recreate as a leisurely walk what was the oddest thing about the design – that the main Dover road went right through it, splitting it into two blocks which were originally connected only by a single bridge. In the museum itself there is one masterpiece, the Royal Barge[4] of 1732 [78] which was designed by Kent and carved by James Richards, who succeeded Gibbons as King's Carver. Kent was never less constrained, and his fancy-free decorative flair led him off into a riot of witty marine allusions combined with a twinkling parody of the Palladian style – e.g. in the way in which the handrail around the stern has an enormous egg-and-dart moulding for a soffit. Richards matched this with a technique which made each mythological beast into a powerful symbol and a person. The bowsprit is a Viking dragon, and lions with tails gambol over the bows; the King's cabin has quintessentially fishy consoles, all different, all with the rudest expressions. What a romp.

Another thing worth looking out for is Orchardson's famous painting of Napoleon on the *Bellerophon*. Instead of a stodgy story-picture, it is very near Manet in the effect of space and the emotional conviction.

4. i.e. Prince Frederick's barge.

Greenwich Hospital   80 6E–81 6F

John Webb, 1664 onwards
Sir Christopher Wren, 1699–1703
Sir John Vanbrugh, 1728
William Newton, 1789

A perfect example of what the English can do with formal design when they feel like it. The axis [38] is one of the best in Europe, but the regularity is far from simple. As much as anything else it depends on Wren's observatory, with its almost Jacobean outline, rising off-centre on the hill behind. So nature has the last word after all. The parts all carry a different charge: the Queen's House in the middle, burning bright; John Webb's blocks by the riverside, which keep Jones's Roman intensity and apply it on a grander scale; and in between, Wren, acting as the perfect go-between, providing a link which is by a long way the biggest part of the composition, yet always allows precedence to the older and fiercer parts. Considered by themselves, Wren's domes and colonnades may seem unexciting and limp (and the twentieth-century copies from the Old Bailey onwards certainly are). But as the lubricating oil which makes the whole engine go, they are incomparable. The detail on Webb's riverside blocks is superb and gives a powerfulness to the heavy elevations which any Continental designer would have envied. London soot fits it particularly well, by emphasizing the rustications and the undercut pride of the capitals, so that the cleaned portion looks particularly futile. The best place for a close view is the walk-way along the riverside, which is covered at high tide; but the best place to see the axis as a whole is from the melancholy public garden across the river in the Isle of Dogs, where it seems like a myth of affluence sent to spur on the working classes. And the best way to get there is by the footpath under the river, served by the weird domed pillbox next to the bows of the *Cutty Sark* [87].

After all this congruence, the brick and stone parts designed by Vanbrugh to fit the back of the axis (they face you as you walk towards the chapel or along Romney Road) are quite a surprise. They would have wrecked the main elevations, but they are perfect as rearward trimmings of the wildest kind. For Vanbrugh here is sending up the whole classical world: stretching some of the rhythms unbearably across heavy plain brickwork, then cramming carved detail on to a single overcrowded linking bay – a koala bear between two elephants. Because there is so much serene classicism around, the joke comes off perfectly; and because Vanbrugh was always creative, the design succeeds on its own topsy-turvy merits as well.

The Painted Hall and Chapel are opposite each other, under Wren's pair of domes. You are allowed in, somewhat on sufferance, and it might be better if there were naval guards at a place with such overwhelming naval traditions. The two buildings make a good comparison in extrovert design: the Painted Hall decorated in 1707–26 by Thornhill to Wren's design, the Chapel done over after a fire in 1779 and designed by James Stuart and his assistant William Newton.

But, apart from nice comparisons, the Painted Hall is superb. Wren's amplitude found an exact complement in Thornhill's decoration, whereby the whole scheme depends on the sober brown and gold of the side walls and the near blackness of the grisaille panels. Only against these can the brighter colours of the main ceiling float away convincingly. And only having experienced the overwhelming solidity of the main space – a domed vestibule, then the long hall – can the viewer discard his reservations and revel in the painted box at the far end where the High Tables are, reached through a huge arch and adorned with *trompe l'œil* windows. It is exactly like the classical theatre: a contract, nobly observed, to suspend everyday standards. But every piece of paintwork enhances rather than disguises the architectural shape: like a setting for the Mass which is ornate yet at every point gives deeper meaning to the words. This is one of London's high points, and compared with it the run of painted decoration – e.g. Verrio at Hampton Court – is laughable.

The chapel is not at the same level. The decoration never transcends the big box-like room and there is none of that almost mystical excellence which makes the visitor feel that he has walked into another dimension altogether. But it is grand by any other standard, with an impassive main design combined with a frenzy of pretty ornament: in wood on the underside of the side galleries, in stone on the superbly carved organ gallery. It has an impersonal and rather chilling sense of power that does not feel English at all; perhaps it might be more at home in Leningrad.

River walk, Blackwall to Greenwich[5]   81 3G–5F and 2H

This unknown and unnamed riverside path is the best Thames-side walk in London. It beats all the embankments and water-gardens hollow. Best in this direction, because then the walk has a climax: the domes of Greenwich Hospital beckoning round the bend of the river, and a splendidly unselfconscious free house, the Cutty Sark. The entrance certainly takes some finding: to get there, fork left facing the southern entrance to the Blackwall Tunnel with its pretty Art Nouveau gatehouse. About two hundred yards along, on the left, a passage leads down beside the Delta Metal Co. It zigs and it zags, but it doesn't give up, and eventually comes out at the river. The start is now a sizeable belvedere, but the path soon takes on much more exciting forms: between walls, or unfenced above a slide down to the water, or wandering past timber wharves, under cranes and in one case nipping around the back of a boatyard. Never the same for a hundred yards at once, a continuous flirtation with the slow-flowing river, choked with working boats. The first houses come in at the Cutty Sark (Union Wharf): then there is a final exciting stretch past Greenwich Power Station and the astonishing contrast with the Trinity almshouses next door, another good riverside pub (the Yacht), and the climax of the footpath in front of Greenwich Hospital. Not just a walk, but a stressed walk – mostly by accident. God preserve it from the prettifiers.★

The river can also be reached east of Blackwall [58], from the end of River Way. A straightforward path winds off towards Charlton,

★ Or the blind. 'They' are trying to close it. Walk it as you would a country path, till they are sick to the guts.

without any of the exciting ins and outs of the Greenwich walk. But the Silvertown skyline opposite is much more exciting, beginning with Tate & Lyle's complicated concrete engineering, and continuing with all the ocean liners in the Victoria Docks.[6]

5. The footpath now starts a hundred yards or so inland from the Blackwall Tunnel gatehouse, opposite the gasholder, and winds between the Molassine Co. Ltd and the Victoria Deep Water Terminal before coming out on the river bank. The boatyard and timber wharves have gone, along with the working boats on the river.

6. The Tate & Lyle factory at Plaistow Wharf, opposite River Way, has been extensively modernized, and there is nothing but water in the Victoria Dock.

The Thames Barrier, on which the future of much of the contents of this book depends, is visible downstream. At this distance it is rather Wellsian, like an invasion fleet of Martian submarines riding at anchor. It can be seen close to farther east, down Eastmoor Street: a heroic sight, even though the stainless steel cladding on the piers looks oddly battered and flimsy. (1974–82; consulting engineers Rendel, Palmer & Tritton.)

[Vanbrugh Castle, Maze Hill, Greenwich   81 6G
Sir John Vanbrugh, 1717–c. 1726

Historically, a fascinating building. For here, for the very first time, medieval grimness was produced as a romantic fancy rather than sheer need. Sir John actually built an estate of tiny castle-villas as well, and the last of them has only just been demolished – and that for hideous neo-Georgian flats, which is cruelly ironic. The trouble is that Vanbrugh's fancy, unlike Hawksmoor's, could not change gear; and what is superbly expressive in a classical style at Seaton Delaval turns here into a bulky, limp brick envelope with a few machicolations on it: an over-large Christmas parcel which you know is going to be a disappointment. But for all that, it ought to be seen.]

Blackheath   97 2H, etc.

For a flat stretch of open space, Blackheath has remarkable personality. It is never quite flat, and there are queer enclaves such as Blackheath Vale crammed into what looks like an old quarry. More to the point, the whole heath is slightly convex, tipping over into views down to the Thames or across to Shooter's Hill. The edges, heavily built up, bounce the space back into the centre, where it is reinforced by the grave parade of lorries and red buses down Watling Street. It is the opposite of London Fields or Mitcham Common or all the other dull areas of amenity inflicted on London. Here there is tension between the middle and the edges: no faint winter sun-shaft but will catch on stucco somewhere around the perimeter. Apart from the Paragon, the houses, Georgian or later, are no more than a backcloth to this surprising exposition that two and two can equal five. But Ferrey's preposterous church [81] gives just the kind of hilarious *bonne bouche* that Blackheath needs. Prickly, sit-up-and-beg Gothic, stuck down on a corner of the grass like a postage stamp as if to say: if I weren't here it would all blow away. This kind of preposterousness in people or places is very hard to resist; any of the preserved bits of Blackheath would be missed less than this pipsqueak.

Blackheath Park (south-east of Blackheath Station)
Eric Lyons, 1957–date   97 3H–J

Blackheath Park is a private estate (the Cator Estate) which began to be built up in the 1820s and 30s: pretty houses, big gardens, plenty of trees. Every variety of villa followed, but never enough to smudge the original patrician stamp. Then in the mid 1950s Span appeared and has been deftly slipping in slices of weatherboarding and tile-hanging. The original leafy layout has received another dimension, absent from almost everywhere else in London: the exhilaration of new and old together when both are good.

The main cross-roads of the estate (Blackheath Park and Foxes Dale) is a perfect blend, at the moment. North-east is a very pretty original group with a new flat slipped in between two old houses. South-east is Span (Hallgate) at its crispest. North-west is the original estate church, St Michael [80], by George Smith, 1830, far more individual than the usual run. The pinnacles here are something more than a studious crib from a pattern-book, and certainly no pattern-book would advise the highly successful eastern tower which means that there is a double east window.

Finally the south-west is modern again, one of the best new single houses in London – not by Span but by Peter Moro, 1960. The garden side is especially fresh and vivid with an outside iron staircase, well worth a peering over the fence in Foxes Dale to see.

The best Span site here is The Priory, a few yards south, off Park Gate. This was actually the first to be built at Blackheath, and keeps the same dream-like floating space as Parkleys at Ham Common. But The Priory is on a slight slope, so there is one marvellous moment where one lush square dissolves into another, downhill, like drowning in a sea of Samuel Palmer's vegetation. The later sites are crisper, more matter-of-fact, and the romantic moment seems to have blown away. Perhaps it has done for the whole country.

The Paragon, Blackheath   97 2J
Michael Searle, 1792

It is very just that the best of all London's surviving eighteenth-century schemes should be by an estate surveyor rather than Adam or Chambers. Men like Michael Searle and his humbler anonymous partners were the real builders of Georgian London. Here he hit on an idea as good as anything in Bath – which is to say as good as anything in Europe at that time. Paragon is a just name for it. Seven identical four-storey units linked by colonnades face the heath in a shallow segmental curve. With an infallible instinct Searle resisted the temptation to split the composition by making an even number of units, resisted also the temptation to accentuate the central house as a Frenchman might have done. Resisted even the temptation to trick out the blocks with pretty detail as Adam would have done. The result is that the taut curve speaks straight out to the lawns and trees: perfect urbanity and perfect rurality meeting head-on. It is the Royal Crescent at Bath wearing a South London grin, the ends beautifully finished without artificial emphasis by small lodges: cockney panache too. Beautifully restored after war damage by C. Bernard Brown.

Charlton House
1607–12

82 6B

Charlton has the spark that so many more famous Jacobean houses lack. The curly detail means something, the irregular outline has real spirit, gleaming in the sun at the end of the humdrum suburban road from Blackheath. It is like finding an epigram in the middle of an official report. And the three-storey frontispiece sizzles like a firework, the stone crackling out into violent grotesque faces [82] or ornamental sprays or strapwork chipped out against the sky. With the big glass windows it looks like a stray from some Baltic waterfront, and this is no accident, for the actual ornament, as well as the urgency, is more German than anything else of the date in Britain. The language that engendered so much heavy melodrama suddenly erupts into sinister poetry: Duchess of Malfi, S.E.17.

Rotunda Museum, off Repository Road
John Nash, 1814–19

82 5D

Alias the R.A. Repository, or Nash's tent. Surely, by now, the oldest tent in the world. Nash put it up in St James's Park as part of the premature arrangements to celebrate the first defeat of Napoleon, in 1814. It was presented to the R.A. in 1819 and equipped with a lead roof, an inner skin, and a socking great Doric column in the middle. Between the two skins the original sailcloth is apparently still there. So here is this elegant concave shape, rocking on a captivating arcade of Doric columns and stretched arches, like an extra room from the Brighton Pavilion, all full of guns, some of them very odd pieces indeed. One of London's most endearing, least known museums.

Woolwich Barracks
1775–1802

82 5E

No need to go to Leningrad. Come to Woolwich instead, and see the yellow brick march out for a quarter of a mile or more [64]. A few stucco columns for inflection, otherwise nothing but London's own material, facing south ready to catch the oblique sun. It won't stand up to a close look, but the first astounding view in enfilade – from either side (strictly, the only proper public viewpoints) – is worth all the subsequent disappointment. In mist or winter sunlight it is haunting: a perpetual Last Post floating as the backcloth to the great parade ground.

Woolwich   83 4F

The reference books say that this is one more of London's boroughs. Your eyes tell you that it is a provincial centre that has got embedded in London by mistake. It has more independence than many towns fifty miles from London (Aylesbury, for example, or Bedford). Powis Street, a commercial gold mine from end to end, has come down from the Midland cities, and in the process lost its Midland drabness and taken on alertness and *savoir faire*. It ends in Beresford Square, opposite the main gate of the Arsenal, where an open market flows all over to the despair of buses accustomed to more docile suburbs.[7] Thumping self-centred vitality; complete freedom from the morning train to Town. It is always being rebuilt, as it must be – that is its nature; but I hope that Sam's in Plumstead Road has many more years of life. It sells Government surplus, has been there sixty-five years already, and would be very nearly my favourite London shop. The fascia is completely hidden by boots, capes, jackets: the tiny entrance leads to a very long shop packed with goods, receding into the distance like a hall of mirrors.[8] Cornucopia, like the whole of the centre of Woolwich: stuffed with goods, yet never impersonal. Window-shopping here is really fun.

7. Powis Street and Beresford Square have been successfully pedestrianized.
8. Still going strong, still overflowing, but not a very long interior these days.

Abbey Wood   84 5D

Astonishing that one wood can be full of character whilst another is just a collection of trees. Abbey Wood has a personality as sharp as a country market place. Between Woolwich and Erith, on a two-hundred-foot slope down to the Thames marshes, crumpled into innumerable rises and dells, owned by the L.C.C. but touched with nothing more urban than a wood fence. There is always one more slope dotted with the boles of lopped chestnut trees when reason says that there should be a line of semis. This is the only park inside the Green Belt where it is really possible to feel cut off from the city: on Hampstead Heath it is always visible; even in Richmond it is always implicit, if only because of the strangeness of the landscape. But Abbey Wood feels as though it would go on for ever. Yet it is only a mile wide and less than half a mile deep. (The best way to get there is from New Road, which bisects it.)

NORTH SIDE

St Mark, Silvertown   82 1B
S. S. Teulon, 1861–2

A hard punch right in the guts. Sombre and compact, brooding over the bizarre landscape of North Woolwich, funnels instead of tree-tops. Teulon's style has stopped being merely original, has become fused into glittering poetry, all knobbly with harsh polysyllables. Apse builds up and into stair turret, gabled clerestory builds up and over to gabled tower. Imploded, savage inward raids into the heart's essence, an architectural imagination the size of Blake's. The church is locked but still used; it must be kept.[9] It is the nearest thing to a mystic's revelation that London has.

9. It became redundant, was abandoned, and finally the roof was burnt. Now being restored for use as a museum of Victorian life.

North Woolwich   82–83 1B–F, etc.

A twin to the Isle of Dogs, that is a loop in the river with docks cut across the neck. Here, though, all the contrasts are wilder and more expressive. The ships in the Albert Dock seem bigger (superb perspectives of a whole fleet from the two road bridges [89], Connaught Road and Manor Way).[10] The south bank at Woolwich seems leafier, the little terraces seem cosier, the riverside warehouses are more impressive. Beckton Gasworks complicates the skyline, every street corner holds a new surprise. All the tension that is absent at Tilbury is super-abundant here. Oddest of all is the Gallions, a huge pub in Norman Shaw style off Manor Way. It is really bizarre, the Bedford Park Hotel transplanted to haunted mud-flats with no other building near, only cranes and funnels.[11] A good private place to hatch a revolution; and when the plotting has finished you can walk under the Thames on a subway just like that at Greenwich. This feels right out of England, never mind out of London – something from another planet.

10. The Royal Docks closed in 1981. The recently-opened London City Airport may represent the beginning of a new era, but there is still dereliction all around.
11. It has been abandoned, with corrugated iron over the windows, and is quite extraordinarily eerie.

Beckton Gasworks   67 5–6F–G

Gasworks City, a magic world of plant and pipes, holders and small hills of coal – even wharves and funnels, for good measure, at the far end. It has all happened by accident: already exciting, it could be stressed to become one of the showplaces of London. All the 'interest' which modern architects try to tickle up in blocks of flats is here for the asking. Snooty phrases like 'about as romantic as a gasworks' would rebound here: it is one of the most moving bits of industrial landscape in London.[12]

12. The landscape is sparser than it used to be, while Beckton ticks over quietly, waiting for North Sea gas to run out. It is popular with film companies, but not open to the public.

Barking Church, Back Lane[13]   67 1G

A happy rambling town church that has never been tidied up. One of
everything, from a fragment of a Saxon cross onwards: you could have
a good game of hide-and-seek around the four lines of arches. Two
tombs make it worth a special visit. In the chancel, Sir Charles Montague (d. 1625) in a faery scene: a camp before the battle, Sir Charles
seated and pensive, a ferocious rifleman on either side, tents fading
away into the back of the picture. Yet he died at his home, aged sixty-
one. Is it all allegorical, man waiting reflectively in purgatory for the
battle at the Last Judgement? This is what it feels like, extremely
atmospheric and poetic and a huge reproach to all the hack-work which
passes for early-seventeenth-century sculpture in Britain.

The other monument is in the north-east chapel; as brilliant and
extrovert as the other was delicate and complex. A mason's tablet to
John Bennett (d. 1706), a shipowner of Poole. Far better than the court
sculptors would have made it, with wonderful attack and verve in the
ringlets of Mr Bennett's wig, his outstretched fingers, his four-square
goddam face; and most of all in the reliefs at either side, fully rigged
ships in a high sea. The rest of Europe has nothing like this: better
individual sculptors, maybe, but not this astonishingly high level of
perhaps a hundred anonymous men.

13. It now lies back from the Broadway in a green space which also contains
the remains of Barking Abbey, and which has been enlarged (unusually) so
that Back Lane and Heath Street have disappeared under grass. But the
windows are covered by thick metal grilles, it is a struggle to fend off graffiti,
and casual requests to see inside are not greatly welcomed.

Barking Station   51 7G
B.R. Eastern Region, 1961

British Railways has recently rebuilt most of the stations on the Tilbury
line. Most of them are small neat boxes, not worth a special visit. This
one is much bigger, the size of a terminus in a country town, and one
of the noblest new buildings in London [84]. A cranked concrete
canopy is continued inside as the roof of the tall luminous booking
hall.* It draws you in, where most stations repel. From there heavy
concrete roof beams carry you through to the platforms. Easy, straightforward, wonderfully free from arty affectation, the perfect building
to represent a modernized railway system. And unlike some other E.R.
stations (especially the freakish smart-for-a-minute Harlow Town) it
is wearing well. For the first time in a hundred years, the centre of
Barking has been given a chance.

Eastbury Manor House, Eastbury Square, Barking   67 1K
1572

When London's flood-tide flowed over the Essex marshes, a few old

* The same idea as at Rome Termini. And why not?

buildings were caught up in it. Sometimes they make more of an impression by shock in their new surroundings than they would have originally; this grim red-brick manor-house is the wildest possible contrast to the placid council houses neatly arranged around a square so as to leave it a strip of lawn on its island. A real Bleak House, still fortified in spirit if not in fact, bunched together around its chimneys and polygonal stair turrets (one intact, one crumbling[14]). Not wicked, just very forbidding indeed, ready made for hauntings and screams out on the mud-flats. (Between A122, Dagenham–Barking, and the main Tilbury road. You get a glimpse of it from this, fighting mad above the uniform roofs.)

14. It has crumbled.

Dagenham Church   53 6J
William Mason, 1800

Marvellous nonsense [86], the work of a man who had Gothic fantasy in his blood. William Kent would have been proud of this one: William Mason obviously was, because he signed his name as architect all the way round the arch above the west door. A riot of curly details and a riot of materials too: rag, stock brick, and flint. Pure froth, without a care in the world; it is difficult to guess which Dagenham is the more alien to it: the original bleak village in the marshes, or the present chaotic spilling over of London's spare parts. (Reached along Church Street from the west, Crown Lane from the east. About a mile north of the Ford works.[15])

15. Now reached along Church Lane from the south.

The Merry Fiddlers, Dagenham   53 2G
Redecorated by Ind Coope's Architectural Department, 1962

From the outside, this is one of those neo-Georgian palaces which brewers put up in the 1930s to cover up the awful facts of drinking. Inside, one bar is still impeccably polite. But the Saloon has been forcibly propelled into the teenage world of the 1960s.[16] The big, blank space has been divided into nooks and corners with beams and baulks made deliberately rough: a kind of packing-case bar. At first it seems like an assault; but there is more here than exhibitionism. The demonstratively crude details are sending up themselves as well as the easy target of the original platitudinous space. This wry, self-conscious honesty matches the spirit of young Dagenham very well, and the place is a roaring success: on a Tuesday night, the bar was packed out by nine o'clock and I was the oldest person in it. (Junction of Wood Lane and Whalebone Lane, near the 'Civic Centre'.)

16. The left-hand bar is kitted out with little wooden balustrades. The right-hand bar is a cavernous room with a sunken floor, full of pool tables. Nobody in either bar remembers anything about the 1960s.

9   South London:
Battersea to Bromley

This is the cockney kingdom – though traditional areas like the Old Kent Road are depleted, now, and there is more vitality out at Mitcham or Lewisham. It seems more friendly and humane than North London, the natural domain of corner tobacconists and cheerful pubs, and it shades easily into the respectable middle-class layer which washes up the reverse slopes of the North Downs, sometimes almost to the crest and sometimes – around Purley and Coulsdon – with quite dramatic effect. Big estates do not fit in here, and the post-war attempts of Croydon at New Addington and the L.C.C. at St Paul's Cray are a depressing reminder of this. There are few highlights, but there is not much monotony either, and a few odd places stand out: Dulwich as a kind of southern Hampstead; Croydon as an old town which had one rapid change with the railway a century ago and has had a much more startling transformation in the last ten years; and one tiny, remarkable piece of real countryside at Chislehurst which is completely surrounded by houses.

BATTERSEA TO PECKHAM AND DULWICH

Battersea Old Church (St Mary) and Heliport   92   1-2B

A bit of real working riverside, with Lots Road Power Station directly across, Fulham just downstream, and the dumpy, eighteenth-century, yellow-brick church with its fan of mutilated trees in the foreground.[1] It has survived the transition from village to grim industrial suburb because of its classless, unselfconscious honesty, something which the nineteenth century could never understand. A Victorian church always bears the stigmata of the exact social layer it was built for.

Upstream a bit farther, off Lombard Road, is Westland Heliport. It is not public, but you may be allowed in;[2] and the place is certainly worth a journey. This tight little square of ground, usually with a gleaming helicopter on it, has all the excitement and immediateness which London Airport so blatantly lacks. Here, though nobody has thought about designing it, is one of the remarkable places of today's London, as typical of 1960 as the railway stations were of 1860.

1. The trees have grown out to a decent shape. The World's End housing estate is conspicuous in the view across the river.
2. There is, in any case, an excellent view through the perimeter wire.

Battersea Power Station[3]   77 6-7F
Sir Giles Gilbert Scott, 1932–4

This is one more London building that sticks in spite of the architecture rather than because of it. The timid fluting on brickwork and chimneys, novel at the time, would have made Telford or Rennie throw up; but the bricks themselves take over. Immense plumes from the chimneys, lurid floodlighting: stage scenery for a riverside opera [57], splendid in mist or with winter sun behind it; if there is such a thing as industrial melodrama, this is it: the C.E.G.B.'s Meyerbeer.

3. The power station finally went out of use in 1983. The company which runs Alton Towers is planning to turn it into a 'leisure and theme park'.

Church of the Ascension, Lavender Hill   92 3E
James Brooks, 1873–83

Plain bricks outside, which is often the sign that there will be something worth-while inside the door. And there is: a grand upstanding space, purged of the offhand detail which mars so many of Brooks's London churches: perhaps because it was unfinished, and completed later by J. T. Micklethwaite. Tiny aisles, and tiny ambulatory behind the great apse; with no niggling mementoes of the thirteenth century to spoil the brickwork, this gives an incredibly strong sense of the central space, which can survive even a melodramatic rood and reredos – not bad in itself, but out of key here. Often locked, especially at the week-end, but worth hunting out the key.

Granada, Mitcham Road, Tooting   108 5D
Cecil Masey, 1931

The outside is any old cinema with a grandiose front and mean flanks. The foyer is like a cross between Strawberry Hill and the Soane Museum; for once the fantasy of films has been matched by fantasy in the cinema. To argue that it is plaster deep is like arguing that *La Règle du Jeu* is just a strip of celluloid. Ninety-nine cinemas may be a shoddy counterfeit and so may ninety-nine films: but this is the hundredth. Gothic arches are all around in the auditorium, dimly lit by reflections from the screen. When the lights go up there is Aladdin's cave; and if you walk to the front for a choc-ice or orange squash and turn round suddenly, the view may literally make you gasp. Pinnacle after gilded pinnacle, to the back of the gallery: one of the sights of London. Miss the Tower of London, if you have to, but don't miss this.[4]

4. It is now known that the fabulous Gothic interior was designed by Theodore Komisarjevsky. Sadly, the Granada closed as a cinema in 1973 and is now a bingo club, open to members only. But membership is free to anybody over eighteen years old, so if you live in the area it may be worth joining just to see the inside from time to time.

King's Head, Upper Tooting Road   108 3D
1896

A great, lucid, late-Victorian pub between Tooting and Balham. It has kept all its bar divisions intact, with scrolly woodwork and incised glass; and surely in this case because they are still as convenient and appropriate in 1960 as they were in 1890. The plan is a *tour de force*, with a central elliptical bar counter and the relative bar areas worked out so that there is never crowding or claustrophobia. Wren might have calculated them: this is a St James Piccadilly among pubs. And just as that is a proper church, this is a proper drinking place, though a completely different sort of drinking fom the Red Lion in St James's. Now that it has survived this far, the brewers (Truman's) must surely preserve the King's Head; especially as Tooting is just the kind of vigorous yet stratified cockney place that gives the divisions a common-sense use (more perhaps now than when the pub was built and its clients were Pooters-south-of-the-river). And if all this sounds very rational and discriminate, why, that's the kind of pub it is.

Clapham Old Town   93 4G

This is one of London's missing villages. On the surface it seems irredeemable. But the bones are still there, and more than anywhere else in London it is a place to sense what might and still could be. The main space is a wedge; the old village centre, now used as a turn-round for 88 and 137 buses (that thing you waited for so long at Oxford Circus ends up here) – not a bad transcription, for it gives the place an up-to-date city identity as well as a ghostly village one. The blunt end, with a good pub in it, points at Clapham Common, just a few yards away, and the Common plays an enchanting game, dancing in with foliage from two directions without breaking up the space. This is the perfect recipe for a neighbourhood: shops, open space, houses, a natural centre, and even a Georgian church (Holy Trinity) just around the corner. Now nobody cares much; it is all dog-shit and bus tickets. But it could easily be marvellous.

Museum of British Transport,[5] Clapham High Street

This is a big shed, with the right kind of unselfconscious steel roof, cram full of locomotives, buses and trams. All that mechanical energy halted into atmospheric stillness, with sparrows walking about on the floor and quiet, enthusiastic attendants. Many of the visitors have a far-away look in their eyes: for although the buses and trams are museum-pieces, the locomotives, mostly from 1890–1920, represent man's ingenuity and self-respect at one of its highest levels. Supreme art because free from all thought of 'art' or 'industrial design': the art of a co-ordinated animal. This is a noble zoo.

Even if this admiration seems quaint, there is a special reason to go to Clapham. Queen Victoria's carriage, built in 1869, is one of the loveliest sequences of rooms that the nineteenth century ever created. Richness without a hint of ostentation or oppressiveness, elegance and force matched, everything in its place, not merely functionally but for all time – Chairs, not chairs; even Lavatory-Seat. It feels like one of the railway designers creating for his Queen with the same pressure that he used for his engine-drivers. An awful declension from this to Edward VII's carriage in the next row, mostly refitted under the supervision of Queen Mary in the 1910s: taste and thought have replaced being and feeling.

The far-away look in those other visitors' eyes holds something more durable than nostalgia. Like *Quattrocento* architecture, Jacobean poetry, German Baroque sculpture, this was It.

5. Closed in 1973. The railway exhibits are now in the National Railway Museum, Leeman Street, York. The London buses and trams are in the London Transport Museum, Covent Garden (p. 69), after a brief sojourn at Syon.

St John the Evangelist, Clapham Road   93 3J
T. Marsh Nelson, 1842

Just a simple brick box with a portico on the end; but that portico is detailed with a discrimination and refinement that is up to the best in London. Where so many Greek revival buildings were offhand, the designer here felt for each column and door, each moulding on each column. He used the resources of cast stone to make a surface that is as tight and elegant as Wyatt's. The date is astonishing, and because of it the building has slipped through the net of architectural books on London. It is not 'Georgian' in name; yet nothing could better express classical sensibility.

Electric Avenue, Brixton   94 4A

Electric, all right, and high voltage too. A whole area east of Brixton Road, opposite the jolly town hall, where the ground floor has dissolved and re-formed as a magic cave of people and goods. Stalls everywhere, arcades everywhere, diving through buildings and under the railway. Meat, fish, nylons, detergent: an endless, convoluted cornucopia. Compared with it, Petticoat Lane is synthetic; this cockney centre has kept all of its Victorian vitality. And it is the twentieth-century New World that has saved the bacon of the Old; for more than half the faces are one shade of brown or another. There is of course a Grand Plan out for this unplanned sky-rocketing power-house. With luck, it will be so grand that it is deferred until planners can understand what makes this place tick. It lives by free growth, like a great hedgerow tree. And as a tree depends on leaves, this vast emporium depends on the humble light bulb. Naked and without frills, binding the whole place into a web of stars at eye level. Electric.[6]

6. The riots happened just around the corner, but the market seems cheerfully unruffled. The Grand Plan remained on the drawing board.

Christ Church, Christchurch Road, Streatham   109 IK
John Wild, 1842

Noble, strong and sensitive. This is how nineteenth-century church architecture could have gone if Pugin had not dashed in with his inspired lunacy. Wild designed this when he was twenty-eight, and lived for another fifty years while his talents gradually curdled. Unlike even the best Gothic Revival churches, this is expressive directly, not by some kind of association. This is partly due to the unselfconscious style, rather like an engine shed or a waterworks, but much more to Wild's own ability. A simple basilican front looks down Christchurch Road to one of London's busiest junctions (Brighton Road and the South Circular). In front, two noble yellow-brick obelisks; at the side a mighty tower, sheer brick right up to the belfry. The detail close to is incredibly delicate and completely original – the best German architects were doing something like this at the same time. On the aisles, the voussoirs are alternately deep yellow and straw yellow; the front has a very slight batter to counter the upward perspective; every window has some spare refinement of carved and cut brick to underline it. This is something much deeper and finer than a load of copied crockets.

The inside seems to have less mastery – to have gone a little flabby in just the same way as the interiors of those German churches of the 1840s. But it is whitewashed now, and whatever resilient effects Wild intended have been smoothed over with a genteel 'beg pardon'. They ought to be recovered, for this is not a building to be tampered with. Wild made his materials live as much as any sculptor.

Tulse Hill School (1956) and L.C.C. Old People's Home (1958), Upper Tulse Hill and Roupell Road   94 7A-109 IK

What was intended as an architectural comparison became transformed for me by accident. These two buildings, utterly different, comprise most of the good things in British modern architecture. The old people's home is cosy and kindly, two-storeyed weatherboarded wings around a central courtyard. The school is a nine-storey slab, built in those few years when the L.C.C. Schools Division seized hold of real grandeur. Four colossal staircase towers look downhill into London; the other side has a sheer glass wall, fading but renewable, with the concrete piers behind; structure and surface expressed as clearly as any modern theocrat could have wished – a system to live up to.

The accident was that of arriving at one thirty on a week-day afternoon. The old people were just finishing their lunch. The school-boys had finished theirs, and had spilled out on to the lawns by the literal hundred. Here, spanned from end to end, is the new London: and whatever may have been done in the East End, there can be no doubt that here there is an enormous improvement on the sniffy self-contained Victorian villas – themselves a crude speculation – which formerly colonized Tulse Hill.

Loughborough Junction 94 3B

No performance, so far, but tremendous promise. This place is a busy road junction in the centre of a triangle of high-level railway lines. Each road has a bridge a few yards along it. This unique signature could so easily be an enrichment instead of an embarrassment, the bridges accentuated and dramatized instead of disregarded. It is a natural centre, so that there would be no fear of tickling up an artificial relationship.

By contrast, the L.C.C.'s well-publicized Loughborough Road Estate, just beyond under the western railway bridge, is all artificial relationship. Most individual buildings are well detailed, the slabs look marvellous from the air. But on the ground, where it matters, the estate is no more than an arid geometrical exercise masquerading as a place.

St John, Vassall Road, Kennington 78 7B
G. E. Street, 1870

Street's overwhelming fault was heartlessness. But this marvellous building suggests that the trouble was not simple absence of feeling but an inability to feel except through the intellect. Here, he had a spatial theorem to resolve, almost a mathematical puzzle, and he did so not only successfully but with majesty. The church, aisled, has an eastern apse and two square-ended chapels. The nave had to be wide from function, the apse had to be narrow for effect. So Street canted in the end bay of the arcades, thereby giving oblique views through to the side chapels as well. The result is exactly right, the church as law-giver; and every other detail in it shows the same assurance which comes from having unravelled the puzzle. Red brick and stone, with every single ornament telling; it settles beautifully into the yellow late-Georgian streets around, which are as husky as Sid James. It was blitzed in the War and superbly restored by H. S. Goodhart-Rendel to mark Street's intentions even more clearly than before.

Sacred Heart Roman Catholic Secondary School, 94 1C
Camberwell New Road (just west of the railway bridge)

This is the small weekly saving that adds up to a fortune in the end. It is an honest, straightforward modern school that is weathering into nobility in the same way that the old warehouses did. I have seen it probably two hundred times, and it never fails to give a small, sure kick on my ammeter. You can get along from day to day without masterpieces, but you can't get along without this kind of quiet humanity, and lack of it is what makes most American cities into such desperate places.

St Barnabas, Calton Avenue, Dulwich   94 6E
Oliver & Leeson, 1894

Just round the corner from the careful arcadia of Dulwich Village, this
suddenly blows you two hundred miles north. St Barnabas is by
Newcastle architects, and has all the scale and freedom from pettiness
that the Gothic Revival meant up there. Even the materials are unexpected: red sandstone, and bricks the colour of the Ruabon startlers,
violent and vermilion. The inside sweeps you away with long arcades,
high aisles, and no division between nave and chancel. The style is
accurate Perpendicular; but the church is less concerned with style in
the self-conscious sense than any other of its time in London. By
comparison, every building by Bodley or even Sedding seems to be
settling points of detail in a weary, cultured voice. St Barnabas has the
same delicacy, but about five times the life-force.

Crown and Greyhound, Dulwich Village   94 7E

Think of all the things which you have been told don't make a pub:
wrought iron, leaded lights, plastic flowers, olde woodwork. Put the
whole lot in a big Victorian pub and you have a masterpiece, due
entirely to the superb life and taste (true taste, not 'good taste') of the
arranger – surely in this case the landlord or landlady. It is an act of
love, it bursts out all over – and has the same reverberating effect as
an untouched nineteenth-century pub, because it is set off by a similar
gusto. The reflections, the intricacy, the richness and depth, are all
there, achieved by means which are normally attached to gentility. It
is a wonderful place to be in, which is enough; but it is also a wonderful
torch to carry through the dark alleys of self-consciousness, fashion
and academism. Really be your real self, like this, and nothing can go
wrong. There is a mirror here with leaded lights on it. *Olé!*[7]

7. The exuberant mid-1960s décor has gone, but the pub's ample Victorian
proportions must have contributed generously to its atmosphere, and they still
do.

Dulwich Art Gallery, Gallery Road   94 7E
Sir John Soane, 1811–14

One of Soane's most original, least satisfying designs. For once, the
miraculous inventiveness is not connected up to an emotional purpose.
It remains an intellectual solution, a beautifully played game of chess.
It was severely damaged in 1944, and the restoration, though exact, is
oddly unsympathetic. It emphasizes the aloof man-hating part of Soane
which was dominant in the design anyway. So Dulwich is a great
curiosity, not a masterpiece.*

The collection is completely conventional but of high quality: the
kind of selection that would appear in any big country house but

* If you don't agree, and would like to look up an opposite view, read Sir John
Summerson, in *Georgian London*. It is one of the most incisive and brilliant descrip-
tions of a building that has ever appeared in print.

without the same distressing proportion of duds. And occasionally amongst the talent there is a real masterpiece like Watteau's *Bal Champêtre*, where the familiar portentous melancholy is screwed up to an unexpected pitch by flecks and gleams of light on the grey dress of the central figure.

Dulwich College, College Road   110 1–2E
E. M. Barry, 1866

This apparition is a fair candidate for the wildest nineteenth-century building in the whole of London [88] – and there is certainly some competition. It was designed by a son of Sir Charles Barry, and what father would have said is hard to imagine. Fragments of all styles and scales are thrown at each other with a kind of nihilistic joy. The central block has a tiny Jacobean lantern, enormous Gothic parapets above round-headed (Renaissance? – Romanesque?) windows. The corner turrets are quite soberly classical and several times too small. Hundreds of other buildings did this at the time, but this one has a crazy Dostoevskian gleam in its eye. It fixes you, and you feel uneasily that the architect has been driven to this by forces outside himself.

Opposite the main gate is Pond Cottages, the best part of old Dulwich, a mixture of brick and weatherboarding. The other pretty bits are too isolated, and the spaces in between too swamped with fussy chain-link fencing, to make the village into South London's Hampstead.

Sydenham Hill Station   111 3F
This is the quintessence of true suburbia, the illusion of rurality more effective here than the real thing would be. From College Road there is no sign of platform or signals, just a tiny entrance surrounded by trees. This is a covered way which drops down through a steep wooded valley to the station itself, the unlikeliness of the site reinforced by self-conscious boarding in. Only the walls and roof keep tigers from eating late passengers for the eight fifty-seven. At the bottom, the modest wooden platform buildings are part of a complete private world, even though buildings are peering over the side. A huge elliptical tunnel bores through towards Penge East, and God knows what animals live in *there*. Best in summer, naturally, but astonishing at any time.

Rye Lane, Peckham   95 1–2G
Now that the East End has been gutted by bombs and the wrong sort of rebuilding, Rye Lane is one of the few cockney streets left inside the county of London. Cockney life has gone outside instead – to Mitcham or Slough or Romford, where the pressure of kind people trying to live your life for you is not so strong. But Rye Lane must always have been one of the best [59 to 62]. It is an old road, hence

narrow and with a few bends in it, and unquenchable vitality has pulsed through it for ninety years. It is not only the Victorian detail that is full of life, but the jazz modern and the dayglo'd window displays. Everything fits except timidity, and a Rye Lane shopfront of 1933 matches a Rye Lane shopfront of 1963 better than either resemble their prototypes.[8] In the same way the display on a coster's barrow, a supermarket and a jeweller's shop are all part of the same family. It is not a dying family; in fact with luck it is a forecast, not a relic. A shoe shop advertises 'If it's new, we've got it'. And I was once in the Hope public house when a stallholder ordered a vodka and tonic, because it was the fashion. His mates stood around and chanted the *Volga Boat Song*, because all fashions are a bit of a giggle. That's the sort of place it is; and if this mixture is the Londoner's reaction to the high- and lowbrow pressures we are offered as a standard of living, then we're going to be all right.

8.   Today the standardized fascias of the multiples are much in evidence. Small businesses keep up a brisk trade, but do so, in many cases, behind cheap and shoddy shopfronts. Coster barrows and a market are hanging on in nooks and crannies.

Sceaux Gardens and The Denes, Camberwell
Borough Architect's Department, 1957–63   94 IE and 95 IH

These two should be seen together: they are about half a mile apart on the north side of that clogged main road that runs from Camberwell Green to New Cross.* Both are by Camberwell Borough Council's architectural department. They have the individuality and sense of place for lack of which most L.C.C. estates become abstract exercises. Many of the designers came in fact from the L.C.C. and clearly must have found that a smaller organization gave them deeper freedom. Sceaux Gardens is a good sensitive example of a conventional layout – high slabs, medium masionettes and a few low houses. What makes it special is the thick landscape which was taken over. It is not fenced in, either, but given over to the kids. So instead of geometry-and-lawns there is a living undergrowth, and the concrete slabs peer out like prehistoric animals. The kids will beat it down in the end, I fear, but meanwhile the magical transformation has happened, and an estate has turned into a place.

   The Denes by contrast would need a herd of elephants to demolish the landscape. It is an immense sequence of interlocking squares, with tall blocks to Peckham High Street and a nest of two-storey terraces behind. All the low squares are tile-hung, sometimes with joins that are apparently extraordinarily crude: yet the result is not a botched job but something amateurish and lovable. There is less do-it-yourself about the tall blocks, and one surpassing effect. The flats, forming a

* Sceaux Gardens at Peckham Road and Southampton Way; the Denes at Peckham High Street and Carlton Grove.

double square, are raised on stilts so that the ground floor is open. Inside the squares there is a formal landscaping on different levels: motion downwards. Diagonally, there are views out: motion sideways. And beyond on the south side there is the continuous traffic in Peckham High Street: motion back-and-forwards. Out of the central squares grow thin birch trees, echoed in the thin concrete supports all around: motion upwards – or rather, all other motion stilled and intensified to a vertical line. The flats, after this, seem weightless: the tyranny of a Dolphin Square transformed to a futurist dream. And not for the aesthetes and the clever boys, nor for an earnest social purpose, but just for the joy of it.[9]

9. Twenty years later, battered, littered, and vandalized, neither of them looks like a lasting success.

Licensed Victuallers Benevolent Institution, Asylum Road
1827 onwards 79 7H

Benevolent indeed, the most affable of London's many Grecian public buildings [63]. The designers knew when to stop, and did not try to belabour the passer-by with their knowledge of Attic precedent. Light pilasters and a singing wooden portico in the centre; the rest is left to the London stocks. More important, it gives each house a basic solidity and dignity. The scale is huge, but it never overpowers. Instead, the big windows and wide stretches of yellow brick radiate serenity and tranquillity. It must be a good place to retire to; and there is a pub just across the road if you feel homesick.

WANDSWORTH AND ROEHAMPTON

Wandsworth Common
92 6B

The edge of tomorrow's landscape, seen across the railway from Windmill Road [65]. A big, spiky Victorian school, which should never be demolished, framed by trees and by a collection of L.C.C. point blocks of the mid fifties. Trees in the foreground too, and a grassy bank running down to the rail tracks – the main line out of Waterloo, with a continuous shuttle of electric trains without heads or tails, like long green worms. An exciting place is just below the surface here – the combination of relevant elements into a unique signature which is the common ground of Blackheath, Bath and Stonehenge.

Mayfield School, West Hill and Portinscale Road, Wandsworth
91 5H
Powell & Moya, 1955

One of London's best new buildings, a place to see a hundred times and not tire of [66]. Yet the programme sounded like a short cut to lunacy, for it involved expanding an existing girls' school into one of the L.C.C.'s educational factories, catering for two thousand girls at a time. Powell & Moya managed to make the job seem effortless, with three-storey blocks fitted in amongst the existing trees and all the colours deep and mellow. It is easy and likeable, yet never leaves you in doubt for a moment of its inner strength.

Oatlands Court, off Park Side, Wimbledon   107 1F
L.C.C. Architect's Department, Housing Division, 1953

Just south of an awkward roundabout called Tibbets' Corner, at the north end of Wimbledon Common or the south end of Putney Heath – in other words a thoroughly shook-up site. When the L.C.C. came to these suburban roads in the 1950s they stirred up the social pudding properly and now the place doesn't know where to turn. This is the very first of the L.C.C.'s point blocks, and still one of the best: compact, not too tall (eleven storeys), with one of those plans, immediately lucid, which architects dream of, fuss over, but rarely achieve: T-shaped, with the staircase in the join. Each arm = one flat, Q.E.D. But the charm and humanity and, above all, the modesty, is not automatic but a personal contribution. To see what happens when it is left out, go half a mile south along Park Side. On the left is the same plan, the same number of storeys, but without the personal touches.[10] It looks awful.

10. Bisley House. Strictly it is two storeys taller.

Alton West Estate, Roehampton   90 6A–7C
L.C.C. Architect's Department, Housing Division, 1957–60

Go and look first, before you read anything about it. In the country of the blind the one-eyed man is king, and Roehampton is just that. The eye of technique and elegance in individual buildings is wide open; the eye of understanding and feeling for a total place is firmly shut. Architecture, like patriotism, is not enough. The estate has taken le Corbusier's ideas of buildings-in-landscape and the style le Corbusier used in his Unité blocks at Marseille and Nantes. Considering the density, they have been used with extreme cleverness; considering the total human situation, they are just a mechanical puzzle dressed up. Nothing grows and flows, nothing feels like London. There is just one moment where the vision really works – and, after having said all this, it is only fair to say that this is such a majestic setpiece that it is worth a special visit. Half way along Danebury Avenue, the main road through the estate, the ground rises on one side into a triangular green with big old trees, part of the landscape taken over from the old Roehampton. Around it, in magisterial order, are five of the Corbusian slabs – identical in design but not in appearance, because each is seen at a different angle. Here, and here only, the magic works. It could have worked everywhere.

EPSOM – CROYDON – BROMLEY – ELTHAM

[Epsom   O.S. 176 21:60

A terrible disappointment, both in its Georgian houses and its market place. A lot is due to twentieth-century stupidity, but faceless neo-Georgian buildings cannot explain everything. Neither the aristocratic associations of the Spa nor the earthy associations of the racecourse ever seem to have been properly expressed.]

Epsom Downs   O.S. 187 22:58

The ingredients are unbeatable, but man has done damn-all to help them along. Open downland – the first out of London, after all those little houses. Britain's best-known racecourse, on top of the hill, hence strings of horses in training, hence horsey pubs scattered around the heath like sultanas and vivid horsey customers to go in them. On the other side, there is a sweet Southern Railway terminus, at Tattenham Corner, and on a clear day there is a view as far as Westminster. Magnificent; an open space charged up with more vitality than most town centres. Yet the terrible drear grandstand of the 1920s almost kills it: if ever a building suffers from shell-shock, this does. Recover your spirits in the Downs Hotel, next door: small and genuine, not pretentious as you might think from the name, and a free house.[11]

11. Now the Rubbing House; still unpretentious nevertheless.

Cheam Old Church,[12]   131 6G
Lady Jane Lumley (d. 1577)

Cheam Old Church is only a fragment, left like an outsize potting shed in the churchyard of a nasty Victorian piece of work. Open the door, step on the threshold, and turn half right. Here, for once, is Elizabethan sculpture up to the level of Elizabethan drama: Lady Lumley, facing the altar kneeling on a hassock, backed by an exaggerated architectural perspective, the hands and face in bolder relief than the rest, growing out of the slab. Everything is balanced with Mozartian elegance and precision in this century of pudding effigies and ostentation. Move round and it falls to pieces; the design is composed to be seen from the west only, looking towards the altar. It feels like a stage set, special for just one moment in one position; but, then, really special.

12. Now known as the Lumley Chapel. 'Information about permission to visit the Chapel may be obtained well in advance of desired visit', says a notice on the door, circumspectly. The telephone number given is 01–642 0810. But Lady Jane can be glimpsed through a small grille in the door.

Beddington Lane   133 1–J etc.

A forlorn, atmospheric place south of Mitcham Common. Six grand cooling towers [68], the first battered farm out of London, pylons everywhere, houses all round the horizon, light industry in the foreground.[13] Yet out of these unexpected ingredients comes a poetry which is missing from most of the preserved villages around London. It is always four o'clock in late November here; but in the same positive way as in *Peter Grimes*. It is the inevitable counterpart to a million well-mown lawns and family saloons: a respectable suburban housewife surprised straining painfully on the w.c.

13. The cooling towers have been demolished. The area is a large, gloomy, low-density industrial estate.

St Michael, Poplar Walk, North Croydon[14]   134 1C
J. L. Pearson, 1871

Perfection is rare anywhere and perfection due to a reasoned balance rather than an inspired leap is maybe rarer still. So North Croydon is worth a visit if you don't look at any other buildings for the rest of the year. J. L. Pearson in his later buildings had the rare gift of being able to take the hackneyed theme of a late-thirteenth-century church and restate its essence exactly, with complete natural sweetness. That a hundred people had tried before and failed makes no difference; any achievement as good as this is beyond relative values. Perhaps the best of all his churches: red brick outside, pale yellow brick inside, apsed and vaulted, burning with a completely steady, cool flame. Off the south transept, Pearson built a chapel, a church within a church, with a complete octagon of columns – a devotional toy. Stand inside the octagon, and look out: every relationship between the multitude of arches, vaults, shafts and mouldings is completely harmonious. It is a Gothic cathedral, re-created without magic by the century which discovered evolution.

14. Open, other than for services, on Thursdays, 11.30–2.00.

Croydon Town Centre   134 2–3C–D

Worth seeing to sense two flavours which don't depend on any piece of architecture or planning. First, in being a city quite distinct from London yet depending on metropolitan tastes: the kind of atmosphere that you get much more strongly at Brighton. Typical, somehow, that the main station, which carries an enormous number of commuters, should be called contemptuously East Croydon and given a mean front, as though it was nothing to do with the town centre.

Second, the astonishing growth of tall office blocks in the last five years. Even the rebuilt deserts of central London have nothing like this wholesale transformation of rather staid Victorian lumps into rather shoddy modern boxes. Whatever the result, the flux itself is exciting; and there is potentially a magnificent new city waiting to be expressed here. Accidental clues to it can be picked up in the way that the new blocks crowd around the Victorian church of St Matthew in George Street, near the station.[15]

15. St Matthew's was finally crowded out and demolished. An office block called St Matthew's House marks the spot. A similar jostle has developed around St Michael's.

St Mary, Canning Road, Addiscombe   135 1F
E. B. Lamb, 1868

From outside, it looks like another twisty, small-scale Victorian neurosis. But the designer was E. B. Lamb, and here as at Gospel Oak he was obsessed with a huge timber roof. It looks as though what he was after was a colossal cruck construction with no walls at all, for the woodwork begins as low down as it possibly can. At the west and especially the east ends the walls are tolerated and harmonized. But in the transepts there is open war. The hammer-beams start low and cut across the stone gables; the gables reply with colossal detached marble columns. Meanwhile the timber lantern, the real centre of the church, looks down, unwinking, on it all – more like a freemason's symbol than anything Christian.

Eros House, Catford   96 7D
Owen Luder, 1962

A monster sat down in Catford, and just what the place needed. No offence meant: this southward extension of Lewisham High Street badly wanted stiffening. Now there is a punchy concrete focus ('you know, that funny new building') both close to and at a distance, from the desolate heights of the Downham Estate, where it stands straight up to the afternoon sun. Rough concrete is put through all its paces, from convex eaves on Sainsbury's[16] to a staircase tower which is either afflicted with an astounding set of visual distortions or is actually leaning. Again, no offence meant. Unlike many other *avant-garde* buildings, particularly in the universities, this one is done from real conviction, not from a desire for self-advertisement. The gaunt honesty of those projecting concrete frames carrying boxed-out bow windows persists. It is not done at you, and it transforms the surroundings instead of despising them. This most craggy and uncompromising of new London buildings turns out to be full of firm gentleness.

16. Now a Lewisham social services office.

68, 70, 72, 74 Wickham Road, Beckenham   126 3D
Francis Hooper, 1897

Four large houses of the eighteen-nineties, in a leafy part of South Beckenham. The architect or builder started with Norman Shaw's style at its prettiest, all tile-hanging and tiny oriel windows. Superimposed on this he rang the changes on half a dozen styles – big bow windows with plasterwork, curved bargeboards and one of those rude Tuscan porches that sprouted on libraries and police stations about then. It is beautifully done, with the sort of gusto that created Baroque churches; and there is more than that, for No. 74 is almost pure Shaw and as surely massed as Shaw at his best. Redevelopment is going on all around; it would be tragic if these houses went whilst there is so much that could happily be replaced.[17]

17. Nos. 68 and 70 went shortly after this was written. Nos. 72 and 74 have survived.

Bromley   127 2–3J

A battered milestone in the High Street says *London Bridge 10 miles*,[18] so you know what the score is, in general. The details turn out to be unexpected. Where most old towns near London have been swamped, and a few have maintained their shape against all comers, Bromley has metamorphosed into an appealing suburban fussiness – the cheerful disorder of a village shop blown up to serve a population of 70,000. The High Street widens into a small square (Market Place), and the middle is completely filled by a blubbery bit of pre-war half timbering. The style could not be worse – it is really horrible, not fun in any sense – yet in an odd way it fits because it bumbles along, complicates the views, and makes every corner into a fidget. Dunn's shop, opposite, translates fuss into concern, with a building (by Bertram Carter, 1956) which though purely modern has exactly the right feel for Bromley; unemphatic and undemanding, full of funny corners.[19] It includes the temporary war-time shop like the kernel in the nut.

Unfortunately, all this close-built fairyland is part of the A21 from London to Hastings. The through traffic must be taken out or bridged over before the road-wideners get abroad and bust the whole thing. Farther south the High Street is already a wide shopping parade, so that Bromley has the best of both suburban worlds side by side. It is worth going down to Harrison Gibson's, just off the west side,[20] to see how a design can be flashy and sensitive at the same time – there are plenty of fine-meshed extroverts in life. It was built in 1960, designed by Forrest & Barber. With luck it will not date, just as the Victorian pub doesn't date, and for the same reason: that both have caught the essence of display, which doesn't alter from century to century.

18. Gone.
19. Now split between Lasky's, Brentford's, Wallis and Jaeger.
20. In Ringers Road. It is now the Army and Navy furniture store.

Swan and Mitre, High Street, Bromley   127 2J

The Saloon Bar here is an Edwardian period piece, renovated (and largely re-created) by Ind Coope's architectural department, which is one of the few to be seriously concerned about keeping the character of old pubs. It teeters all the time on the brink of preciousness, but never quite falls in: and the tension is invigorating. Exactly mid way between tea shop and gin palace, with pretty fretwork patterns on the mirror frames and pretty brass tops to the velvet screens which split up the wall seating. Here is a real suburban pub (the sort of thing that the Bedford Park tavern ought to be but isn't). The notice requesting you not to take draught beer into the lounge, which at first seems to be an inexplicable convolution of English gentility, is in fact topographically just: this really is the place where you drink with your little finger crooked.[21]

21. Some of its gentility has gone along with the notice and the velvet screens.

Chislehurst
129 1G, etc.

This place is all interaction, not static vignettes. The static observer sees a triangular common with Victorian intrusions, and nothing composed or picturesque in a static way. But start taking diagonal walks through the scrub and everything comes to life. Grisly gabled white brick looms above birch trees and is marvellous, because of the shock. Anything can be round the next corner. At the south end, Chislehurst turns into real countryside. Opposite the parish church, a lane leads past a typical Chislehurst mixture (and a coarse modern school that makes you want to brain it for thick-skinned crassness). Just beyond the Catholic church, the ground ripples and falls away and Chislehurst meets an improbable rurality with gracious minglings, as though fields were round the corner of every suburban street. It is the suburban dream come true. In one sense it is illusion, for this is a tiny island of greenery, walled in by Petts Wood, which is nobody's idea of rural life. But, if you like, a flat horizon is an illusion too; here, as far as you can see is unspoilt fields, and that is enough. There is none of the draggle-tailed desperation that makes much of the Green Belt into a parody; this is proper, full-blooded coexistence. With care there could have been oases like this all over outer London, for this repository of a million dreams is about half a mile square. But it is the real stuff, not merely a green colour on somebody's map.

Chislehurst Church,
Lord Thomas Bertie (d. 1749) monument
129 1G

A dull done-up church; and this Palladian monument in the north aisle looks dull also, at first. But under the inscription is the most exquisite relief of a sea-battle, all foamy and fluffy. Rococo waves lap around a man-of-war carved with understanding as well as technical brilliance. Two others appear left and right, one in the lowest possible relief, the other made up of incised lines fading into the marble. It is the same pattern that created funny, lively vignettes at the feet of stuffy late-medieval effigies. One was done out of duty, the other out of joy.

King's Head, Bexley
101 7H

Instant attraction, like someone you meet at a party. You make a bee-line for it in the battered narrow street, the remnant of an old village, carrying ten times as much traffic as it should do. It feels exactly right:

unforced fresh-faced prettiness without any of the coyness or false sophistication of so many suburban pubs. A big weatherboarded cottage, with square Victorian extension at the front and modern dining-room at the back: all additions, not sweeping away. Public, Private and Saloon, just as they should be, straightforward and natural.[22] Of a lunch-time, the whole of Bexley seems to flow through it: the complexity of a place that is part suburb, part old local centre, part sharing the new autonomy of London's outer edges. You could film the town without ever stepping out of the door.

22. All one class now, as in most London pubs these days.

Hall Place, Bexley   101 6J

An astonishing place to find a few yards from the Dartford By-Pass and right beside a busy road (A223, Crayford–Bexley) full of industrial traffic. Facing the road, a demure Tudor courtyard, squared flint and brick.[23] Another courtyard of rustic seventeenth-century brick was thumped down on the back of it. On the south side there is a mad topiary garden that is like an exhibition of modern sculpture gone vegetable. There it all is, snoozing away as though the twentieth century had never happened. Greater London has a lot of miscellaneous manor houses scattered among the semis, and many of them aren't worth crossing the street for. But not Hall Place.

23. The good eighteenth-century gates were being restored when this entry was written.

[Red House, Bexleyheath[24]   100 4E
Philip Webb, 1859

A very famous building – William Morris's house, commissioned from the young Philip Webb as a deliberate reaction from everything implied in mid-Victorian design, a shock as big as Butterfield's first churches. But the achievement is nowhere near All Saints, Margaret Street. Webb simply could not make his volumes real enough or forceful enough. It is clearly a beautifully thought out design, honest and sensitive, but it stays in two dimensions. Photographs or drawings can give it a solidity which does not exist in the flesh, so its final influence matched the worthy intentions, which is perhaps fair enough. Anyone who makes a visit may get more of a shock from the mean subtopian[25] surroundings than from the building – Bexleyheath would be nobody's first choice as the ideal London suburb. It is in Red House Lane, south of the main street (A207).]

24. You can write for an appointment to visit on the first Saturday or Sunday in the month: Mr and Mrs Hollamby, Red House, Red House Lane, Bexley-heath (send stamped addressed envelope).
25. The word was coined by Ian Nairn in his special *Outrage* edition of the *Architectural Review* in 1955.

Eltham Lodge[26]   98 7D
Hugh May, 1663

Nothing great, but worth at least a sentimental journey to see the
grandfather of all Georgian brick boxes. The style here has been
imported almost straight from Dutch buildings like the Mauritshuis;
May had actually been with Charles II in Holland before the Restoration. Wren and his friends were to modify it and make a national
style of it. Here, for the first time, the ordinary country gentleman
shook off his gables and scrolls. A century and a half of genteel plainness lay ahead.

26. It is the clubhouse of the Royal Blackheath Golf Club, off Court Road, to
the east.

[Eltham Palace, Court Yard   98 7C
A lush hammer-beam roof of the 1470s, and two lush vaulted bay
windows. But also, a perfect example of the ornate heartlessness of
much mid-fifteenth-century architecture, especially court architecture. It was built for Edward IV. War Department property, open
only on Thursdays and Sundays.]

St Saviour, Middle Park Avenue, Eltham   98 6B
N. F. Cachemaille-Day, 1933

Apart from Greenford, the only good inter-war church near London.
Whereas that is idiosyncratically English, this could fit easily among
the best in Germany or Scandinavia. A dark, tense, springy hulk
amongst the semi-detached houses, projecting solidity where most
modern churches radiate emptiness. The squat oblong 'tower' at the
east end is actually the choir roof, taller than the nave. This is commor -
sense, and much more satisfying than the symbolic vertical features
which are in vogue nowadays. The effect inside is magisterial: spatial
movement finally brought to a grave halt around the altar, backed by
four narrow vertical strips of blue glass. Apart from the dark brown
of the bricks this is the only colour in the building, and no more is
needed. The rhythm of bricks laid zigzag runs through on various
scales as powerfully as the pointed arch does in a Gothic church:
literally in the wall-piers, pulpit and reading desk; metaphorically in
the cranked rhythm of the nave walls outside. Every bit of it seems to
be impelled and inevitable.

Well Hall Estate, Eltham   98 3C, etc.
Sir Frank Baines and others, 1916

This extraordinary place was designed in seven days as a rush job to
house war-workers for Woolwich Arsenal. It seems an odd recipe for
one of the best housing estates near London. Perhaps the architects
simply did not have time to air their preconceptions, and the local
officials their disastrous application of by-laws. Comfortable, cottagey

design, slate and stucco, taken out of the rarified atmosphere of the garden cities, always trying to see streets as entities rather than collections of units. The best part is Ross Way, running west from Well Hall Road at the junction of Rochester Way. This curves round a gentle slope with a raised footpath on one side and uses every possible trick of gables and end walls. Half way along, footpaths run off under archways as part of a fairy-tale composition which by an irony is more like a German village than anything else.

10 North London: Hampstead to Watford

Long grim terraces, four-storey shaking out to two, then to semis, and finally to everyone's castle: separate, garaged and privet-ringed. But all of it has a slight edge in monotony and gracelessness over the southern suburbs. This cuts across class divisions, and is equally evident in the old slums of Seven Sisters Road and the drawing-room cosiness of Finchley. It is as if all the northern qualities of scale and size had come south to become as aggressively alien as a Scotsman in the West End. Embedded in this flow is the unexpected rolling wildness of Hampstead Heath and its attendant villages: Highgate (true metal, tarnished), Hampstead (alloy), and the Garden City (well-intentioned repro). North London's main asset is the set of whale-backed ridges which run east to west from the Lea valley to the highish ground at Stanmore. Hampstead and Highgate depend on them; so do the period charm of Muswell Hill and the preserved prettiness of Mill Hill.

South-west of this, the land flattens out towards the Thames valley, with Harrow an isolated hummock; the suburbs become more friendly. Wembley is like a chirpy sparrow; Ruislip and Eastcote, farther out, are almost gracious.

HAMPSTEAD AND HIGHGATE

St Dominic's Priory (Roman Catholic),   44 5D
Southampton Road
John Chessell Buckler, 1874–83

The outside says little except that the building is very big and honest. The inside is magnificent: a real working-class cathedral, free from all the petty quibbles that beset nineteenth-century architects. Purpose came before style, here, and the effect is exactly that of one of the medieval Dominican churches in Italy – a transfigured meeting place. Very long and tall, with a simple wood vault and a lot of exposed yellow brick. The most impressive evidence of its personality is the way that the nineteenth-century fittings are part of it. The prickly reredos augments the apse instead of spoiling it; the sweep of the vault is underlined by the long iron walkway under the clerestory, just like the gallery of a reading room. It makes the Brompton Oratory seem petty.

St Martin, Vicar's Road, Gospel Oak   44 5E
E. B. Lamb, 1866

The outside, like Addiscombe (p. 183), is mildly odd. The inside, like
Addiscombe, has one of Lamb's crazy timber roofs capering all over
the crossing and coming down on to four free-standing clustered piers
like elephant paws. The roof itself seems more animal than mineral,
an entirely benevolent circus performer that has got out of hand but
won't savage the trainer. The result is luminous and happy, not in the
least strained.

Gospel Oak housing estate,[1]   44 5E
Lamble Street and Grafton Road
Powell & Moya, 1954

The architects made their reputation by winning the competition for
the vast Churchill Gardens estate in Pimlico. For all its virtues, that
is not a real place, whereas this much smaller group is. It uses just one
of the tall slabs of Pimlico, sited on a mound of made-up earth. At the
bottom, as though huddling for protection, are three sweet two-storey
terraces: proper houses with proper back gardens that are a riot of
rose-bushes after ten years. With the simplest of means, here is a real
relationship, not an arrangement on paper.

1. Now known as Barrington Court; part of the Lamble Street estate, which
in its turn is part of the comprehensive redevelopment south of Mansfield
Road.

Parliament Hill Secondary School, additions   44 4E
L.C.C. Architect's Department, Schools' Division, 1956

It is quite a job to see this at all. The old building blocks off the view
from Highgate Road, trees and a fence screen it from Parliament Hill
Fields at the back. A long raking view is possible from Lissenden
Gardens, to the south, and it is enough. The classroom block expresses
real personality instead of the drab group-work of later L.C.C. schools.
Showing wear and tear, but the basic force of the design will never be
dissipated.

Holly Village, Highgate   45 2F
H. A. Darbishire, 1865

An endearing group of hedgehogs in the angle between Swains Lane
and Chester Road. Built for Baroness Burdett-Coutts with all the
child-like bravado of Darbishire's late lamented Columbia Market
behind Shoreditch Church. Through the archway on the corner [69]
and there is a different world: eight very spiky houses, all different,
around a central green space. The idea comes from Nash at Blaize
Hamlet near Bristol, and the design has hardened, but also broadened
and toughened. Children romp about in the artfully planted traffic-
free space in a way that would disrupt the gentleness of Blaize. The

cottages in their preposterous angularity must be like having outsize toy animals around the playground. The plan is as sensible and convenient as a London square with its central garden; a whole suburb could be built up of units like this.

Highgate Cemetery
Stephen Geary, 1838

44 1E

There are better reasons for going here than to look at the grave of Karl Marx. This is the creepiest place in London; no Dickensian stretch of the river can match this calculated exercise in stucco horror, now itself decomposing.[2] The entrance is well downhill in Swains Lane, and at first the landscape is ordinary. But as you wind up the hill it becomes more and more overgrown, choked in winter by dead fronds with an unnerving resemblance to spanish moss. The landscape looks less and less like London, more and more like Louisiana. Then, with a shock like a blood-curdling scream, the Egyptian entrance shows up. Beyond it, the Catacombs, a sunken rotunda lined with stucco-faced vaults, gently deliquescent, crumbling away. Inside them, coffins on ledges. A familiar name like Carl Rosa on one of the vaults seems to accentuate the terror. Nothing seems real but death at its greyest and clammiest. The cemetery closes well before dark, and a good job too.

2. Karl Marx is in the eastern part of the cemetery. Admission to the older western part, described here, is by guided tour only, every hour on the hour, 10–4 daily in summer, 10–3 in winter.

Highgate Village

44 1E

Potentially a wonderful place both for spaces and buildings – and in a cheerful London way, too, with Georgian politesse and Victorian rudeness side by side. But ruined by traffic and by a weary flow of municipal 'improvements' – asphalt and crazy walling – which is at its worst in Pond Square. The place could be transformed without altering anything but the surface of the floor.

The Archway, Archway Road

45 1G

Nash's farewell to London, slung across the Great North Road on the Hornsey boundary. The arch itself has been rebuilt, so that the main-road traveller does not get much fun. But from the top, along Hornsey Lane, it is spectacular. An apparently ordinary suburban road crosses a small, apparently ordinary bridge. But instead of rail tracks there is a leafy chasm with heavy lorries roaring along at the bottom of it, plus a view over the whole of Central London. Accident has helped Nash's Midas touch by putting St Paul's smack on the axis of Archway Road, and this is the most surprising and exhilarating distant view of it in London.[3]

3. It is still visible, but has to contend with a seemingly solid block of City skyscrapers to its left.

Highpoint 1 and 2, North Road   28 7E
Tecton & Lubetkin, 1936 and 1938

Famous names, with pictures in every history of modern architecture. The reality is a bit different. Highpoint 2 now seems to be just a trial run for the kind of confused pattern-making that ended up in the Festival Hall. But Highpoint 1 can still provide, a little diminished, the thrill of the thirties, where its contemporaries now provide nothing at all. This is what it was like to build fresh and new and fight the forces of reaction: an emotion transmitted directly, through the repeated ripple in the concrete facings to the balconies. Highpoint 1 would be a decent building in any style, for deeper reasons. One of them is that you can infer the bones of the building directly from the building without ever looking at a drawing: a Lorraine cross, with staircases at the two joins serving a flat in each arm. The crazy roofline of TV aerials adds our own comment on the brave new world, but the building can take it.

Mansfield Heights   28 5D
Metropolitan Police Architect's Department, 1956

A group of police houses and flats, at the north end of Archway Road where the pattern of North London finally disintegrates. The site is an awkward wedge sloping up from Aylmer Road to Great North Road. It has been treated like a person, a living partner in the architectural process. So the result is a living place, where Roehampton by comparison is a clever bit of clockwork. Best to start at Aylmer Road with two-storey houses near the road, beautifully grouped. In the centre, a path leads up through the site, first past three-storey flats, end on, then to a six-storey block at the top. So everything builds up naturally. The whole scheme was implicit in the site all the time and grows out of it like rocks and trees.

Hampstead Garden Suburb   27 5–6H–K
Sir Raymond Unwin, c. 1910

The suburb mostly lives up or down to its reputation, insufferably cosy details allied to a central blankness of imagination which shuffled the shops out to the edges, then refused to build a pub and filled the Central Square with churches and institutes. But when Sir Raymond Unwin finally got around to recognizing that man had got to satisfy some of his material needs somewhere, he (or one of his assistants) provided a masterpiece. The shops are in Finchley Road (about No. 800) on the west edge of the suburb, a block on either side of Hampstead Way. Neo-Tudor, but with all the conviction and solidity that the twee private houses lack. Tall hipped gables like crane-hoists tower above the road, and the side elevations to Hampstead Way are brilliant asymmetrical compositions. This side of the northern block (Temple Fortune House), with its low tower, is one of the finest pieces of design in the whole of London: sensitive, finely balanced, yet never for a moment losing hold of common sense. It has all the ingenuity of Philip Webb's Red House but this time truly carried out in three dimensions.

St Jude, Hampstead Garden Suburb 27 6K
Sir Edwin Lutyens, 1908

By Lutyens, like the rest of that bird-brained Central Square. The church is full of coy perverseness which ruins the inside and makes the outside unbearably giggly – 'Look at me, I'm mixing Gothic and classical, look at me, look at me.' You want to give Sir Edwin's precocious bottom a good clout. Yet out of it all, this puzzling child produced a magnificent steeple, building up strong and sure through the belfry to an octagonal top and a bulky spire. It stamps the suburb from any angle and any distance; the way in which styles and details are subordinated to and sublimated by the total idea of steeple is up to Hawksmoor's level – yet there is no attempt to copy Hawksmoor, no precedent at all. But what about the frippery of the rest? Was it a necessary fetish, like high-heeled leather boots?

The Spaniards 44 IB

Hampstead pubs are usually not much fun: they are like a private society whose performance is not worth the entrance fee – the intellectual equivalent of the Soho strip-tease club. But The Spaniards, at the very top end of the Heath, gets a solid butt from its cockney visitors, at least in fine weather. The mixture shakes down very well; the warren of dark rooms, the big gardens, and this mingling of ages and classes make it more like a German beer-garden than anywhere else I know in London. The atmosphere has all grown together, just like the slap-happy brick and weatherboard walls of the pub. The one thing which will kill it is wholesale redecoration. Good beer, the serious drinker's standby in foreign parts: Draught Bass and Worthington E.

The Spaniards would be a memorable place anyway: opposite the pub is a small square tollhouse, now a splendid obstruction. It reduces a busy London cross-route to a single car-width at a blind bend. The road, all of a sudden, is not everything: and so far from being wished away in the name of progress, local opinion wants to keep it. The cars, of course, sort it all out, as they will if they are given the chance and not beaten into bloody-minded truculence with too many rules.[4]

4. The Spaniards has kept its atmosphere, its tollhouse and its Draught Bass.

Heathbrow 44 IB
Higgins & Ney, 1961

A few yards nearer Hampstead is a gravelly lane, hard to pick up, called Spaniards End. Down it, on the left, is Heathbrow, one of the best recent houses in London. The concealed back and sides are for living in: the front is a masterly sliding together of brick shapes, almost blank. Vanbrugh would have been proud of this one.

Kenwood House   44 1C
Robert Adam, c. 1766
George Saunders, c. 1795

Adam in his fiddling, over-cultivated mood, languidly sketching in a pilaster or two, a nice set-off for the landscape. The library, at the moment closed for redecoration, is a sugary masterpiece that in anyone else would have become over-ripe.[5] Adam used his favourite trick of screening an apse with columns to splendid effect here, providing an ante-room which means that you are in the same space yet separated at the same time. The other memorable space in the house is utterly different – the Marble Hall, part of George Saunders's additions of 1795: a beautiful crisp bit of neo-classic design. The vaulted ceiling is pierced to give a circular gallery on the upper floor and reveals a circular top-light far above that.

The collection (the Iveagh Bequest) is a long way removed from a country-house job lot. There is one of Rembrandt's most grandiose and level-headed self-portraits, and a Romney (*Lady Albemarle*) which balances exactly on the knife-edge of tender sympathy without sentimentality. Above all, there are two drumroll full length Gainsboroughs, in the Orangery. One (*Lady Briscoe*) is in his party-piece style: imperious figure, glistening grey dress, wonderful landscape behind in dashed-off diagonal brushstrokes. In the other (*Countess Howe*) figure and background are treated with equal sympathy and the result is a wonderful to-and-fro like the relation between house and park in a Repton landscape garden. Diaphanous wrap matches diaphanous trees, the honest face matches the honest clouds. A wonderful performance, as completely English as the Heath.

5. It has been deliciously restored in pink and blue.

Hampstead Village   44 3–4A

Hampstead is a bit of a joke, though many of its inhabitants are deadly serious about it. As soon as a picturesque street or alley gets well started and you can begin to live the refined life, along comes a great hospital or board school or block of tenements. Clatter and thump, you pick up the pieces and start again. It is not an amusing or exciting contrast, either, just head-on conflict which ends in stalemate. But socially, it has undoubtedly saved Hampstead from becoming intolerably precious.

The maze of alleyways and passages is still all there, behind the heavy through traffic in Heath Street, but only once does it add up to something. This is in Holly Mount, and the way to get to it is up a set of steps between 73 and 75 Heath Street, near the Cruel Sea.[6] The staircase winds round, giving you a tiptoe peep down Rosslyn Hill, and then deposits you in a tiny hilltop square, apparently a hundred miles from the lorries, with a good pub (the Holly Bush) which has been left alone by the bright boys. Here, the traditional idea of Hampstead really comes alive. But a few steps farther, towards Mount Vernon, and the colossal bulk of the National Institute for Medical Research[7] shatters this highly-strung small-scale elegance. The whole place is a china shop with a good many wild bulls in it.

6. Now the Nag's Head.
7. Now, more sinisterly, the National Institute for Biological Standards and Control.

Church Row, Hampstead   44 4A

Here is the complete freedom which results from submission to a common style. A rough gentleman's agreement about heights and size – nothing so rigid as a fixed street line or fixed cornice level – and you can do what you want. Most of these houses of 1720–50 did it in brick, but No. 5 is outspokenly bow-windowed and weatherboarded, and fits in perfectly. As a setpiece, a bit of stage scenery running up to the spiky tower of the church, the Row suffers from too many parked cars, maybe also from the line of trees up the middle which breaks the space. But the sides are just about perfect. The south side is austere and formal, and still with a great variety of detail. No need for standard front doors, or fear that the owners' curtains will 'destroy the architectural composition'. The north side is much more ribald: more like the sergeants' mess, that is, what with that No. 5 and the equally odd No. 8, which is only two bays wide but taller than anything else.

39 Frognal   44 5A
Norman Shaw, 1885

Shaw built very many houses in London, and all bar this one have their inventions vitiated by a cold-hearted manipulation and unconcern whether the artful counterchanges of surface had any feeling in them. This one is quite different – easy and unpretentious, growing naturally and informally at the owners' convenience. Prettily tile-hung, windows at all angles and of all shapes, yet underneath it a keen eye for the relation of all these apparent accidents. Appropriately enough, it was built for Kate Greenaway.

St Stephen, Rosslyn Hill[8]   44 5C
S. S. Teulon, 1876

Here he is again, weaving another tapestry full of his strange ideas. Purple brick, here, and three kinds of stone: a great hulk on a sloping site with a brooding and bulgy central tower made into a macabre Gothic dirge, moody and flashing with unexpected poetic juxtapositions: weathered sandstone columns, or a gristly roundel of sculp-

ture, or cheesy voussoirs eaten away so that they are now inset to
the bricks. It seems to be locked, nowadays, but the inside is worth
seeing if you get the chance: all Teulon's perverse elements combined
in a harsh Hallelujah, raw with life to the top of the notched and
horseshoe-shaped chancel arch.

8. Disused, derelict, and boarded up. Plans for its future are uncertain.

Downshire Hill and Hampstead Heath   44 4B–C, 3A–B, etc.

The best bit of Georgian Hampstead. Inflected half way down by the
delightful front of St John, which strides out from the wedge-shaped
corner site as though it had arrived fresh that morning from Naples.
Built in 1818, and still a proprietary chapel: the sunny, uncomplicated
charm has affected the stucco and yellow brick around and it manages
to escape the bijou archness which bedevils so much of Hampstead.
The special thing about Downshire Hill is that the Heath is beckoning
at the end of it, grass and trees shaded in like a Gainsborough, curving
uphill out of the view, promising release ...

... and providing it. This is the best entry to the Heath, because
you lose the houses straight away. No wonder it is well-loved and
well-used: the romantic abrupt scenery, a bit like the hilly parts of
Shropshire, provides maximum effect in the smallest area. It is useless
to nibble at the edges, because you only get the inevitable tatty feeling
of over-used turf, and maybe disappointment that there are no spectacular views over London. Instead there is Nature fitting you like a
glove, never uncomfortable, just made for healthy walks and happy
dogs. If you go from south to north, the walk can end in the climax of
the lawns of Kenwood House – nature smoothed over for a few yards,
but with thickets and boskiness always ready to encroach. Then west
to the Vale of Health, to find an epigram of what makes the Heath part
of London: a nest of houses with grass all around, crammed into a fold
of the ground under Heath Street. Alleyways burrow into the middle
and the cul-de-sac road winds round the outside as best it can. But as
well as the studios, there are brash Victorian terraces and the
fairground. Like the Spaniards pub just up the road, it belongs to the
cockneys too.

NORTH-WEST LONDON

St Augustine, Kilburn (corner of   59 2K
Rudolph Road and Kilburn Park Road)
J. L. Pearson, 1879

Pearson was a clever architect and knew it; sometimes his technique
for creating instant piety tempted him to substitute the latter for the
spirit. But not here; in this weightless and fragile building every part
has had pride honed away like surplus flesh. Everything that is left is
truly humble and reverent – a remarkable thing in such a big building

which uses such a showy style, shafted and vaulted. Spatially fragile, too; what seems to be a single space turns out to have transepts, disguised by a walkway which runs across the entrance, that are almost small churches in themselves. Passageways tunnel behind the altar, a luminous screen and rood is stretched across the entrance to the chancel. It is all membrane, purged of grossness but not of the common touch. St Augustine is in a poor area at the back of Kilburn High Road and could easily have tried to put one over on the shabby streets, as so many London churches do. But instead, everything is comfortable and welcoming outside. It is a kind of guarantee that the ethereal glitter inside is not spurious.

The Crown, Cricklewood Broadway   43 4F

The bones of a splendid place. Buses turn round in the pub forecourt, and the pub itself is big enough to take in customers by the busload – a huge Victorian gin palace, well kept up by the brewers (Ind Coope) and full of Irishmen. This is a relationship every bit as valid as the old country group of church and manor-house. So far, here, it is just happy accident, but it could be more.[9]

9. Buses no longer turn in the forecourt (they would crush the parked cars), and the pub is still only bones – big, raw, basic, and male. Unlikely to be developed, unless as a steak house.

Wembley Park   41 4G–H, etc.

The 1951 Festival has almost disappeared, but Wembley, of 1924, lingers on. They built those exhibition buildings to last. Quite apart from the stadium, the site is full of concrete ancillaries as bull-nosed as a 1920 Morris, now full also of light industry and warehousing. One is still called the Palace of Arts. And there's more: on the left of Olympic Way, the main avenue to the stadium, a concrete bridge moulders away among weeping willows and beer cans. Crisp and angular, it must be one of the best things we did in the twenties – true English modernism, not an echo of Maillart – and it deserves a better fate. Behind, in Third Way, a street of conglomerate smells and squalid fantasy – shot-silk and mud – the G.E.C. Hirst Research Centre turns out to be gravely pedimented with the royal arms on top and Wembley lions guarding the entrance – six of them.[10] It is worth a visit anyway, for the *frisson*: it could be an outstanding place, the fantasy world of the international exposition matched by the fantasy world of modern electronics – and enlivened by those bloody-minded Middlesex 'factory operatives' who are the despair of politicians because they persist in voting for their own ends instead of someone else's beliefs. They're all right, Jack.

North of the grounds is Wembley Park station, an easy tube-step from Baker Street. North of this again, the Wembley Town Hall and a really lively new pub, the Torch, which is as good a place as anywhere in London to feel the real temper of 'ordinary England' in the 1960s.[11]

Very nice it is too. The whole area has the dimensions, scale and potentiality of a city, a natural for comprehensive redevelopment where so many aren't. What Wembley thinks today, Parliament is going to have to legislate for tomorrow.

10. The Palace of Arts and the Palace of Industry are still living their half-life of industrial decay on one side of Olympic Way. The other side has been taken over by big, gaudy, cash-and-carry warehouses. The concrete bridge and the gravely pedimented building (once the British Government Pavilion) have been demolished, although two of the Wembley lions have found their way to the wildlife park at Woburn Abbey. Only the stadium has both survived and prospered.
11. Still there, big and quite friendly, but its heady days in the 1960s are only a memory.

Harrow-on-the-Hill   39 IJ

At large, Harrow means one thing – the school. And alas, in this ridge-top part of a very large borough, you can never get away from it. Eton College strikes a balance with the High Street: Harrow swamps its village with Victorian buildings as ponderous as company reports. The result is far from ugly, but it has muddled the *genius loci* to a point where it will probably never be sorted out. On a flat site it would hardly matter. Here, there is always a haunting might-have-been.

Basically, Harrow is a hill town, and the main street snakes along the top of the ridge up to the church. School buildings have broken the chain, and only fragments are left. Spectacular fragments, though: the medieval lead spire surrounded by trees, sudden views through archways across ten miles of suburbia (the archway that leads to the Bursar's office points straight at Earls Court).

The college asked all the right people: Burges, George Gilbert Scott, Herbert Baker. Yet somehow they always got the wrong answers. Only one building is worth seeing, and from the first glimpse of it you can see what went wrong with the others: they are just large shapes with curly detail stuck on. The quiet integrity and bricky solidity of E. S. Prior's Music School of 1891 puts them all to shame; Philip Webb's style, done by a man with more architectural talent than Webb. You get to it down Football Lane, which is on the map but has no street name,[12] only a signpost indicating a public footpath to Watford Road. On the way, Basil Champneys's Butler Museum at least wears its stuck-on detail with a swagger: the oriel windows high up on the downhill side are a fine bit of buccaneering.

12. It has now.

Houses, corner of Buck Lane   25 5K
and Highfield Avenue, Kingsbury

That an Englishman's home is his castle is one rather contemptuous justification of suburbia. The sneer rebounds here, because the four dwellings at this road junction are highly castellated. In a quiet semi-detached part of Kingsbury, some splendid eccentric heard the call of the folly. So there are stuccoed battlements, baronial steps, and also much wilder details that would not be out of place in Gaudi's Barcelona. Like most true follies, more than a joke and more than a whim: a real expression of the dreams of individuality which sent people flocking here in the 1920s along with the Underground.

Little Stanmore Church, Whitchurch Lane 12 7A
John Price and Louis Laguerre, 1715

It looks like an ordinary suburban road with an old village church left high and dry. But this is no ordinary church, inside. A long dark tunnel, flickering with *grisaille* paintings, the organ at the east end behind the altar, framed in a gorgeous wooden arch just as though it were in a theatre. Behind that, painted clouds, and indirect light coming in from one side. It is a true Baroque illusion, dark and lustrous, where Germany would have been all white-and-gold and Italy would have drowned the effect in a welter of gilt paint. To call it Handelian would be more than a cliché: this was in effect the private chapel of Canons, whose site was about half a mile to the north, and that most English of Germans often played here. What an illusion that must have been, the superb square-cut phrases and tender improvisations coming apparently out of the clouds.

If you turn left just before the altar, you reach an ante-chapel and then the mausoleum of the builder of Canons. James Brydges, uncomfortably Roman, displays himself in an unfeeling big monument by Grinling Gibbons, who had no flair for stone. One of the mourning ladies now holds a posy of plastic flowers, which is fair comment. But detailed criticism takes no account of the incredible atmosphere of tatty grandeur, the slapdash but convincing frescoes. The grand illusion works, and works in a British way – deep, solid, reverberating. I wish we had more like it.[13]

(The paintings were done by Laguerre, far better here than else-where: the shell of the church was designed by John Price, but his other buildings suggest that the decorative scheme would have been beyond him.)

13. The church has been beautifully and lovingly restored: no more tattiness, no more plastic flowers. Open (other than for services) only on Saturday and Sunday afternoons, when you are guided round by immensely knowledgeable members of the congregation.

Stanmore Old Church 11 5G

Stanmore, even now, seems to be more trees than houses. Behind a mean-minded Victorian church, the ruins of the old one are dissolving away in gentle melancholy. It was built in 1631 by Archbishop Laud to be the old religion revived, very Gothic, though using up-to-date bricks. Now it is roofless, with a mouldering Victorian tomb in the nave, and a triste churchyard around. But lovable, not horrible: brambles and roses growing up to the walls and over the mass-produced headstones: soft, tender dissolution, the kind of end that most people would wish for. This seems to be recognized, for this is a controlled wilderness, with a winding path scythed through [70]. Long may it stay so. Gray's *Elegy* should have been written here, instead of at Stoke Poges.

Grimsdyke
10 4B
Norman Shaw, 1872

Harrow Weald is a leafy place but suburban, with concrete lamp standards peering out between the shrubbery. Nice, but nothing to bite on. Just north of it, on the Bushey road (A409), there is a pub, the Hare. Turn left, along a lane called Old Redding, and you are suddenly right out in the country. It is pure illusion, for this ridge-top is mid way between Harrow and Watford; but it is proper woods and open fields, not the horrible compromised pylon-mesh of the so-called Green Belt east of Watford. There is a proper country pub, the Case is Altered, and a gravel standing to look back at Harrow-on-the-Hill. And, on the other side, facing north, is Grimsdyke itself, one of Norman Shaw's best early houses, now a rehabilitation centre.[14] Tile-hanging and half-timber are manipulated in a mechanical way, but the parts mean something even if the whole doesn't.

14. Now the Grimsdyke Hotel.

Lululand, Melbourne Road, Bushey
O.S. 176 13:95
H. H. Richardson, 1885

Melbourne Road runs off the London road a little south of the centre of Bushey. A few yards along it, on the left, is the local British Legion headquarters: a great entrance door and a stretch of wall. It is all that is left of the house designed for the successful Victorian painter Herkomer by H. H. Richardson. He was the best American architect of his generation and this fragment is his only work in Europe. Straight away, from this one superb doorway, you can feel genius rather than an extreme talent such as Norman Shaw's. The bumpy sandstone voussoirs are expressing every arch as well as this one: the lintel with its vibrant interlace ornament represents every support as well as this particular one. All the parts are emblematic, related to life, not to professional expertise.

Watford
O.S. 176 11:96

Here is the first stop on the Birmingham line versus a quiet country town. No doubt which was bound to win through in the end: the surprise is that Watford, which became a suburb in the 1870s, stayed countrified until the 1950s. Now the old parts are going under and the town is unhappily in-between. The new parts are despicable in the

High Street,[15] and just bearable in the office blocks which now line the long avenue to the main line station (Clarendon Road).[16] Yet for all the desperate results, there is no way back. Watford must, now, become another Croydon, a small city embedded in the big city. It is no fun to look at, yet an exciting feeling to experience, the culmination of a long groundswell which was inevitable from the first day that fast trains ran from Watford Junction to Euston. It is quite different from the indiscriminate rape of places like Hornchurch.

The church is one of those dreary case-hardened flint jobs which dog the Home Counties. But inside, in the north chancel chapel, are two famous early monuments to the Morison family by Nicholas Stone, fresh air blown into the stale trade-union atmosphere of the Southwark carvers. Like the first modern buildings, they were more important for what they did than for what they were; they look bleak enough and official enough now, overall. But the kneeling figures at the side of the earlier (right-hand) monument, made in 1619, are the kind of sheer poetry that burst out of Stone intermittently throughout his life: sparkling mannered poses, allegory and person at the same time.

15. The commercial part of the High Street is partly pedestrianized, partly limited access, with a one-way system whizzing all round it. In general, the post-1966 innovations are pleasanter and more interesting than those of slightly pre-1966. An engaging touch is the way Exchange Road skims over the pedestrianized part of High Street at not much more than head height.
16. They now include a post-modernist building, prominently dated 1982, with a pitched roof and polychrome brickwork to harmonize with the Victorian-Byzantine Baptist church next door – a sign of the times.

Moor Park
Sir James Thornhill, 1720 onwards   o.s. 176 07:93

A terrible design, thick and blundering, the kind of thing which gave Baroque architecture a bad name. Lord Burlington's restraint would be a relief after this. But worth going to see (on Monday afternoons in the summer) for the glorious painted and stuccoed entrance hall, the whole height of the house. Painted rooms in England are usually a joke: gloom and gilding and vapid goddesses. There is plenty of this here for comparison in the saloon (by Thornhill)[17] and the stairwell (by F. Sleter of Venice). But the hall is sparkling, the arabesque ornament flowing from marble to stucco to wall paintings, everything heightened, not depressed, by the colour scheme of gold, white and royal blue. There is no attempt to make the room itself move: this stucco embroidery reinforces the shape instead of dissipating it, so that this is in the grand four-square English tradition of the Double Cube room at Wilton. Yet the artists were all Italian: Artari and Bagutti for the plasterwork, Amigoni for the painting, which was done c. 1730. Here for once is something which can really stand up to eighteenth-century palaces on the Continent.[18]

17. Now known as the Thornhill Room.
18. Open to the public Mondays to Fridays, 10–4, and Saturdays, 10–12 noon (inquire at reception).

Rickmansworth Aquadrome   O.S. 176 05:93

This is the kind of thing that living in a city-region could mean. London needs not one or two such but several hundred. The Aquadrome is a pair of lakes formed from worked-out gravel pits in the Colne valley just south of the friendly, nondescript little town. A municipal aquadrome sounds like a vast outdoor public bath. In fact these lakes are unspoilt, leafy places where you can sail or fish or bathe:[19] land already industrialized, reclaimed, and made into something more than a paper amenity. The process could go much farther – landscaping to screen the few urbanized views, for astonishingly enough the east side of the Colne valley is still green; extension north and south to make a complete linear chain of riverside and lakes. Meanwhile, here is the idea, all complete, like a ripening seed; and God bless Rickmansworth for not larding this place with asphalt paths and notices.[20] Two or three crude touches would destroy this delicate balance.

19. A prohibition on bathing was imposed in 1986.
20. There are a few near the entrance, but they peter out.

BARNET AND ENFIELD

Muswell Hill Broadway   29 3F

Very much of a place, though it may take some getting used to. At first it seems like any other late-Victorian centre in North London. Then the naïve charm of the shopping arcades seeps through, each announcing itself to the central roundabout with a pompous little flourish. The straight part is just the right length and the church at the end is just the right height. All of the streets seem to be called Muswell Hill Broadway. The Express Dairy, dated 1900, is Art Nouveau and a delight.[21] And most of all, any of the streets on the south side lead to a steep drop, a hundred and fifty feet down to Crouch End and then up to the heights of Finsbury Park. A period piece of unruffled cheerfulness; when the suburbs were new, there were green fields next door and war was still rather jolly.

21. Part of it was a tea shop, which has been converted, not entirely sensitively by the look of it, into the Swiss Chalet public house.

Hendon Place, Parson Street, Hendon   27 3F

This mix-up could only happen on the edge of a big, old, complicated city. At the back of a plain eighteenth-century house[22] is a huge pediment, done with the utmost richness: this certainly came from Wanstead, and is supposed to have come from Canons – a Rolls-Royce handed on from millionaire to millionaire. On one side of it is a half-timbered gable, very 1930s. On the other, some new flats, by Owen Luder (see Catford, p. 183), whose chunkinesses look as though they derive from the needs of the flats rather than the aesthetic fads of the architect. The combination of these three is hilarious and desperate at the same time: a tragi-comic modern play which displays our situation exactly and tellingly but doesn't offer any glimmer of a way out.

22. Now the Hendon Hall Hotel.

Mill Hill
13 5J

A lot of pretty things, but they only come to something around the pond.[23] Here, after a continuously urban ride, you come upon an unspoilt piece of unsophistication cared for by sophisticates. It plays shepherdesses very prettily. Or almost: the weatherboard cottages next to the low brick almshouses are derelict, and will be replaced instead of being done up by television producers. If the new buildings are badly done this little place will be destroyed, like a boor destroying a delicate conversation with platitudes.[24] Will Mill Hill survive? There's certainly enough lolly on this ridge-top to preserve a dozen villages.

23. i.e. Mill Hill village, by the junction of the Ridgeway and Milespit Hill.
24. The cottages were replaced by new houses. They were designed to fit the village, but are already looking like 1960s period pieces.

Totteridge
14 1A–C

More of a phenomenon than a village. It is a ridge-back south-west of Barnet, and the views are green in both directions. North Finchley should show up on the southern skyline, but doesn't, and the miracle of the Green Belt has worked again. The country here has the same bones as Enfield Chase and in fact is far better than the bedraggled fields farther out, sprinkled with pylons, motorways and the chimneys of loony-bins.

Totteridge village, at the east end of the ridge, is restrained, expensive, and not really remarkable except for the sweet weatherboarded tower of the church, built 1790 and not looking a day over eighteen. It is what happens west of this that is astonishing. A strip of green winds along the ridge: wavy sides, big trees, sometimes five yards wide and sometimes fifty. There is a long pond. Behind are the houses of a hundred drawing-room comedies: 1910-ish, big, comfortable and in fact very nice indeed. And this dream goes on for a whole mile.[25] The curtain is always rising on the maid setting the table for tea. In Wimbledon there is no more than this, and it remains a social document. Here there is a contract with the landscape and it becomes a marvellous place, unlike anywhere else near London. Signposts for crows would read Barnet 1, Edgware 2.

25. And still goes on today, more or less, give or take the occasional very expensive new house. But the dream is not entirely untroubled, to judge from

the incidence of locks, chains, gate-phones, warning notices, and guard dogs which stand four feet high at the shoulder. Stroll around here too inquisitively, and you might be arrested or savaged, if you aren't mown down by the ceaseless traffic first.

Monken Hadley   4 2C–E

Barnet is a hill town with an imposing church, but has never found itself, perhaps due to the traffic. At the north end the shops stop suddenly and with the first countryside out of London the landscape changes dramatically into a long diamond-shaped green – Hadley Green. The west side is wavy with enough big trees to contain the suburban houses behind; the east side is firmer, with a mellow selection of Georgian houses. This would be enough; in fact it is only the beginning of Monken Hadley. The east side curves round, narrows, sheds the grass and becomes a village street, leading up to the church tower. There, it skips round past a disarming set of Gothic cottages and opens out again to something completely different – Hadley Common, big and shaggy, with a wood at the end and big houses hidden behind trees on the sides. All the time, Common and Green are balanced in the mind's eye, this which is so *here* was done differently *there*. A path through the churchyard short-circuits the road and winds the tension even higher. Hadley's last flourish is the oddest of all. Take the right fork at the beginning of the Common, going east. It leads eventually to a point where the forward road is a cul-de-sac and you have to turn right through a gate with a signpost to the Hadley Hotel. Lush private grounds? No; bang, immediately into the streets of Victorian Barnet. This is diving straight into London with a vengeance.

This is one of the most eloquent village sequences in England, let alone within fifteen miles of London. What will wreck it is false pretension. Three neo-Georgian puddings have been put up here in the past few years, screened by trees and walls, but still bad enough. Any more would be a disaster.

Enfield   7 3H–J

Enfield is quite different from the rest of Middlesex. It feels like a country town, and not even a country town close to London. To go with it is a cantankerous country-town shape which would be memorable anywhere. There is a short busy shopping street with a small square market place at one end. Behind it is the church, and behind the church, reached by an alley, is a pedestrian's world of trees, school buildings and Victorian cosy cottages. Holly Walk runs around the back of the whole town to meet up with the northern end of Gentleman's Row. This is Enfield's West End, and is one of the best sequences of town houses anywhere near London. The path runs between house and front garden, a mesmeric blend of leaves and old stock brick. It leads back to the other end of the High Street, so that the whole plan is tied in a knot, or given a signature. There are many tourist centres that would be lucky to have as much to them as this.

And yet, incredibly, this unique place is in danger. One arm of a ring road is proposed to run right across Holly Walk, sever the tendons, and leave the parts useless and inorganic. Alas, this is done with good will in an attempt to make the High Street pedestrian. To give Enfield an artificial centre, we propose to destroy the real Enfield. Blind.[26]

26. The ring road was never built, and the main street was never pedestrianized. Enfield settled instead for a one-way system and a pedestrian shopping precinct.

[Waltham Cross   O.S. 166 36:00

Cruelly sited and cruelly restored, nothing like the Eleanor Cross at Geddington in Northants. The frankly Victorian detail of Charing Cross hurts much less. Be careful when taking a look, otherwise buses will run over your toes.]

11 West London: Kensal Green to London Airport

BEYOND PADDINGTON AND KENSINGTON

Holy Trinity, Latimer Road[1]   59 7F
Norman Shaw, 1887–9

Norman Shaw's church in the rough north-west corner of Kensington
is locked up now, its congregation gone to a pathetically flaccid post-
war building. Only the great curvilinear east window hints at the
inside, which was Shaw's best, free of the fussiness which plagued
Bedford Park: a long plain room like a friars' church. It must be kept.

1. Latimer Road has been chopped in two by the Westway–West Cross flyover
junction. In the blighted southern half, renamed Freston Road, is the church,
converted into a youth club, run by Harrow School. There is a painted mural
on the flank wall, and a ground floor has been inserted, with ugly windows.
But the gymnasium on the first floor is majestically framed by Shaw's roof and
lit by Shaw's great window.

Kensal Green Cemetery   58–59 3–4E–F
1833 onwards. Chapel by Sir J. D. Paul

A fantastic private world, open to all for the price of a bus ride down
the Harrow Road. The main avenues are trim, the by-ways are a
winding wilderness with tombs of every size and style peering out
from the grass and trees. And all the time, the skyline is made up of
gasholders and factories, just across the Grand Union Canal. It is such
a friendly piece of melancholy, dust to dust in the gentlest sense, with
ragwort and cow parsley covering up all those nineteenth-century
bones. Nothing eerie, and none of the sense of being buried by numbers
which you get in today's cemeteries: the original designers knew what
they were doing both in the Picturesque layout and more unexpectedly
in the Grecian chapel, up to the best academic standards of the time
and designed by the chairman of the General Cemetery Company. It
seems a hundred miles away from Harlesden.

All Souls, Station Road, Harlesden   58 2B
E. J. Tarver, 1875–9

Nothing outside. But inside, to roof the central octagon, the architect
put an amazing timber cage on top of his mean walls: a temple inside
a temple, the intensity making an absurdity of the weary Gothic detail

underneath.[2] This architect's other buildings are just as weary, so perhaps this was the one marvellous thing in his whole life. It is enough.

2. The large nave, still there in the 1960s, has been demolished, leaving only the octagon, and giving the timber cage pride of place.

Grand Union Canal towpath, Park Royal   57 2K–58 3A

This should be one of the sights of London. Instead you have to slip on to it furtively from Acton Lane or Old Oak Lane. Cooling towers, steaming engines, chimneys, black corrugated-iron sheds: a new industrial excitement every few yards, mellowed and bound together by the water in the foreground and the grass on the banks. The complete walk out of London from Paddington to Uxbridge, which I have never done, must be tremendous. Even a short sample is enough to get you hooked on the neglected world of industrial landscape. After it, everything else seems a bit pallid.[3]

3. Industrial landscape is not what it was – fewer dark satanic mills, more small prefabricated factories, waste ground, and general mess – but the cooling towers have survived here, along with a girder bridge. The path is narrow and precarious in places, and the canal looks black and turbid, so take care.

Du Cane Estate, North Hammersmith   58 6B
(around Du Cane Road)
L.C.C. Architect's Department, c. 1910

Fifty years old, but an object lesson in how to design cottages. It was built by the L.C.C. in the first flush of enthusiasm for the garden cities, and in fact beats them at their own game – more friendly, less contrived, a happier mixture of formal and informal. The happiest designs are in Fitz Neal Street, but every road has its pleasant surprise. Erconwald Street runs through the middle, slightly uphill, and seems to point at endless countryside. In fact it bursts out on to Wormwood Scrubs, an immense flat field. Around it, the prison, Hammersmith hospital, chimneys and some of the most rewarding rail sheds in London. Could it be a marvellous place to grow up in? – if you think I am speaking ironically, then remember your own childhood, and what really interested and enthralled you, as opposed to what the grown-ups thought you ought to like.

Ministry of Pensions, Uxbridge Road   74 1A–B
and Bromyard Avenue, Acton
Ministry of Works, 1914

God knows what was in the mind of the designer (nominally Sir James West of the Ministry of Works). One colossal monolithic block, with bleak concrete aggregate walls, forty bays of windows on the long sides. No projections, no concessions, just a heavy lid and gaunt big porches with a good deal of Vanbrugh to them. This is something far more than warehouse impassivity: an active leviathan, the ideal Gestapo headquarters twenty years before the Gestapo was invented. Yet it doesn't hurt; the horror has been generalized and abstracted. The date perhaps tells everything, the time when the whole world wanted war. In an odd way this is a futurist building come out askew, the equivalent of Nevinson's war paintings.

The notice pasted at regular intervals round the walls is worth commemorating. It says:

Attention is drawn to the fact that these lawns are Crown property. The public is requested to please refrain from using them for recreational purposes or for the exercising of animals.

Goldsmiths' Almshouses, East Churchfield Road, Acton
Charles Beazley, 1811 73 1K

Acton for felicity? You mightn't think so. But Charles Beazley, uncle of the theatre architect, did the place proud. Rather like a birthday cake, with icing here and there and plainer stuff in between. The stucco centre is as tricky as Soane; the stucco ends to the wings are as deft as Nash, and really beautifully done. In between is old yellow brick; but two huge cedars[4] in the angles take up the interest and prevent the stuck-on parts seeming silly. What a professional standard, when an out-of-the-way architect could produce this for what was then an out-of-the-way place.

4. Now only one.

Queens Drive, W.3
Built in 1932–3 57 6F–G

Strung between two geographical improbabilities called North Ealing and West Acton. This is a half-timbered square mile, and marvellous nonsense. Go and see!

[Pitzhanger Manor, Ealing
Sir John Soane, 1801–2 72 1D

This was Soane's country house, before he moved to Lincoln's Inn Fields. It is now the Borough Library, on a site just off the restless, flavourless Broadway.[5] The original design, built in 1801–2, is now hedged about – in particular by a stupid new lending library which has gone classical out of false respect – and the surroundings are hopeless; but more than this would be needed to wipe away Sir John's idiosyncrasies. It is not really happy: exhausted of energy, like his church towers, and made into a composition of squares which is playing an even more obscure private game than usual. The interiors are full of pointers to what he was to do later and better, and they sit around very oddly in the inevitable overcrowding of a municipal library.]

5. Recently restored, and opened to the public as a museum and adult education centre. To be found in Walpole Park, or by walking down a passage out of the New Broadway, called Barnes Pikle. The library has moved across the High Street to the Ealing Broadway Centre, London's most confident display to date of quasi-neo-Victorian post-modernism, opened in 1985 (architects Building Design Partnership).

St Mary, Ealing   72 2D
S. S. Teulon, 1866–73

The architect on the razzmatazz, out for a day in the suburbs. Not compelling and realized, like Silvertown or St Stephen, Rosslyn Hill; instead, an experimental whistling through the teeth that is even wilder, one of the most bewildering buildings in London. It began as a pretty eighteenth-century box, and it looks as though Teulon with grisly sense of humour kept the tower and wrought it about. The inside defies description. It could be an agricultural hall, with cast-iron columns. It could be a nineteenth-century copy of Cordova, with all the striped horseshoe arches. There are fish all around the bottom of the pulpit, and the horseshoe-shaped baptistery opposite is a complete space in itself, electrified with Teulon's astonishing life-force. Who? What? How? A rag-bag with enough ideas for a dozen churches: and a splendid place for a boggle.

Hanwell Church and viaduct   71 1H

From east or west along the Uxbridge road, Hanwell is an apparition of meaning after miles of chaos. Behind a green field, the W.R. viaduct spans a small valley with eight superb elliptical arches, the shape coiling and storing energy like an acrobat. Behind, the ground rises gently, still green, to the spire of the small Victorian (George Gilbert Scott) church. All of a sudden, things relate to one another instead of being scattered around the place. Best not to go close, because the effect slips away; but the first astounding main-road view is enough.[6]

6. Visible opposite Ealing Hospital.

Horsenden Hill, Ealing   40 6-7A

This is a low, flat-topped hill which was somehow left alone when the building flood hit Middlesex between the wars. So now it is a public park with a truly astonishing view right round the compass, of housing stretching as far as the horizon in every direction. The 'city-region' stops being an academic phrase: here it is. A very special kind of public park: the borough (Ealing) has miraculously let well alone and so this is still real rough grass, unblurred by notices and asphalt paths. One thing like this right in the middle of an urban area is worth miles of landscaped amenity.

Perivale Church   56 3A
Near enough to Western Avenue for the traffic to be a continuous
buzz, yet invisible. Even from the local road (Perivale Lane) there is
only a footpath and a lych gate on the south side: still invisible. A few
yards down, among thick trees, you almost stub your toes on it: petite,
unspoilt, the tower weatherboarded and the rest decently whitewashed.
Since the rectory was demolished the surroundings have gone rank,
and, if anything, this adds to the contrast of this modest, cared-for
building.

Greenford Churches   55 2H
New church, A. E. Richardson, 1939
Just off Western Avenue,[7] like Perivale, and almost as unexpected.
Not one church but two: the sweet old building and a new one, at right
angles to it, which at first looks like the weakest kind of shilly-shally,
a religion to offend nobody and inspire nobody. The inside is quite
different (if it is locked you can get a fair idea of the quality from the
band of clear glass at head height). All timber, centrally planned with
an aisle all the way round, the construction is without period style
altogether, and hence genuine. It makes the surface trimmings seem
all the sillier: but even with them, this will last when most of our pitiful
attempts at modern churches have been shown up.

7. Down Oldfield Lane South, off the slip road on the south-west side of the
Western Avenue/A4127 junction.

Northolt Church   38 7E
The picture of old Middlesex, from Western Avenue: a couple of fields
and the little church behind, brilliant tile roofs, white walls, and a
sparkling wooden bellcote. A cameo to sustain you for the ride into
London.[8] And best to leave it like that, for the poor thing has had a
waspish doing-over recently, meanly rendered where it should have
had a mellow coat of plaster and whitewash. The last remnants of the
Reigate stone in the big mid-thirteenth-century windows – the same
style as the Abbey – are crumbling away, too.

8. Visible beyond the Northolt golf range.

Harefield Church: O.S. 176 05:89
reredos and Derby monument
In fields; the only rural parish of West Middlesex. But the houses are
peeping over the horizon from every side: the Green Belt here isn't
much fun, with broken-down farms and every lay-by full of dumped
rubbish.[9]
   Nothing like that in the church, though the chancel certainly does
look like a box-room, in the nicest sense. Monuments all over the

place, dominated by the dramatic, Baroque reredos and altar rails, one
florid guttural unit, intertwined foliage leading to two angels bending
submissively before the commandments written on translucent glass.
It came from Belgium, and the impersonal nobility is utterly unlike
England in 1700 with its roguish cherubs and the feeling that every
swag of fruit was carved especially for you.

On the right-hand side, this is jostled by some petticoat frills and a
pair of uncompromising black shoes. This is the bottom end of the
Countess of Derby, who died in 1636. Her tomb is one of those rare
images which when they do pop up are worth all the exploration of
Jacobean and Caroline hack-work. Individually, the parts may not be
remarkable; together, they lock into place like the lines of a sonnet. A
four-poster bed, in effect, with the curtains looped back. Lady Alice
lies still, her ringlets rippling away from a pallid face which is the
opposite of empty: pregnant, waiting for the Last Trump. The black
pall hangs down over the side in wrinkled folds above kneeling ladies
with more ringlets, at which the sculptor was something of a dab hand.
All the colours are rich and deep – gold, black, brick-red and alabaster.
The connexion with a Caroline poem on death is as direct as that by
which poets wrote epitaphs for their bread and butter.

9. The farms are, happily, no longer broken-down; they are prospering, and
the area looks very spruce.

Uxbridge
O.S. 176 05:84

The faint coaching flavour of the High Street is ebbing away, but
Uxbridge could still be a memorable place. The centre is a triangular
space on to which church and market hall have been crammed, literally
only inches apart. One flint, late Gothic, the other brick and Georgian,
an angular node of contraries in the middle of all the commercial
change. It now does duty as a traffic island, but if the through traffic
were taken out the High Street could be closed and paved across to
the Underground terminus: a centre of some power would be created.[10]
This Underground station of Holden's, built in 1938, is a queer fish.
The outside is really terrible, foreshadowing his post-war disasters, a
grandiose yet ineffective piece of symmetry. It could and should be
disguised. But the inside is one of Holden's most luminous and elegant
concrete inventions. As a terminus the booking hall leads directly on
to the shed over the tracks, arranged like a nave and aisles with
canted frames running the length of the platforms. It feels more like
Amsterdam than London, with everything smooth, precise and utterly
civilized.

10. The High Street is now closed to traffic, except for the station approach.
It is worth a stroll to the far end to see the Hillingdon Civic Centre (1970–78),
a spectacular response by a distinguished team of architects (Robert Matthew,
Johnson-Marshall & Partners) to the public's nostalgia for brick, tile, intricacy
and hipped roofs.

Cowley Church
O.S. 176 06:82

South of Uxbridge: Old Middlesex, and incredibly pretty. The little weatherboarded belfry, painted cream, sits up inimitably on its hipped gable. When the sun is out the vermilion roof tiles glow so brightly that the colour is unlike anything else in Britain. The rest of Cowley is New Middlesex, and worth a curse or two.

Harmondsworth Tithe Barn
O.S. 176 05:77

An astonishing village, to start with, only half a mile from London Airport's runways: a tiny green with too many rose bushes on it, two village pubs and a simple village church. The grandeur is behind the church, in the ancestor of all the hundreds of tile and tarred-weatherboard barns that survive around London. A hundred and ninety feet long, probably fifteenth-century; the tiled roof is so big that it fills the whole view as you come to it from the churchyard. Inside, twelve great luminous bays, timber-framed, with no attempt to make the beams Gothic, and all the more memorable for that. Timeless: and the word is not a careless superlative. With no real greatness in any of the Airport hangars, here is a five-hundred-year-old shed which could hold light aeroplanes almost without alteration, and with complete understanding of the strange ecstasy of flying.[11]

11. It is not open to the public; there are metal gates and barbed wire to emphasize the point.

London Airport
O.S. 176 07:76

Squalid, messy, cluttered, a sea of cars, a depressing introduction to London ... maybe. Certainly, London Airport is a confused tangle, and the various terminal buildings only add to it, with their air of wanting to be country houses instead of all this nasty business of modern living. But the spirit of the place has taken over and reduced architecture to an irrelevance. The 'main feature', as the P.R. boys say, is the nest of high-level lamp standards around the car park. They are on the same scale as the tails of Boeings and Vanguards which peer round and sometimes over the droopy buildings. London Airport has been breech-birthed into a kind of greatness; this huge tangle of uses and purposes, and the undeniable nobility of the aircraft themselves, on a site which is a bowl with the sides always visible, far away: Harrow and Runnymede and the North Downs. The whole thing can be watched from the roof gardens, which are a small town in themselves – tricked out with all the inappropriate fussiness that England can summon up (new-style, not olde. The leopard doesn't change its spots). Yet, again, the final effect is to augment the impact of those astonishing 600-m.p.h. packages, each one costing as much as Coventry Cathedral. This is still all raw material, like Clapham Junction or Tilbury Docks. But to realize it will take an imagination miles removed from the traditional idea of architecture.

In spite of the obvious advantage of the roof gardens, the best place to feel the excitement of the airport is on the south side, on the by-road from Stanwell to East Bedfont. You can park on a strip of ground between the canalized Longford and Duke of Northumberland rivers and look across at the whole sweep of hangars and runways. Because of the water jump there are no fences or warning notices, and beyond it the foreground is still cabbages, not asphalt. The landscape is stripped down to essentials, just like the jet airliners.[12]

12. Twenty years later, Heathrow Airport, as it is known both officially and generally, is a vast sprawl of buildings, car parks, roads, and runways, four times the area of the whole of the City of London and in a perpetual state of change. Since 1966 it has acquired a spacious new Terminal 1 (opened 1968) and a Terminal 4 (on the south side of the airport, opened 1986). During the same period, short-term parking has gone up into central multi-storey car parks, while acres of long-term ground-level parking have been banished to the hinterlands. All this has given the central area a roughly symmetrical diamond-shaped layout with Terminals 1 and 2 on the east side, the two Terminal 3 buildings on the west, and in the centre the surprisingly modest control tower, the bus and underground stations, a vortex of traffic, and a radar scanner ceaselessly rotating on its tall concrete plinth.

You cannot park between the canals any longer, and anyway there is not much to see from the Stanwell–East Bedfont road because of the clutter of perimeter buildings. The exciting views are now all inside the airport. Parking for spectators is currently in the long-term car parks: aim for one on the western part of the Northern Perimeter Road, and take the free bus-ride to the viewing area. You won't see any Vanguards these days, but there are Boeings in abundance, now in the company of (among others) TriStar and, of course, Concorde.

Postscript: London Beer

The state of London beer is a telling microcosm of London itself. The old small breweries have largely been swallowed up and their individual tastes have been replaced by mass-produced flavours, which in London tend to be unpleasantly tinny, without any bouquet. The stuff is undeniably strong, but whoever drank beer just to get drunk? Of the big breweries the best is Whitbread's – very good when on form, but be careful, because not all Whitbread pubs sell Whitbread bitter. From the smaller breweries, the best beer by far, to my taste, is Fuller's London Pride, brewed next to Chiswick Church and sold over a wide area of West London. But when in doubt, go for the two Burton standbys, Draught Bass and Worthington E. One will give you more kick at the time and one will give you less kick the morning after and I suggest you find out which is which.

All this refers to proper draught beer. If you are forced into drinking keg, which is a kind of bottled beer in big cans – some London pubs sell only keg, especially if they want to put on airs – then my advice is the same: Canister Bass or Canister Worthington E, and also Flower's Keg, which comes from Stratford-on-Avon. Draught Guinness, from Park Royal, is of course in a class by itself. Good drinking!

LONDON BEER 1988

The battle between tradition and modern mass-production has been fought over London beer at least as fiercely as over London buildings. One result has been a great increase in the variety of beers available in London pubs, with such regional names as Adnams, Brakspear, Wadworth, and Samuel Smith ranged alongside the London and national brewers, and a small chain of pubs – all called the Something & Firkin – brewing their own beer on the premises. Another has been that proper draught beer has regained its ascendancy over keg, to such effect that any pub wishing to impress today will hide its kegs and lay on an ambitious selection of Real Ales. Much of this is due to the traditionalists' vanguard, the Campaign for Real Ale, founded in 1971, which routed the big breweries, and their keg beer and corporate imagery, in just a few years, with resounding success.

Among London beers, Fuller's London Pride is still very highly rated by serious drinkers. Whitbread no longer brews in London, and its beers generally appear under the names of subsidiaries: Flower's (from Cheltenham), Fremlins (Faversham), and Wethered (Marlow), all of which are well regarded. Young's (brewed at Wandsworth) was not one of Ian Nairn's personal favourites, but he respected it, and it has always enjoyed a strong following and remained consistent and reliable. Draught Bass is generally thought to be not what it was, but is still a good standby.

Worthington E survives only as keg. Keg is pasteurized and fizzy; on the other hand it is easy to handle and should arrive in your glass in good condition. And it is worth bearing in mind that London draught Guinness, still brewed at Park Royal, is all keg, and always has been.

Specialists' Portmanteau

This extra index is a short means of hunting down your particular fancy, whether it is Wren churches or new flats. But, more seriously, it can be used to try and see London at a particular point in time. The fifteenth century, for example, has left us a lot of mementoes of one kind or another, but they are widely scattered: it seems worthwhile to try and gather them together. In the same way, old villages are embedded in every part of the city, and even the Thames itself can be bewilderingly hard to follow. Entries like this start on page 224.

Harmondsworth Tithe Barn   probably C15   212
[Eltham Palace   *c.*1470   187]
Hampton Court, Wolsey's buildings   Henry Redman, 1520s   135–6
Hampton Court, Henry VIII's buildings   John Molton, 1530s   135–6
St James's Palace   mixed   52

Renaissance monuments
Westminster Abbey, Lady Margaret Beaufort   Pietro Torrigiani, 1511–13   36
Westminster Abbey, Henry VII   Pietro Torrigiani, 1512–18   34
Public Record Office, Dr Yonge (d.1516)   probably Torrigiani   74–5
Westminster Abbey, Lord Hunsdon (d.1596)   33
Cheam, Lady Jane Lumley (d.1577)   181
Westminster Abbey, Queen Elizabeth (d.1603–7) etc.   Maximilian Colt   33
Harefield, Countess of Derby (d.1636)   211

Elizabethan–Jacobean country houses
Eastbury Manor House, Barking   1572   168–9
Charlton House   1607–12   165

Seventeenth-century churches
St Katharine Cree   1628–31   13
St Paul, Covent Garden   Inigo Jones, 1631–8   68–9
[Stanmore Old Church   1631   199–200]

Early-seventeenth-century monuments
Watford, Morison family   Nicholas Stone, 1619   201
Guildhall Library, Edward VI, Charles I, Elizabeth I   Nicholas Stone, 1623   21
Westminster Abbey, Duke of Lennox and Richmond (d.1624)   Hubert Le
   Sueur   34
Barking, Sir Charles Montague (d.1625)   168
Westminster Abbey, Lord and Lady Cottingham   Hubert Le Sueur, 1635   33
Westminster Abbey, Sir Thomas Richardson (d.1635)   Hubert Le Sueur   37–8

Seventeenth-century fittings, pre-Wren
St Helen Bishopgate, doorcases   *c.*1640   11–12

Wren
St Mary-at-Hill   1670–6   18
Monument   Wren and Hooke, 1671–7   17
St Stephen Walbrook   1672–7   6
St James Garlickhythe   1674–87, steeple 1713   16
St James Piccadilly   1676–84   60–61
St Benet Paul's Wharf   1677–85   14–15
St Martin Ludgate   1677–87   2
St Peter Cornhill   1677–87   11
St Mary Abchurch   1681–6   7–8
St Mary Aldermary   finished 1682   5
Chelsea Hospital   1682–91   117–18
St Mary Somerset, tower   1686–94   15
St Michael Paternoster Royal   1686–94, steeple 1715   16
St Margaret Lothbury   1686–1701   8
Christ Church, Newgate Street, steeple   finished 1704   22

Wren–Baroque fittings
St Margaret Lothbury, chancel screen, pulpit, font   8–9

St Mary Abchurch, reredos (Gibbons), pulpit 7
St Benet Paul's Wharf, doorcase 14–15
St James Garlickhythe, iron columns 16
St Mary-at-Hill, woodwork, pulpit, sword-rests 18
St James Piccadilly, reredos Gibbons, 1684 61
All Hallows, Barking, font cover 1689 19
St Magnus Martyr, clock 1709 17
Crown Jewels, Tower of London mostly 1660s 20n
Hampton Court, carving, east front Cibber, c.1695 136
Harefield, reredos Belgian, c.1700 210–11

City companies' halls
Apothecaries', Blackfriars Lane mostly c.1780 14
Skinners', Dowgate Hill William Jupp, c.1790 16–17

Late-seventeeth–early-eighteenth-century monuments
Fulham, Viscount Mordaunt (d.1675) Bushnell 127
Westminster Abbey, William Morgan and Thomas Mansel c.1685 31
Fulham, Elizabeth Limpany (d.1694) 127
Barking, John Bennett (d.1706) 168

Seventeenth-century public buildings
Banqueting House Inigo Jones, 1619–25 47
Queen's House, Greenwich Inigo Jones, 1619–37 160
Greenwich Hospital John Webb, 1664 onwards; Wren, 1699–1703 160–2
Chelsea Hospital Wren, 1682–94 117–18
Hampton Court Wren, 1689–1700 135–7
Kensington Palace, orangery Wren(?), 1704 113

Seventeenth-century town houses
229–30 Strand 1625 74
21–22 College Hill, City, doorcase c.1680 16
41 Cloth Fair late C17 23–4
Schomberg House, Pall Mall 1698 51

Late-seventeenth-century country houses
[Eltham Lodge Hugh May, 1663 187]

Eighteenth-century churches
Spanish and Portuguese Synagogue, Bevis Marks Joseph Avis, 1700 12
St Paul, Deptford Thomas Archer, 1712 158–9
St Anne, Limehouse Nicholas Hawksmoor, 1712–30 143
St Mary Woolnoth Nicholas Hawksmoor, 1714–30 7
St Mary-le-Strand James Gibbs, 1714–17 71–2
St George-in-the-East Nicholas Hawksmoor, 1715–23 142
St Michael Cornhill, tower Nicholas Hawksmoor, 1718 10
St George, Bloomsbury Nicholas Hawksmoor, 1720–31 95
St Martin-in-the-Fields James Gibbs, 1722–6 54–5
Christ Church, Spitalfields Nicholas Hawksmoor, 1723–9 148
St Mary, Islington, steeple L. Dowbiggin, 1751–4 152
St James, Pentonville Road A. H. Hurst, 1787 152
Greenwich Hospital Chapel James Stuart and William Newton, c.1789 161–2
St Anne Soho, tower S. P. Cockerell, 1802–6 57

Pelham Crescent   George Basevi, c.1840   110
Syon, greenhouse   Charles Fowler, c.1830   132

Grecian churches
[St Pancras Church   W. and H. W. Inwood, 1819–22   88]
All Souls, Langham Place   John Nash, 1822–4   78
St Peter, Regent Square   W. and H. W. Inwood, 1824   90
Bethnal Green Church   Sir John Soane, 1825–8   146–7
Kensal Green Cemetery Chapel   Sir J. D. Paul, c.1833   206
St John the Evangelist, Clapham Road   T. Marsh Nelson, 1842   173

Clubs
Travellers' and Reform, Pall Mall   Sir Charles Barry, 1829 and 1841   51
City Club, Old Broad Street   Philip Hardwick, 1833   9–10

Victorian churches
Christ Church, Streatham   J. Wild, 1842   174
All Saints, Margaret Street   William Butterfield, 1849–59   77–8
St James the Less, Pimlico   G. E. Street, 1860   43
St Mark, Silvertown   S. S. Teulon, 1861–2   166–7
St Martin, Gospel Oak   E. B. Lamb, 1866   190
St Mary, Ealing   S. S. Teulon, 1866–73   209
St Columba, Kingsland Road   James Brooks, 1867–71   149
St Mary, Addiscombe   E. B. Lamb, 1868   183
St John, Kennington   G. E. Street, 1870   175
St Michael, Croydon   J. L. Pearson, 1871   182
Ascension, Lavender Hill   James Brooks, 1873–83   171
St Dominic's Priory, St Pancras   J. C. Buckler, 1874–83   189
All Souls, Harlesden   E. J. Tarver, 1875–9   206–7
St Stephen, Rosslyn Hill   S. S. Teulon, 1876   195–6
St Augustine, Kilburn   J. L. Pearson, 1879   196–7
St Cuthbert, Philbeach Gardens   H. R. Gough, 1884–7   120–1
Holy Trinity, Latimer Road   Norman Shaw, 1887–9   206
Holy Cross, Cromer Street   J. Peacock, 1888   90
St Barnabas, Dulwich   Oliver & Leeson, 1894   176
St Ignatius (Roman Catholic), Tottenham   B. Williamson, 1894   150

Victorian chapels
St Paul's Presbyterian Church, Millwall   T. E. Knightley, 1859   144
Westminster Congregational Chapel   W. F. Poulton, 1864   45
Welsh Baptist Church, Eastcastle Street   Owen Lewis, 1889   78
Agapemonite Church, Clapton   Frank Morris, 1895   150

Victorian public buildings
Licensed Victuallers' Benevolent Institution   1827 onwards   179
Apsley House   Benjamin Wyatt and John Harper, 1828–30   65–6
Goldsmiths' Hall   Philip Hardwick, 1829–35   21–2
Houses of Parliament   Sir Charles Barry and A. W. Pugin, 1835–60   40–1
Dulwich College   E. M. Barry, 1866   177
Albert Hall   Captain Fowke, 1867   111
Law Courts   G. E. Street, 1868–92   72
St Ermin's Hotel   E. T. Hall, 1887   46
Scotland Yard   Norman Shaw, 1888 and 1912   46

Modern shops, offices and public buildings

Royal Festival Hall   L.C.C. Architect's Department, Special Works Division, 1948–50, 1963–4   99–100]

Dunn's and Harrison Gibson's, Bromley   Bertram Carter, 1956; Forrest & Barber, 1960   184

Peter Robinson, Strand   Denys Lasdun, 1957–9   68

Daily Mirror Building   Sir Owen Williams etc., 1957–60   90

Eastbourne Terrace   C. H. Elsom, 1958   77

Financial Times Building   Sir Albert Richardson, 1959   5

Route Eleven or South Barbican   City of London planning office, begun 1960   24–5

County Hall, Addington Street Extension   L.C.C. General Division, 1960   99

New Zealand House   Robert Matthew, Johnson-Marshall & Partners, 1960–2   54

Royal College of Art   H. T. Cadbury-Brown, 1961   112

Portland House, Victoria   Howard, Fairbairn & Partners, 1962   44–5

Eros House, Catford   Owen Luder, 1962   183

Chelsea Barracks   Tripe & Wakeham, 1962   117

The Economist Building, St James's Street   Alison & Peter Smithson, 1964   63

Modern industry

Mallinsons' Timber Yard, Parnell Road, Victoria Park   144–5

Sheds, Ferry Lane, Tottenham   150–1

Modern engineering

Waterloo Bridge   Sir Giles Gilbert Scott, 1940–5   100

Barking Station   B.R. Eastern Region, 1961   168

Hammersmith Flyover   127–8

M4 Extension, Chiswick–Langley   Sir Alexander Gibb & Partners, 1964   130

Modern flats and housing schemes

Oatlands Court, Wimbledon   L.C.C. Architect's Department, Housing Division, 1953   180

Lawson Estate, Southwark   Sir John Burnet, Tait & Partners, 1953   105

Golden Lane   Chamberlin, Powell & Bon, 1953–64   24

Gospel Oak housing   Powell & Moya, 1954   190

Parkleys, Ham Common   Eric Lyons, 1954–6   126

Boundary Road housing   Armstrong & MacManus, 1954–6   88

Highbury Quadrant   L.C.C. Architect's Department, Housing Division, 1955–7   151

Mansfield Heights, Highgate   Metropolitan Police Architect's Department, 1956   192

Cluster blocks, Bethnal Green   Denys Lasdun, 1956–60   147]

Roehampton   L.C.C. Architect's Department, Housing Division, 1957–60   180

Sceaux Gardens and The Denes   Camberwell B.C., 1957–63   178–9

Hide Tower, S.W.1   Stillman & Eastwick-Field, 1957–60   43

Blackheath Park   Eric Lyons, begun 1957   164

Langham House Close, Ham Common   Stirling & Gowan, 1958   125–6

Tulse Hill Old People's Home   L.C.C., 1958   174

26 St James's Place   Denys Lasdun, 1959   52

24 Hereford Square   Colin Wilson & Arthur Baker, 1959   119

Park Close, Melbury Road   Colin Wilson & Arthur Baker, 1960   114–15

Farley Court, Melbury Road   Julian Keable & Partners, 1961   114–15

Index

232　INDEX

Christian, Ewan, 55
Churches (Outer London parish
　churches appear under the name of
　the place, not under the dedication)
Agapemonite Church, Clapton, 150
All Hallows Barking-by-the-Tower,
　19
All Saints, Camden Street, 88, 90
All Saints, Margaret Street, 77–8,
　145, 186, ill. 27
All Saints, Petersham, 125
All Souls, Harlesden, 206–7
All Souls, Langham Place, 78
Ascension, Lavender Hill, 171
Barking Church, 168
Battersea Old Church, 170
Bethnal Green Church, 146–7
Blackheath Church, 163–4, ill. 81
Brompton Oratory, 110, 189
Cheam Old Church (*Lumley
　Chapel*), 181
Chislehurst Church, 185
Christ Church, Newgate Street, 22
Christ Church, Spitalfields, 26, 143,
　148, 149, ill. 53
Christ Church, Streatham, 174
Cowley Church, 212
Dagenham Church, 169, ill. 86
Esher Old Church, 138
Fulham Church, 127
Great Synagogue (*mosque*), Fournier
　Street, 148–9
Greenford Churches, 187, 210
Hanwell Church, 209
Harefield Church, 210–11
Holy Cross, Cromer Street, 90
Holy Trinity, Brompton, 110
Holy Trinity, Clapham, 172
Holy Trinity, Latimer Road (*Freston
　Road*), 206
Holy Trinity, Marylebone, 80, 146
Holy Trinity, Southwark, 105
Islington Church, 152
Leyton Church, 155, ill. 85
Little Stanmore Church, 199
Littleton Church, 140
Northolt Church, 210
Notre-Dame de France, Leicester
　Place, 13
Perivale Church, 210
Petersham Churches, 125
Rotherhithe Church, 103
St Anne, Limehouse, 142, 143
St Anne Soho, 57
St Augustine, Kilburn, 196–7

Churches *continued*
St Augustine, Watling Street, 4
St Barnabas, Dulwich, 176
St Barnabas, Hackney, 150
St Bartholomew-the-Great, West
　Smithfield, 22, 23–4
St Bartholomew-the-Less, 23
St Benet, Upper Thames Street, 14–
　15
St Botolph Aldersgate, 22
St Bride, Fleet Street, 22
St Clement Danes, 72
St Columba (*Christ Apostolic Church
　Mount Bethel*), Kingsland Road,
　149
St Cuthbert, Philbeach Gardens,
　120–1
St Cyprian, Clarence Gate, 80–1, 120
St Dominic's Priory, St Pancras, 189
St Dunstan-in-the-West, Fleet
　Street, 75
St Ethelburga, Bishopsgate, 12
St George, Bloomsbury, 95
St George, Brentford, 130–1
St George-in-the-East, 42, 142, 143,
　ill. 52
St Helen Bishopsgate, 11–12
St Ignatius, Tottenham, 150, ill. 7
St James Garlickhythe, 16
St James the Less, Moreton Street,
　43, ill. 28
St James, Pentonville Road, 152
St James Piccadilly, 55, 60–1, 172, ill.
St John, Bethnal Green, 146–7
St John, Clapham Road, 173
St John, Downshire Hill, 196
St John, Kennington, 175
St John, Smith Square, 41–2, 158, ill.
　14
St John, Stratford, 155
St John, Waterloo Road, 101
St Jude, Hampstead Garden Suburb,
　193
St Katharine Cree, 13
St Lawrence Jewry, 2
St Luke Chelsea, 119
St Magnus Martyr, 17
St Margaret Lothbury, 8–9
St Margaret, Westminster, 28, 29
St Mark, Silvertown, 166–7
St Martin, Gospel Oak, 183, 190
St Martin-in-the-Fields, 54–5, 152
St Martin Ludgate, 2, 4²
St Mary Abchurch, 7–8, ill. 2
St Mary, Addiscombe, 183, 190